W9-ARL-869

GOLF'S GREATEST MOMENTS

GOLF'S GREATEST MOMENTS

by ROBERT SIDORSKY

GENERAL EDITOR

HARRY N. ABRAMS, INC., PUBLISHERS

CONTENTS

PAGE 2
The 9th hole at Cypress Point Golf Club, Monterey, California

FORE WORD
and ACKNOWLEDGMENTS

Golf, as all golfers know, is a great game but also a fickle and complex one, which makes us all the more devoted to it. The aim of this book is to depict the moments that define golf's greatness in the words of the game's finest writers. I have tried in making the selections for this anthology to convey the extraordinary range and depth of outstanding writing about golf, while focusing on the key areas of the game—the great players, the great courses, and the great virtues of golf—that collectively make the game what it is.

Golf is a sport with a particularly rich and diverse literary tradition. As George Plimpton points out in the selection from *The Bogey Man*: "No other sport can offer such fine reading." Baseball is a strong contender, and Plimpton offers the possible exceptions of exploration, or game hunting, but golf is the sport that has attracted and inspired the broadest spectrum of superb writers.

There are many reasons why the literature of golf has been of such a high standard. To begin with, golf is a very old game and one that has proven truly international in its appeal, spreading from Scotland throughout the British Empire, across to Continental Europe, and then to America. This unique combination of longevity and popularity in so many lands explains in some measure why golf has developed such an extensive and first-rate literature.

There are other compelling reasons as well. Golf, like baseball, is an intellectual game. It involves a considerable amount of strategy and thought, looks simple to play but is maddeningly difficult in practice, and offers plenty of time to ponder and reflect. It is also a game of the great outdoors, with courses in varied and captivating landscapes, and therefore appeals to the close observer of nature and those interested in the artistic challenge of shaping the natural landscape. These are also factors that have undoubtedly contributed to golf's attraction to accomplished writers.

Golf is the most individual of games, and the great golfers over the game's history have been exposed in their moments of triumph and failure to a greater degree than in other sports. The character and fortitude of the game's top players is always on display and is constantly tested. This intense individual challenge makes for a particularly interesting and sophisticated brand of writing about the game's champions.

Above all, more than any other sport, golf is a participatory game that can be played by each of us for many years, long after we have consigned the glove to the attic and hung up the spikes. The individuality of golf, and our ability to continue playing the game, however frustratingly badly, also explains its hold on the literary imagination. More than any other sport, it provides a sense of personal escape and fulfillment that is reflected in the autobiographical writing of so many of the contributors. When we put all of these considerations together, it is no wonder that golf as a sport has engendered such fine writing and that the literature of golf continues to flourish.

In organizing this anthology, I have concentrated on each of the main aspects of the game and its historical development, exploring the essence of golf's appeal, the great courses on both sides of the Atlantic, and the game's enduring champions.

Chapter One addresses the fundamental question of what makes golf the greatest game of all. Chapters Two, Four, and Six are devoted to the legends of the game, ranging from Old Tom Morris and the Great Triumvirate to the golden era of Bobby Jones and Walter Hagen, to the post World War II dominance of Ben Hogan and Sam Snead. Chapter Three covers the glorious, brooding links courses of Great Britain and Ireland, from the venerable Old Course at St. Andrews to Aberdovey in Wales to Royal County Down in Northern Ireland. Chapter Five traces the development of the classic American courses, from the fiendishly difficult Pine Valley to the mesmerizingly beautiful Cypress Point to the modern masterpiece at Whistling Straits. The psyche also plays an important role in golf, and so Chapter Seven analyzes the subject of golf dreams and golf remembered. Chapter Eight profiles the greatest players of the modern era, from

Arnold Palmer and Jack Nicklaus to the incomparable Tiger Woods.

Given the scope and quality of lively writing about golf over the years, making the selections for this anthology was no easy task. Many of the articles and essays included are by the cream of American sportswriters: Grantland Rice, O.B. Keeler, Red Smith, Al Laney, Charles Price, Jim Murray, Dan Jenkins, Dave Anderson, Frank Deford, Tom Boswell, and Herbert Warren Wind. No book about great golf writing would be complete without several selections by the greatest golf writer of them all, Bernard Darwin, who for over forty years was the golf correspondent for *The Times* (London). There are essays by other distinguished British golf writers as well, including Henry Longhurst, Pat Ward-Thomas, and Peter Dobereiner. The younger generation of outstanding golf writers is well represented by David Owen, Curt Sampson, Jaime Diaz, John Paul Newport, and Michael Bamberger.

Many well-known writers and poets have also been drawn to golf, although they made their mark pursuing other literary passions. The literary lions who have found themselves humbled on the course include John Updike, A.A. Milne, George Plimpton, Siegfried Sassoon, and Ogden Nash. Many of the leading golfers have also been highly accomplished authors. In some instances they were working with topnotch coauthors, but the high caliber of golfing autobiographies reflects the inherent intelligence and good sense of so many of golf's champions over the years, which is another hallmark of the game. The selections include writing by J.H. Taylor, Harry Vardon, Tommy Armour, Walter Hagen, Bobby Jones, Glenna Collett, and Jack Nicklaus.

An important and unusual feature of this anthology is that the pictures are integral to the text, and also demonstrate that golf has been a source of artistic inspiration. For many of the same reasons that golf has produced the finest literature of any sport, it has also given rise to a remarkable photographic record and an impressive array of fine painting, works on paper, and landscape photography. I have sought to use a variety of illustrations, including rare archival photographs and panoramas by the world's leading golf course photographers, to convey and enhance the theme of each of the selections.

I hope that you will enjoy reading these selections by so many wonderful writers and looking at the accompanying illustrations as much as I did when choosing them.

There are a number of people to whom I owe a debt of gratitude and without whose help and encouragement I would never have been able to produce this illustrated history by the game's finest writers. I am particularly grateful to Margaret L. Kaplan, Editor-at-Large at Harry N. Abrams, Inc., for helping me to conceive this book, for her sound and unerring judgment throughout the editorial process, and especially for showing faith in me. I would also like to thank Gary Tooth and Carrie Hamilton of Empire Design Studio for their commitment, creativity, and the esthetic sensibility that has resulted in an exuberant design that positively shouts fore!

I am truly indebted to my research assistant, Amber Reed, for her great care, efficiency, and thoughtfulness in preparing the manuscript, as well as to Denise Rodriguez and Lenora Glass for their reliable and dedicated assistance.

I would also like to thank all of the photographers who provided the enchanting scenic photography and vivid historical images for the book, including Larry Lambrecht, Matthew Harris, Phil Sheldon, Aidan Bradley, John and Jeannine Henebry, Russell Kirk, Mike Klemme, and Leonard Kamsler. Everyone at the United States Golf Association's Museum and Library went out of their way to help me with my photo and editorial research, including Rand Jerris, Executive Director, Tanya Steffan, Patty Moran, Nancy Stulack, and Maxine Vigliotta. Mark Morosse did a consummately professional job in photographing the images from the USGA's collection.

Finally, I would like to thank my parents for their unflagging encouragement, my sisters, Gina Bartlett and Emily Kronenberg, for their enthusiasm, and, most of all, my wife Hilary for her support while I was consumed with this project. My son Alexander was too young to contribute in word or deed, but was a great source of inspiration nonetheless.

Robert Sidorsky
NEW YORK CITY, MARCH 2003

WHAT MAKES GOLF GREAT

CHAPTER ONE

WHAT MAKES GOLF GREAT

Any book about golf, but particularly an anthology that covers the game, must confront the seminal question: What makes golf the most elusive, maddening, and all-consuming of passions? What makes golf the greatest game has intrigued writers for well over a century now. Those who have taken up the gauntlet to provide answers include a surprisingly eclectic cross-section of the literary world, all of them golfers but many not identified as golf writers. In exploring the secret of golf's appeal, it becomes apparent that the game's attraction lies not in one thing but in many, and that the whole is greater than the sum of the parts.

Golf is the most individual of sports. We can compete against our playing partners on the course, but ultimately we are playing against ourselves. This aspect of golf makes it both intensely exhilarating and exasperating, and because golf is such an individual sport, it tends to magnify our personal character strengths and flaws.

We have all experienced, however infrequently, the thrill of the perfectly struck shot. There is some truth to the old adage that it takes only one good shot to bring us back to the course, but the lure of golf goes much deeper. Golf is a game for optimists, or perhaps it would be more accurate to say that it appeals to the optimistic side of our nature while never quite fulfilling it. We keep playing it because, unlike other sports where we know we will never surpass our youthful form, golf is a game of technique and intellect more than of stamina and strength. We therefore convince ourselves—indeed, we are unshakeable in our belief—that we can and will improve.

Golf always offers room for improvement. We are told that even the great Tiger Woods has not reached his peak. There are so many facets to playing golf that even if one area of our game does get better, another invariably slips, so we are always in search of the grail.

PAGES 12, 13
The 11th hole at the
Pacific Dunes Course,
Bandon, Oregon

Whether we are Tiger Woods or Joe Duffer, we need something to strive for. Part of the pleasure is never being quite satisfied, always believing we can play better.

Because golf is a game of hope, it is enjoyed by players of all different levels. In no other sport can players of very different abilities compete against one another, but in golf the handicap system allows for this. It goes beyond that, though. Golf is more about the chase than its attainment. We wish to achieve mastery, but we also view the end of the journey with trepidation, and this is part of the inherent psychological tension of golf. On rare occasions we do play up to our expectations, we do slip into what is known as the Zone. We know, however, that it cannot last, and we know for certain that it will not last if we wish for it too hard, for that is an invitation to the golfing deities to set us up for a fall.

There is also a certain pleasure and camaraderie to be derived from not playing very well. We duffers experience a thrill at carrying a water hazard or making a scrambling par that a pro or scratch golfer will never again know, and we feel a bit sorry for the golfer who can find no joy in these small triumphs.

A central aspect of the game's allure is the vast green landscape. Golf offers us a natural beauty and a scale for competition that no other sport can begin to rival. The length of a football field is a mere chip shot. Golf courses adorn some of the most spellbinding scenery in the world, from the Monterey Peninsula in California to the Mountains of Mourne in Ireland to the Moray Firth in Scotland, and even many modest courses offer momentous views of sea and land.

On top of this, golf is the only sport that offers a personal guide and companion in the form of a caddie. Caddies, although their numbers are dwindling, have played a decisive role in championship golf and have provided a mix of wisecracking wisdom and comic relief that has filled numerous volumes.

Finally, there is something reassuring in knowing that golf has been played for hundreds of years and that, while the equipment and haberdashery have changed dramatically, the intrinsic appeal of the game has not. In reading Sir Walter Simpson writing in the 1880s or John Updike writing in the 1980s, we instantly recognize the same shared experience of golf. The essential fascination and frustration of the game has not changed. Golf has been and will always be a game that teaches us the virtues of determination and humility, and of learning to laugh at our own foibles.

JOHN UPDIKE

THE BLISS OF GOLF

from *Golf Dreams*, 1996*

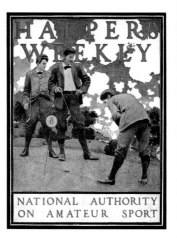

Poster by Maxfield Parrish for
Harper's Weekly, circa 1896

I NEVER TOUCHED A CLUB UNTIL I WAS TWENTY-FIVE. THEN, ON A SHADY LAWN IN Wellesley, a kind of aunt-in-law showed me how to hold her driver and told me, after one swoop at a phantom ball, that I had a wonderful natural swing. Since that fatal encouragement, in many weathers inner and outer, amid many a green and winding landscape, I have asked myself what the peculiar bliss of this demanding game is, a bliss that at times threatens to relegate all the rest of life, including those sexual concerns that Freud claims are paramount and those even more basic needs that Marx insists must be met, to the shadows.

The immensities of space, beside which even polo and baseball are constricted pastimes, must be part of it. To see one's ball gallop two hundred and more yards down the fairway, or see it fly from the face of an 8-iron clear across an entire copse of maples in full autumnal flare, is to join one's soul with the vastness that, contemplated from another angle, intimidates the spirit, and makes one feel small. As it moves through the adventures of a golf march, the human body, like Alice's in Wonderland, experiences an intoxicating relativity—huge in relation to the ball, tiny in relation to the course, exactly matched to that of the other players. From this relativity is struck a silent music that rings to the treetops and runs through a Wagnerian array of changes as each hole evokes its set of shots, dwindling down to the final putt. The clubs in their nice gradations suggest organ pipes.

There is a bliss to the equipment—the festive polyester slacks, the menacing and elevating cleated shoes, the dainty little gauntlet the left hand gets to wear, the leathery adhesion of the grips and the riflelike purity of the shafts, the impeccable luster of the (pre-Day-Glo orange) ball. The uniform sits light, unlike the monstrous armor of the skier or the football player, and cloaks us in a colorful individuality—not for the golfer the humiliating uniforms, cooked up by press agents and tyrannic owners, inflicted upon baseball players. We feel, dressed for golf, knightly, charging toward distant pennants past dragon-shaped hazards. The green when it receives us is soft, fine, gently undulating, maidenly.

A beautiful simplicity distinguishes the game's objective and the scoring. One stroke,

---

* As America's foremost contemporary novelist and man of letters, **JOHN UPDIKE** (b. 1932) is best known for exploring personal relations and midlife angst in suburban America, but he is also clearly a golfer at heart. Updike has written a good deal about golf—both fiction and nonfiction—which is collected in *Golf Dreams*.

count one. William Faulkner's *The Sound and the Fury* opens with an idiot watching a game of golf, and he grasps the essence well enough: "They took the flag out, and they were hitting. Then they put the flag back and they went to the table, and he hit and the other hit." That's how it goes; golf appeals to the idiot in us, and the child. What child does not grasp the pleasure-principle of miniature golf? Just how childlike golf players become is proven by their frequent inability to count past five. There is a lovable injustice, a comic democracy, in the equality, for purposes of scoring, of a three-hundred-yard smash from an elevated tee and a three-inch tap-in. Or, let's not forget, a total whiff—the most comical stroke of all. A ground-out in baseball or a tennis ball whapped into the net is not especially amusing; but bad shots in golf are endless fun—at least the other fellow's are. The duck hook, the banana slice, the topped dribble, the no-explode explosion shot, the arboreal ricochet, the sky ball, the majestic OB, the pond-side scuff-and-splash, the deep-grass squirt, the cart-path shank, the skull, the fat hit, the thin hit, the stubbed putt—what a wealth of mirth is to be had in an afternoon's witnessing of such varied miseries, all produced in a twinkling of an eye by the infallible laws of physics!

And the bliss of the swing. The one that feels effortless and produces a shot of miraculous straightness and soar. "I'll take it," we say modestly, searching about with a demure blush for the spun-away tee. Just a few shots a round keep us coming back; what other sport offers such sudden splendor in exchange for so few calories of expended energy? In those instants of whiz, ascent, hover, and fall, an ideal self seems mirrored. If we have that one shot in us, we must have thousands more—the problem is to get them out, to *let* them out. To concentrate, to take one's time, to move the weight across, to keep the elbow in, to save the wrist-cock for the hitting area, to keep one's head still, down, and as full of serenity as a Zen monk's: an ambitious program, but a basically spiritual one, which does not require the muscularity and shapeliness of youth. What other sport holds out hope of improvement to a man or a woman over fifty? True, the pros begin to falter at around forty, but it is their putting nerves that go, not their swings. For a duffer like the abovesigned, the room for improvement is so vast that three lifetimes could be spent roaming the fairways carving away at it, convinced that perfection lies just over the next rise. And that hope, perhaps, is the kindest bliss of all that golf bestows upon its devotees.

The 16th hole at the Myopia Hunt Club, South Hamilton, Massachusetts

SIR WALTER SIMPSON

THE PRAISE OF GOLF

from *The Art of Golf,* 1887*

Prize of the Silver Golf, a watercolor painted by David Allan in 1787. The Honourable Company of Edinburgh Golfers played an annual tournament for the silver club presented to them by the City of Edinburgh in 1744. The winner had to present a silver golf ball or coin to be attached to the trophy. There are now four such silver clubs on display at Muirfield, the Company's present home course. Allan depicts the annual announcement of the competition, made by a public procession with drums through the city

FACING PAGE

The Golfers: A Grand Match Played over St. Andrews Links, by Charles Lees, 1847. One of the most famous of all golf scenes, it records a match that took place at the Royal & Ancient's annual meeting in 1841

THERE ARE SO MANY GOOD POINTS ABOUT THE ROYAL AND ANCIENT GAME OF GOLF that its comparative obscurity, rather than its increasing popularity, is matter for wonder. It is apparently yet unknown to the Medical Faculty. The golfer does not find it in the list of exercises recommended by doctors to persons engaged in warfare with the results of sedentary habits. He is moved to pity British subjects compelled to stir their livers by walking, horse-riding, or cycling. He knows how monotonous it is following one's nose, or flogging a horse and following it, compared with flogging and following a ball. For the wearied and bent cyclist, who prides himself on making his journey in as short a time as possible, he has a pitying word. Men who assume that the sooner the journey is over the greater the pleasure, evidently do not love their pursuit for its own sake.

With any other sport or pastime golf compares favourably.

With cricket? The golfer has nothing to say against that game, if you are a good player. But it is a pastime for the few. The rest have to hang about the pavilion, and see the runs made. With the golfer it is different. He does not require to be even a second-class player, in order to get into matches. Again, the skilful cricketer has to retire when he gets up in years. He might exclaim with Wolsey: "Had I served my golf as I have served my cricket, she would not thus have deserted me in my old age." How different it is with golf! It is a game for the many. It suits all sorts and conditions of men. The strong and the weak, the halt and the maimed, the octogenarian and the boy, the rich and the poor, the clergyman and the infidel, may play every day, except Sunday. The late riser can play comfortably, and be back for his rubber in the afternoon; the sanguine man can measure himself against those who will beat him; the half-crown seeker can find victims, the gambler can bet, the man of high principle, by playing for nothing, may enjoy himself, and yet feel good. You can brag, and lose matches; depreciate yourself, and win them. Unlike the other Scotch game of whisky-drinking, excess in it is not injurious to the health.

---

* **SIR WALTER SIMPSON'S** *The Art of Golf* is one of the classics of nineteenth-century golfing literature. Simpson, who was a member of the Scottish Bar, inherited his peerage from his father, a physician who pioneered the use of chloroform to relieve the pain of childbirth. As a young man, Simpson became a close friend of Robert Louis Stevenson, then a promising young Scottish writer. They took a canoe trip together in 1877 through Belgium and northeast France that became the basis for Stevenson's first published book, *An Inland Voyage.*

Better than fishing, shooting, and hunting? Certainly. These can only be indulged in at certain seasons. They let you die of dyspepsia during the rest of the year. Besides, hunting, you are dependent on horses and foxes for sport; shooting, on birds; fishing, on the hunger of a scaly but fastidious animal. The pleasures of sport are extracted from the sufferings of dumb animals. If horses, grouse, or fish could squeal, sports would be distressful rather than amusing.

Golf has some drawbacks. It is possible, by too much of it, to destroy the mind; a man with a Roman nose and a high forehead may play away his profile. That peculiar mental condition called "Fifish" probably had its origin in the east of the Kingdom. For the golfer, Nature loses her significance. Larks, the casts of worms, the buzzing of bees, and even children, are hateful to him. I have seen a golfer very angry at getting into a bunker by killing a bird, and rewards of as much as ten shillings have been offered for boys maimed on the links. Rain comes to be regarded solely in its relation to the putting greens; the daisy is detested, botanical specimens are but "hazards," twigs "break clubs." Winds cease to be east, south, west, or north. They are ahead, behind, or sideways, and the sky is bright or dark, according to the state of the game. . . .

The 1st hole of the Old Course, St. Andrews, Fife, Scotland, looking back toward the town

Although unsuited to the novelist, golf lends itself readily to the dreaming of scenes of which the dreamer is the hero. Unless he is an exceptionally good rider, or can afford 300-guinea mounts, a man cannot expect to be the hero of the hunting-field. The sportsman knows what sort of shot he is, and the fisher has no illusions; but every moderately good golfer, on the morning of the medal-day, may lie abed and count up a perfect score for himself. He easily recalls how at different times and often he has done each hole in par figures. Why not this day, and all the holes consecutively? It seems so easy. The more he thinks of it the easier it seems, even allowing for a few mistakes. Every competitor who is awake soon enough sees the necessity of preparing a speech against the contingency of the medal being presented to him in the evening. Nor is any one much crushed when all is over, and he has not won. If he does well, it was but that putt, that bad lie, that bunker. If his score is bad, what of it? Even the best are off their game occasionally. Next time it will be different. Meanwhile his score will be taken as a criterion of his game, and he is sure to win many half-crowns from unwary adversaries who underrate him.

The game of golf is full of consolation. The long driver who is beaten feels that he has a soul above putting. All those who cannot drive thirty yards suppose themselves to be good putters. Your hashy player piques himself on his power of recovery. The duffer is a duffer merely because every second shot is missed. Time or care will eliminate the misses, and then! Or perhaps there is something persistently wrong in driving, putting, or approaching. He will discover the fault, and then! Golf is not one of those occupations in which you soon learn your level. There is no shape nor size of body, no awkwardness nor ungainliness, which puts good golf beyond one's reach. There are good golfers with spectacles, with one eye, with one leg, even with one arm. None but the absolutely blind need despair. It is not the youthful tyro alone who has cause to hope. Beginners in middle age have become great, and, more wonderful still, after years of patient duffering, there may be a rift in the clouds. Some pet vice which has been clung to as a virtue may be abandoned, and the fifth-class player burst upon the world as a medal-winner. In golf, whilst there is life there is hope.

A.A. MILNE

THE CHARM OF GOLF

from *Not That It Matters*, 1920[*]

WHEN HE READS OF THE NOTABLE DOINGS OF FAMOUS GOLFERS, THE EIGHTEEN-HANDICAP man has no envy in his heart. For by this time he has discovered the great secret of golf. Before he began to play he wondered wherein lay the fascination of it; now he knows. Golf is so popular simply because it is the best game in the world at which to be bad.

Consider what it is to be bad at cricket. You have bought a new bat, perfect in balance; a new pair of pads, white as driven snow; gloves of the very latest design. Do they let you use them? No. After one ball, in the negotiation of which neither your bat, nor your pads, nor your gloves came into play, they send you back into the pavilion to spend the rest of the afternoon listening to fatuous stories of some old gentleman who knew Fuller Pilch. And when your side takes the field, where are you? Probably at long leg both ends, exposed to the public gaze as the worst fieldsman in London. How devastating are your emotions. Remorse, anger, mortification fill your heart; above all, envy—envy of the lucky immortals who disport themselves on the green level of Lord's.

Consider what it is to be bad at lawn tennis. True, you are allowed to hold on to your new racket all through the game, but how often are you allowed to employ it usefully? How often does your partner cry "Mine!" and bundle you out of the way? Is there pleasure in playing football badly? You may spend the full eighty minutes in your new boots, but your relations with the ball will be distant. They do not give you a ball to yourself at football.

But how different a game is golf. At golf it is the bad player who gets the most strokes. However good his opponent, the bad player has the right to play out each hole to the end; he will get more than his share of the game. He need have no fears that his new driver will not be employed. He will have as many swings with it as the scratch man; more, if he misses the ball altogether upon one or two tees. If he buys a new niblick he is certain to get fun out of it on the very first day.

And, above all, there is this to be said for golfing mediocrity—the bad player can make the strokes of the good player. The poor cricketer has perhaps never made fifty in his life; as

[*] **A.A. MILNE** (1882-1956) is internationally renowned as the author of *Winnie the Pooh,* but he established his reputation writing humorous essays for *Punch* and other literary magazines. Several of Milne's spoofs feature hotly contested golf matches between fearless protagonists (including Milne himself), who valiantly battle through thick and thin while shooting astronomically high scores. In this essay, Milne explains why golf is the best game at which to be bad.

soon as he stands at the wickets he knows that he is not going to make fifty today. But the eighteen-handicap man has some time or other played every hole on the course to perfection. He has driven a ball 250 yards; he has made superb approaches; he has run down the long putt. Any of these things may suddenly happen to him again. And therefore it is not his fate to have to sit in the club smoking-room after his second round and listen to the wonderful deeds of others. He can join in too. He can say with perfect truth, "I once carried the ditch at the fourth with my second," or "I remember when I drove into the bunker guarding the eighth green," or even "I did a three at the eleventh this afternoon"—bogey being five. But if the bad cricketer says, "I remember when I took a century in forty minutes off Lockwood and Richardson," he is nothing but a liar.

For these and other reasons golf is the best game in the world for the bad player. And sometimes I am tempted to go further and say that it is a better game for the bad player than for the good player. The joy of driving a ball straight after a week of slicing, the joy of putting a mashie shot dead, the joy of even a moderate stroke with a brassie; best of all, the joy of the perfect cleek shot—these things the good player will ever know. Every stroke we bad players make we make in hope. It is never so bad but it might have been worse; it is never so bad but we are confident of doing better next time. And if the next stroke is good, what happiness fills our soul. How eagerly we tell ourselves that in a little while all our strokes will be as good.

What does Vardon know of this? If he does a five hole in four he blames himself that he did not do it in three; if he does it in five he is miserable. He will never experience that happy surprise with which we hail our best strokes. Only his bad strokes surprise him, and then we may suppose that he is not happy. His length and accuracy are mechanical; they are not the result, as so often in our case, of some suddenly applied maxim or some suddenly discovered innovation. The only thing which can vary in his game is his putting, and putting is not golf but croquet.

But of course we, too, are going to be as good as Vardon one day. We are only postponing the day because meanwhile it is so pleasant to be bad. And it is part of the charm of being bad at golf that in a moment, in a single night, we may become good. If the bad cricketer said to a good cricketer, "What am I doing wrong?" the only possible answer would be, "Nothing particular, except that you can't play cricket." But if you or I were to say to our scratch friend, "What am I doing wrong?" he would reply at once, "Moving the head" or "Dropping the right knee" or "Not getting the wrists in soon enough," and by tomorrow we should be different players. Upon such a little depends, or seems to the eighteen-handicap to depend, excellence in golf.

And so, perfectly happy in our present badness and perfectly confident of our future goodness, we long-handicap men remain. Perhaps it would be pleasanter to be a little more certain of getting the ball safely off the first tee; perhaps at the fourteenth hole, where there is a right of way and the public encroach, we should like to feel that we have done with topping; perhaps—

Well, perhaps we might get our handicap down to fifteen this summer. But no lower; certainly no lower.

Golfski by Frank Reynolds. One of the premiere golfing cartoonists, Reynolds began contributing to *Punch* in 1909 and became the magazine's art editor in 1920

ROYAL CORTISSOZ

ON DUFFERDOM

from *Nine Holes of Golf,* 1922*

IT IS A BROAD AND GOODLY LAND, THIS LAND OF DUFFERDOM, ITS LIMITS MARKED ONLY by those of the golf-courses of the earth. Does not its representative figure deserve some consideration? Voltaire would appear to have answered that question as far back as the eighteenth century. To the duffer who reminded him that even duffers must exist he sweetly replied: "I don't see the necessity." There are commentators who stand by that assertion to this day. They are a little too austere. After all, the duffer is a friendly human brother. Suppose he does top his ball. Nevertheless, hath not a duffer "hands, organs, dimensions, senses, affections, passions"? He abounds in error, of course. Mayhap he is fairly steeped in it. But—

> *Errors, like straws, upon the surface flow;*
> *He who would search for pearls must dive below.*

Let us then dive into dufferdom, an adventure which especially appeals to me at the moment, for as I write the welkin is ringing with the exploits of Mr. Jesse Sweetser, winner of the national amateur championship at Brookline. His scores read like the "Eroica." The talk is all of birdies and eagles. If one listens to it long enough one develops the suspicion that golf has been lifted to a Homeric plane and that only Homeric men are fit to play it. But the duffer remains—immovable, monumental. We may turn to him, if only in the spirit of Calverley and his invocation to that "grinder who serenely grindest":

> *'Tis not that thy mien is stately,*
> > *'Tis not that thy tones are soft;*
> *'Tis not that I care so greatly*
> > *For the same thing played so oft:*

"The Agony of the Two-Footer": *Country Club* magazine cover for May 1931

FACING PAGE
Missing a Short Putt in Four Languages by Frank Reynolds

---

* **ROYAL CORTISSOZ** (1869-1948), who provides this homage to the duffer, was a prominent American art historian. He served as art critic for the *New York Tribune* for 53 years, beginning in 1891. Cortissoz was decidedly conservative and Victorian in his artistic sensibility and a notable critic of the work of the Post-Impressionists.

But I've heard mankind abuse thee;
And perhaps it's rather strange,
But I thought that I would choose thee
For encomium, as a change.

I thought sympathetically of the duffer not long since, in the midst of a conversation which seemed to leave him no excuse for being at all. The merits of a certain hole had come up for discussion. It was a hard hole, so hard as to be denounced by some as merely tricky and demoralizing. When I had the chance I submitted the problem to the one august authority in these matters, the wizard and wonder-worker, Mr. Charles MacDonald. He settled it in a saying which I suppose might well be inscribed in letters of gold over the portal of every golf-club. "Well," quoth he, "a golf-course is designed for men who can play golf." How everlastingly true and inspiring that is! It sums up the rigor and the glory of the game. It erects the only authentic standard. To question it would be to speak disrespectfully of the equator. Your golf-course is unquestionably made for the men who can play golf. But, on the other hand, if one may with diffidence hazard a small interrogation: Who on earth keeps it going?

Establish yourself comfortably on the bench at the first tee and watch one foursome after another drive off. Keep careful tally for an hour or so. Then tot up the numbers of those who played golf and the numbers of those who launched themselves blithely into dufferdom. The latter region has, I verily believe, a density of population rivaling that of a Chinese slum. Only, you see, there is nothing in the least slummy about it. On the contrary, its sunny slopes are rich in elbow-room, which is used in ecstasy by happy myriads. Not for them the sublime certainty of a Sweetser. In Grantland Rice's account of that young old master's dazzling triumph I find this tribute to his flawless form: "He reminded you of a well-oiled machine that could continue to send the ball on a straight line for year after year, until the cogs wore out." The duffer's straight line may be, in a sense, an annual affair, but there is otherwise nothing of the inerrant machine about him. He hasn't a cog to his name. But, I ask again, is it the Sweetsers of this world who keep a golf-course going?

What a deadly place a golf-course would be if they did! It might please a Henry Ford to watch the functioning of a long procession of well-oiled machines, and the rest of us would, for a time at least, be so keen about the spectacle that the committee would probably have to cover up the rough with bleachers. But sooner or later the duffer would rebel. He would be first fascinated, then stupefied, and, finally, bored to death. He would want the feel of a club in his hand. For a little while he would shrink from the ordeal of making a birdie whether he liked it or not. He would end by making that hole in seven and glorying in his shame. Driven to bay by an irate committee, he would ask the members if they would not, for one thing, look at the statistics. What these would reveal in the personnel of almost any club I have already hinted. And there are other items that build up a formidable economic total. Who is it that buys and tries every new club? The duffer. Who is it that buys and tries every new ball? The duffer. Who is that enters sweepstakes after sweepstakes, counting his defeats as naught? The duffer. And so on. He is the rock-ribbed foundation of golf. If he were to withdraw, the golf-courses of the country would infallibly bust up. But I would not dwell importunately on his status as an economic factor. Indeed, I would far rather emphasize his traits as a sportsman, his significance as an embodiment of the immortal spirit of the game.

The duffer is nothing if not an artist. To quote my friend Rice again: "In golf there is no man who is ever master of his destiny." That is the artist's point of view. The duffer has it, rejoices in it, and is steadily faithful to it. For him the very mutability of the game constitutes one of its strongest lures. He faces each game as an experiment, just as a painter faces a new

"The Tiller Girl": *Life* magazine cover for November 5, 1931

canvas. The thing may prove a botch. It may prove a jewel. And this artistic conception of the struggle involves a peculiarly exquisite satisfaction in victory, when victory comes off. Rarity, most of us will admit, is one of the supreme blisses of life. The passion for it is a universal attribute of human nature. There are few men who would not exchange a fixed income for a thumping windfall. It must be, beyond all peradventure, a delectable thing to play six holes in succession in authoritative, automatic par, to play them with the assurance of an acrobat sailing over six elephants at a jump. But, frankly, can this trained, rehearsed achievement equal in high emotion the unexpected prowess of the duffer who makes a two where he never made a two before? The question answers itself. It is like painting a composition that has always got confused and suddenly having it resolve itself into perfect clarity.

Think of the moments in a duffer's progress in which he perceives that it really is progress that he is making. He studies Sarazen's grip until he feels like Laocoon in the coils of the serpent, but some fine morning he actually gets the hang of it. He wrestles with his brassie in despair, and then, unaccountably, discovers that it is the best club in his bag, the one with which he can do incredible things. He makes a two-shot hole out of an interminable brute that had previously done nothing but deface his score. And, mark you, he does all this by the process which is the very life-blood of the game, by the process of trying. I never could comprehend the complacent scorn of the Pharisee in golf for the duffer at whom he directs his gibes. When the potentate misses a two-foot putt it is, I suppose, because the solar system shifted just then. The duffer in the same case is assumed to have sounded the depths of ineptitude and receives the opprobrium due to personal guilt. I have seen numbers of very good players do fairly terrible things. We read about them even in historic matches. Nobody is blamed for them. Neither should the duffer be blamed. What he needs is not blame but sympathy.

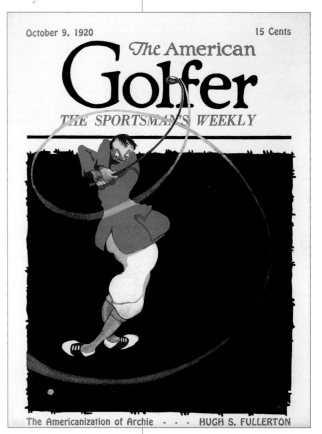

The American Golfer cover for October 9, 1920

If he deserves it for anything it is for the all-essential virtue which he shares with the elect, the virtue of resolution. You couldn't dampen his ardor with a cloudburst. Sweetser, Hagen, Sarazen, Ouimet, and the rest fight on through thick and thin. So does the duffer. That is where he is on all fours with the best of them, though his resources, compared with theirs, are like windblown sparks compared with the roaring flame at the heart of the conflagration. He may top his ball, as I have said before, but he will tackle it again, and again, and yet again. His head is bloody but unbowed. Jocund as the morning, after unnumbered rebuffs, he swings his driver from the first tee and with Gilbert sings:

> Roll on, thou ball, roll on!
>> Through pathless realms of Space
>>> Roll on!
> What though I'm in a sorry case?
> What though I cannot meet my bills?
> What though I suffer toothache's ills?
> What though I swallow countless pills?
>> Never you mind!
>>> Roll on!

H.N. WETHERED

THE PERFECT CHAMPION

from *The Perfect Golfer*, 1931*

POPE, IT MAY BE REMEMBERED, POINTED OUT VERY CLEARLY THE IMPOSSIBILITY OF A state of perfection:

Whoever thinks a perfect work to see,
Thinks what ne'er was, nor is, nor e'er shall be.

This conclusion applies, of course, to the artist as well as to the work he produces. In fact, the quotation of Pope's maxim would be altogether superfluous, if it were not necessary to begin by first eliminating the idea that the perfect golfer has existed or is ever likely to exist.

Joyce Wethered, daughter of writer H.N. Wethered, came as close to achieving perfection as any golfer. Here she receives the trophy for winning the British Ladies' Amateur

Pope's generalization is a valuable contribution to the subject in introducing a point of considerable interest, because it limits us to an abstraction or standard which helps us to judge the greatest that have lived amongst us or the greatest that may appear in the future. At the same time it is necessary to appreciate how disastrous it would be if such an untoward event as the appearance "out of the blue" of the perfect golfer were to materialize.

It is a moot point whether golf takes rank most prominently as a science, an art, or a game. The three things are totally different, yet in one way or another golf combines them all. Whichever view is taken the result is bound to be imperfection, and that is one of the saving factors in the situation.

Regard it, for example, from the point of view of science. I happened to dip casually into Sir James Jeans's *The Mystery of the Universe*, in order to discover what light, if any, modern physics could throw on the theoretical question of perfection, because obviously the universe must be perfect and only man is vile. I innocently thought that such a work would be easily understood by the mediocre intellect, since scientists and theologians have freely quoted from its pages, with equal satisfaction to their convictions. The result, however, was bewildering in the extreme.

* **HERBERT NEWTON (H.N.) WETHERED**, born in 1869, was an English painter and art historian, who wrote about many subjects, including golf, with seemingly limitless erudition and ease. Wethered was also, as it turns out, the father of Joyce Wethered, perhaps the greatest woman golfer of all time, and Roger Wethered, the English amateur champion. In his very original book, Wethered explains the impossibility of perfection in the golfer, and why it is best that way.

Relatively speaking, relativity remained to me a closed book. But there were a number of references to pushes, pulls and twists by which the universe is drilled into obedience to the one universal law that faintly suggested what human effort is up against. It partly explained the difficulties under which even golfers labour. They are impelled this way and that, whirled through space at an immense speed which has been compared with a violent wind blowing through a grove of trees at 10,000 miles a second. We are even told that it would make no practical difference if the speed were a hundred times greater. But when I came to the proposition that "the second should be able to fill the same hole as the first" I stopped, because, so far as golf was concerned, this was inconceivable.

The quest for perfection: Tiger Woods with the Claret Jug after winning the British Open at St. Andrews in 2000

Therefore science in some of its aspects cannot help us greatly. The only feasible conclusion is that in a universe too perfect to be otherwise than mysterious there are factors too insurmountable to allow any human effort, whatever its nature, to arrive at perfection—certainly enough to establish the perfect golfer as a scientific impossibility.

Regarded, secondly, as an art, golf becomes a simpler problem. After Einstein we can refer to Ruskin. We find to our relief that artistically imperfection has actually many claims to assert itself as a virtue. Ruskin went so far as to demonstrate that no good work can be perfect and that the demand for perfection is a misunderstanding of the ends of art. Like all truths that appear at first to be paradoxical, this is an arresting and comforting thought. If we had hitherto imagined that perfection was the ultimate goal of great art we were mistaken: we have to recognize that it is not even an ultimate good. The principle must indeed have a universal application. Golf, being a very distinctive and subtle art, has been distinguished from time to time by the appearance of many remarkable artists; but we have had reason occasionally to congratulate and pat ourselves on the back when we discover that "they are only human after all." That is to say, their human frailty is at once their salvation, our own satisfaction and their great attraction. "Were she perfect, one would admire her more, but love her less."

Should we not after all feel a slight disappointment if any of us were too immaculate? Some people might be disposed to dispute the suggestion; but they would assuredly be mistaken. There appear to be, to outward view, a privileged few who seem so near the ideal as to have reached the very threshold, to have touched the outer fringe, to have brought the cup to the lip. It is indeed the occasional slip which redeems the situation and makes for the very essence and charm of the game. If the ideal executant of shots were to appear on the scene, golf would have ceased to function as a game or to have any meaning as a sport. There would be no fun in it; it would have become a cold inhuman fact devoid of loveliness and abstraction—the last thing to be desired. In order for a game to retain any warmth or jollity it is necessary that it should be a little faulty, full of delicate transitions, an artistic blending of accuracy and error, with just sufficient elusiveness to make us welcome the pursuit and unmurmuringly dispense with the capture. Games are meant to be an exercise of skill not unassisted by the element of fortune. They are, fortunately for us, definitely fallible. They represent a conflict between opposing forces, none of which are quite equal and never completely efficient. There would be no point in playing games at all if there was not at least the remote but glorious chance of the odds being upset and the weaker side occasionally winning. If one side were omnipotent, the result would be a farce. A tiny ray of hope always exists, although it may be the faintest glimmer. The only point of considering

Bobby Jones holds his trophy after winning the U.S. Amateur at Minikahda Golf Club, Minneapolis, in 1927

perfection at all, therefore, is that it has a certain importance as representing a somewhat extravagant ideal, a fleeting fantasy of the mind which, so far as realities are concerned, is eminently enjoyable.

As a more direct and practical illustration of this truth I can recall one of the exhibition matches which the members of the old Triumvirate, assisted by one other rather humbler fourth, used to play with delightful regularity all over the country. Vardon on the occasion of which I am thinking was in such dazzling form that he left the others struggling so far behind that Taylor, in moody desperation, declared with emphasis that this was "not golf." In making this audacious statement Taylor was undoubtedly inspired: he uttered a profound philosophic truth. Such play, if it had been prolonged indefinitely, would have lost any meaning and become a mere negation. If Vardon or any other artist could sustain an uninterrupted sequence of immaculate play whenever he pleased, he would at once have become an anarchist of the deepest dye. The system of the world would have been destroyed and become an offence against nature. We must cut our ambitions to a lower standard altogether. We must content ourselves with occasional joy-rides which can be pleasant enough; but perpetual joy-rides would be a crime and, if generally adopted, would have to be suppressed by Act of Parliament.

ARNOLD HAULTAIN

THE SECRET OF GOLF

from *The Mystery of Golf,* 1908*

XXXIX

BUT THE ULTIMATE ANALYSIS OF THE MYSTERY OF GOLF IS HOPELESS—AS HOPELESS AS the ultimate analysis of that of metaphysics or of that of the feminine heart. Fortunately the hopelessness as little troubles the golfer as it does the philosopher or the lover. *The summum bonum* of the philosopher, I suppose, is to evolve a nice little system of metaphysics of his own. The *summum bonum* of the lover is of course to get him a nice little feminine heart of his own. Well, the *summum bonum* of the golfer is to have a nice little private links of his own (and, now-a-days, perhaps, a private manufactory of rubber-cored balls into the bargain), and to be able to go round his private links daily, accompanied by a professional and a caddie.—It would be an interesting experiment to add to these a psychologist, a leech, a chirurgeon, a psychiater, an apothecary, and a parson.

XL

To sum up, then, in what does the secret of golf lie? Not in one thing; but in many. And in many so mysteriously conjoined, so incomprehensibly interwoven, as to baffle analysis. The mind plays as large a part as the muscles; and perhaps the moral nature as large a part as the mind—though this would carry us into regions deeper even than these depths of psychology. Suffice it to say that all golfers know that golf must be played seriously, earnestly; as seriously, as earnestly, as life.

XLI

But may not also the simple delights of the game and its surroundings, with their effect upon the mind and the emotions, be included under the allurements and the mystery of golf? My knowledge of links up to the present is limited, but on mine there are delights which, to me a duffer, are like Pisgah sights: hills, valleys, trees, a gleaming lake in the distance, a grand and

---

* **ARNOLD HAULTAIN** (1857-1941) was born in India and spent some years in England before emigrating to Canada. Haultain wrote essays, love poems, and a book of aphorisms; but it is *The Mystery of Golf* that endures as a cult classic. In his essay "Golf in Writing," John Updike reserves the highest praise for Haultain, concluding: "Amid the torrents of writing that have entertained golfers, Haultain's essay retains the freshness of a mountain spring."

The Montagu Course at the Fancourt Resort in South Africa, facing the Outeniqua Mountains

beloved piece of bunting lending gorgeous colour to the scene; a hospitable club-house with spacious verandas and arm-chairs; shower-baths; tea and toast; whisky and soda; genial companionship; and the ever-delectable pipe. Has anyone yet sung these delights of the game? the comradeship in sport, the friendliness, the community of sentiment, the frankness of speech, the goodwill, the "generosity in trifles"? Or of the links themselves? the great breeze that greets you on the hill, the whiffs of air—pungent, penetrating—that come through green things growing, the hot smell of pines at noon, the wet smell of fallen leaves in autumn, the damp and heavy air of the valleys at eve, the lungs full of oxygen, the sense of freedom on a great expanse, the exhilaration, the vastness, the buoyancy, the exaltation? . . . And how beautiful the vacated links at dawn, when the dew gleams untrodden beneath the pendant flags and the long shadows lie quiet on the green; when no caddie intrudes upon the still and silent lawns, and you stroll from hole to hole and drink in the beauties of a land to which you know you will be all too blind when the sun mounts high and you toss for the honour!

OGDEN NASH

THE STRANGE CASE
OF THE AMBITIOUS CADDY

from *The Face Is Familiar*, 1940*

Once upon a time there was a boy named Robin Bideawee.

He had chronic hiccups.

He had hay fever, too.

Also, he was learning to whistle through his teeth.

Oh yes, and his shoes squeaked.

The scoutmaster told him he had better be a caddie.

*He said, Robin, you aren't cut out for a scout, you're
cut out for a caddie.*

*At the end of Robin's first day as a caddie the caddymaster
asked him how he got along.*

*Robin said, I got along fine but my man lost six balls,
am I ready yet?*

The caddymaster said No, he wasn't ready yet.

*At the end of the second day the caddymaster asked
him again how he got along.*

*Robin said, My man left me behind to look for a ball
on the fourth hole and I didn't catch up to him
until the eighteenth, am I ready yet?*

Travel poster for Le Touquet, the
fashionable golf resort founded by
British golfers on the coast of
Calais. Circa 1925

* **OGDEN NASH** (1902-1971) was America's virtuoso of humorous poetry and parody, famed for his imaginative and almost
acrobatic rhyming skills. Nash's poems frequently appeared in *The New Yorker*, where he also worked as an editor.

A humorous *Country Club Magazine* cover for May 1930 depicts the caddie's burden

FACING PAGE

Caddie Willie was painted by C.H. Robertson about 1839. The subject is William Gunn, also known as Daft Willie Gunn. He caddied in the early part of the nineteenth century and is shown here at Bruntsfield Links in Edinburgh. Gunn lived in a garret in Edinburgh during the golf season, then returned to his native Highlands. In 1820, he returned to the Highlands and never reappeared. As was customary at the time, Gunn received cast-off clothing from the players for whom he carried, but it was his peculiar habit to wear all the clothes at once. He wore several jackets with the sleeves cut off, three pairs of trousers, and three bonnets sewn together

The caddymaster said No, he wasn't ready yet.

*Next day Robin said, I only remembered twice to take
the flag on the greens and when I did I wiggled it,
am I ready yet?*

The caddymaster said No, he wasn't ready yet.

*Next day Robin said, My man asked me whether he
had a seven or an eight on the water hole and I
said an eight, am I ready yet?*

The caddymaster said No, he wasn't ready yet.

*Next day Robin said, Every time my man's ball stopped
on the edge of the bunker I kicked it in, am I ready yet?*

The caddymaster said No, he wasn't ready yet.

*Next day Robin said, I never once handed my man the
club he asked for, am I ready yet?*

The caddymaster said No, he wasn't ready yet.

*Next day Robin said, I bet a quarter my man would
lose and told him so, am I ready yet?*

The caddymaster said, Not quite.

*Next day Robin said, I laughed at my man all the way
round, am I ready yet?*

*The caddymaster said, Have you still got hiccups, and
have you still got hay fever, and are you still learning
how to whistle through your teeth, and do your
shoes still squeak?*

Robin said, Yes, yes, a thousand times yes.

Then you are ready, said the caddymaster.

Tomorrow you shall caddy for Ogden Nash.

THE FIRST GIANTS

CHAPTER TWO

THE FIRST GIANTS

L ike all men who came first and achieved greatness in their time, the first golfers hold a particular fascination. These were the men who popularized the game, who literally spread the gospel of golf at a time when the sport was just starting to branch out beyond Scotland, and who laid out courses that are still being played and admired today. We cannot help wondering what these pioneers were really like as men and as golfers. In reading about them, we learn that their legacy is based as much on their strength of character as their accomplishments as golfers. The early professionals seem to have been more purely about the game than their contemporary counterparts, not because they were less motivated by material pursuits, but because they appear to have had no existence apart from golf. They were born into the game in the early Scottish acropolises of the sport—St. Andrews, Musselburgh, North Berwick, and Prestwick. They caddied for the gentlemen golfers and became professionals at a time when that was considered at best a semirespectable living. It offered an escape from the traditional trades of their fathers as masons, gardeners, joiners, and laborers, and for many it proved a ticket to emigrate to America.

There is something inspiring in the stories of these men. The greatest of them live on through the writings of authors like Bernard Darwin and Horace Hutchinson, and through images burnished into old glass photographic plates that upon close inspection reveal not only the patterns of their tweeds but also the depth of their characters.

The first of the legendary golfers was Allan Robertson of St. Andrews, "born in the purple of equable temper." Robertson was famed both for his prowess as a player and his skill in manufacturing feathery balls from a tophat-full of boiled goose feathers. In every photograph and painting, the red-jacketed Robertson looks alert of mind and nimble of movement. He died young, in 1859, but his great disciple, "Old Tom" Morris, led a long

PAGES 36, 37

The Tee Shot, dated 1877, is by the golfing artist
Francis Powell Hopkins, also known as "Major
Shortspoon." The painting shows a group of
golfers on the first tee at Westward Ho! (Royal
North Devon Golf Club) and was commissioned
by John Dun, Captain of Royal Liverpool, who is
shown driving. Fourth from the left is Major
Hopkins himself. Hopkins left the army in 1864
and retired to North Devon, where he took
up golf. He was not a particularly good player,
but he proved to be a strong influence on his
young caddie at Westward Ho!, J.H. Taylor

life that spanned the era from Robertson to the prime of the "Great Triumvirate" of Harry Vardon, J.H. Taylor, and James Braid.

Old Tom's importance to the game is difficult to exaggerate. He appears in almost every nineteenth century photograph of St. Andrews. In his younger days, he and Robertson battled the Dunns of Musselburgh in home and away matches that still linger in golfing lore, and later Morris was pitted in famous matches against his archrival, Willie Park. By the time of his death in 1908 at age 87, he had become a revered figure and the very embodiment of golf at St. Andrews.

Morris impressed and inspired generations of golfers with his decency, modesty, and devotion to the game. Charles Blair Macdonald, one of the founding fathers of golf in America, came under Morris's spell shortly after he arrived at St. Andrews in 1872 from his native Chicago to attend the University. Donald Ross, the progenitor of Pinehurst, apprenticed to Morris as a greenskeeper in 1893, not long before Ross emigrated to Boston and went on to design hundreds of courses in the United States. A young Philadelphian named Albert Tillinghast met Morris while spending the summer at St. Andrews in 1896 and struck up a lasting friendship. Tillinghast went on to design such famous American courses as Winged Foot, Baltusrol, Quaker Ridge, and the Black Course at Bethpage.

Old Tom's son, Young Tom, surpassed his father as a golfer, setting the then record of 77 on the Old Course, bettering Robertson's famous 79 in 1859. Young Tom demolished the competition in the Open Championship, earning the championship belt after winning in 1868, 1869, 1870, and 1872. He died on Christmas Eve of 1875, when he was only 24. Legend has it that Young Tom died of a broken heart, grief-stricken at the death of his young bride in childbirth.

These early heroes were clearly extraordinary golfers. They were able to record scores in the upper 70s or low 80s on difficult links courses in the days when the fairways were maintained by grazing sheep. They played with what by today's standards were primitive clubs and with balls made from gutta percha, a Malayan tree gum.

The Great Triumvirate of Vardon, Taylor, and Braid were all born within a few months of one another in 1868-69. They were the Palmer, Nicklaus, and Player of their time. Of the three, Vardon was the most astonishing — the first truly great golfer even by modern standards. Described as of "placid and serene disposition," Vardon was an unlikely genius from Grouville, on the Isle of Jersey. Vardon won six British Opens between 1896 and 1914, a record that still stands. He was so unerringly accurate that an apocryphal anecdote has been handed down that when he played a round in the afternoon, his ball would land in the divots he had taken in the morning's round. In old film clips of Vardon's swing, the folding of the arms on the backswing seems unorthodox by current standards, but his tempo and action through the ball are completely modern and flawless.

Like Vardon, J.H. Taylor came from humble circumstances and rose to great heights, winning the Open Championship five times and finishing runner-up another five. Taylor had a forceful, extroverted personality and educated himself by reading Dickens, Boswell, and Kipling. He never forgot his start as a small caddie on the links of Westward Ho!, one of the first and most romantic golf courses in England, set on the remote coast of Devon. After serving as the professional at Royal Mid-Surrey for forty-seven years, Taylor lived out his days in a bungalow overlooking his beloved Westward Ho! Looking out over the expanse of the course when he was ninety years old, Taylor remarked: "This is the finest view in all Christendom."

Braid was a lanky, laconic Scot who lashed the ball with a power that has been described as "Divine Fury." Braid had a quiet, shrewd wisdom that he dispensed for close to fifty years as the professional at Walton Heath, outside London, until his death in 1950. His cottage down the road from the course was called Earlsferry, after the small village in Scotland where Braid was born. The "Sage of Walton Heath" also designed a number of fine golf courses, most notably the King's and Queen's courses at Gleneagles, and would have designed more but for a fear of sea voyages.

In 1913, the epicenter of the golfing world suddenly shifted from the Old World to the New when Francis Ouimet, an unheralded American amateur, won the U.S. Open at The Country Club in Brookline, outside Boston. Ouimet, a mild-mannered twenty-year-old, had grown up across the street from The Country Club, where he had learned the game as a caddie, following in the footsteps of his older brother Wilfred. What made Ouimet's victory so truly remarkable and revolutionary was that after four rounds of play in regulation, he stood tied with Vardon and Ted Ray, the overwhelmingly favored British professionals. The next day, he vanquished the Englishmen in an 18-hole play-off. This golfing version of David and Goliath was the single most important event in establishing golf as an American game.

In the old photographs, Ouimet looks like a milquetoast standing next to the mature Vardon and the massive, long-hitting Ray, but he had the mental fortitude and inner calm needed to prevail. Ouimet was also a man of principle. His friends urged him to replace his caddie, the doughty, ten-year-old Eddie Lowery, with a more experienced caddie for the final round. Ouimet refused, knowing it would break Lowery's heart. Lowery went on to become a fine amateur golfer. He moved to southern California, became a successful businessman, and sponsored a number of promising young golfers on the pro tour, including Ken Venturi.

While Ouimet's triumph stirred the public imagination, he was not the first American to break the British domination of the game. That distinction belonged to Walter Travis, who won the British Amateur at Royal St. George's in 1904. Travis emigrated to America from Australia, and took up the game when he was thirty-five years old. The "Old Man" was a dour, angular figure with a coal-black beard and an Alpine hat, who hit the ball impossibly straight and spurred himself to victory through a relentless will to succeed.

JAMES BALFOUR

PROFESSIONALS
AND CADDIES

from *Reminiscences of Golf on St. Andrews Links,* 1887*

LET ME RECALL SOME OF THE PROFESSIONALS AND THE OLD CADDIES. FIRST AMONG these was Allan Robertson, the prince of golfers. He and his father and grandfather had been ball-makers, when feather balls were the only balls, for more than a hundred years. He was a short, little, active man, with a pleasant face, small features, and a merry twinkle in his eye. He was universally popular, not a bit forward, but withal easy and full of self-respect. He generally wore a red, round jacket, and played constantly with gentlemen, both in matches of great importance, and in those that were only more or less important. His style was neat and effective. He held his clubs near the end of the handle, even his putter high up. His clubs were light, and his stroke an easy, swift switch. With him the game was one as much of head as of hand. He always kept cool, and generally pulled through a match even when he got behind. He was a natural gentleman, honourable and true. He died of jaundice on 1st September 1859, when only about the age of forty-four, much regretted.

Next to him was Tom Morris, now called "Old Tom." He began by helping Allan to make balls, and was very nearly his match at the game. His style I need not describe, as all golfers of the present generation know it. He still flourishes on the Links, and is still a fine player. He and Allan were together the champions of their day. Tom has always been respected, not only as a player, but for his excellent private character. There is an anecdote told of him, which I have great pleasure in repeating, because it is so honourable to him. On one occasion he was playing with the late Captain Broughton, and when at the high hole Tom's ball was lying in the bents that used then to surround it, the Captain said, "O Tom, you had

A studio portrait of Old Tom and Young Tom Morris, circa 1875

---

* **JAMES BALFOUR** became a member of St. Andrews in 1842, when the links was the preserve of "a few resident gentlemen and some occasional strangers from Musselburgh, Perth and Leith." His slim but resplendent volume of reminiscences provides warm and witty sketches of many of the unusual personalities who frequented the Old Course in the nineteenth century. His son, Leslie Balfour-Melville, was a champion all-around athlete for Scotland, who won the British Amateur in 1895 and was elected captain of the Royal and Ancient Golf Club of St. Andrews in 1906.

Old Tom Morris, with his ever-present pipe, views a ladies' competition at St. Andrews on the putting area known as the Himalayas. 1894

better give up the hole; you are playing three more, and you are in the bents." "No," said Tom; "I'll perhaps hole this." "I'll give you £50 if you do." "Done with you, Captain," said Tom, and he holed it! Next morning the Captain brought £50, and handed it to him. "What is that?" said Tom. "What you won yesterday." "Take it away," exclaimed Tom, "I would not touch it. We were both in fun." This was exceedingly creditable to Tom, and showed real good feeling. If he had taken it, no one could have found fault with him, and £50 offered to a tradesman was a temptation. I had often heard the story from Campbell of Saddel, who was present, and other gentlemen, but I once asked Tom himself about it. He said it was all true, and he laughingly added, "You should have seen the Captain's face when I went in!" Tom, as is well known, is now the Conservator of the Links, and has a large establishment for making both clubs and balls.

His son, "Young Tommy," was perhaps the best player that ever appeared on the green. He was a tall, handsome athlete, and unmatched at all parts of the game. His victorious career began in 1867, when he was sixteen. It continued without a break till his early death in 1875. During these eight years he exhibited as remarkable a display of golf as has ever been seen. When he died, at the early age of twenty-four, he was buried in the ground at the old Cathedral, where a monument has been erected to his memory by contributions from sixty golfing clubs.

Among the older professionals were the twin brothers Dunn of Musselburgh. They were beautiful golfers, and fought many pitched battles with Allan and Tom. They ran them hard, but could not beat them.

Referring to the caddies, there were Sandy Pirie, who carried for Sir Hope Grant, and Sandy Herd, who carried first for Saddell and afterwards for Mr. Whyte-Melville; Charlie Thomson, once a crack player, as most of the others were; and many other most respectable men. But perhaps the greatest character among them was "Lang Willie." He was very tall, about six feet two, with bent knees and a slouching gait, a tall hat, swallow-tailed blue coat, and light trousers. His look was rather stupid, but he was in reality wide awake. He used to insist that he drank nothing but sweet milk, greatly to Allan's amusement, who knew better. He was much taken out as an instructor of beginners, and when one met him and asked him how his pupil was getting on, he had always the same stereotyped answer, "Jist surprisin'," which might mean either very well or very ill. On one occasion he was teaching one of the Professors of the University the noble game. But the said Professor was not a promising pupil. As he hammered away, sometimes "missing the globe," sometimes topping the ball, or cutting up large divots of turf, Willie fairly got out of patience, and said to him, "You see, Professor, as long as ye are learning thae lads at College Latin and Greek it is easy work, but when ye come to play golf ye maun hae a heid!" On another occasion he was carrying in a match, when, at the last hole coming home, the party had to wait till a young man on horseback had passed along the road. The rider was not very steady in his saddle, and Willie quietly remarked, "I think that lad is a wee lowse in the glue"—a phrase which golfers will understand who have felt the inconvenience of their club-head getting rather loose. Willie had more than one stroke of paralysis. I could not help being amused at his description of the first one. I asked him one day what he had felt. He said he felt nothing, but in the morning his sister said to him that his face was twisted. "I said to her, 'Nonsense, lassie,' but when I sat down to my parritch my jaw wouldna work!" At last he was overtaken by a fit on the Links, was carried home in an omnibus, and died in about twenty minutes after.

Hay Erskine Wemyss, Captain of the Royal & Ancient in 1854, tees off at St. Andrews. The young Old Tom Morris is on the far left and Allan Robertson is third from the right. The caddie carrying the clubs is Bob Kirk

ALLAN ROBERTSON:
THE UNBEATEN
from *British Sports and Sportsmen,* 1908*

Allan Robertson, painted by
Charles Lees, in the Scottish
National Portrait Gallery

FACING PAGE
Allan Robertson, "The Prince
of Golfers"

ONE OF THE GREATEST GOLFERS WHO EVER LIVED, ALLAN ROBERTSON WAS BORN AT St. Andrews in 1815. He came of a golfing race, his father and grandfather being professionals and feather-ball makers. He was teethed with a golf-club handle.

In all the details of the game Allan showed remarkable science. He seemed to "play with" the ball. The little "26" he could humour with his toy club as he pleased. His putting was simply marvelous. He would "wile the wether intae the hoose." He used no sand for a tee, and when playing against the wind he would place his ball on the backward slope, and, picking it up clean, would make it skim along, "to cheat the wind," until it ultimately rose, swallow-like, before dropping from the carry.

Unruffled in temper, he could bear anything. Of the game he might say to his partner, "It's aye feching against ye," yet he was of the most cheerful disposition, born in the purple of equable temper and courtesy. To gentle and simple he was the same, as polite as a Brummel and as politic as a Metternich.

Yet he could chuckle when his opponent got bunkered. "It appeals," he would remark, with a twinkle in his eye, "to the higher feelin's o' humanity to see yer rival in a bunker." He was the most artful miser of putts when it suited him. But he played always with his head. With him golf was a passion.

Consternation seized the little man when the boy Robert Patterson showed him the first gutta-percha ball in 1845. He would buy up all the old balls and burn them, for he thought his living was to be ruined. Yet in the end he began to realize that the substitute was surely coming into the game.

Allan Robertson was never beaten—this is a proud epitaph. His matches are classical. When twenty-eight years of age he had to tackle the most brilliant driver of his day, Willie Dunn, of Musselburgh. The match was one of twenty rounds, of eighteen holes each, over St. Andrew's links, each round counting one point. This Allan won by two rounds and one to play.

* The editor of the entries on famous golfers in this two-volume folio of biographies of the great British sportsmen is **HORACE HUTCHINSON** (1859-1932). Hutchinson's home course was Royal North Devon, which is popularly known as Westward Ho!, after the novel of that title by Charles Kingsley. Hutchinson was a leading player in his day, who won the British Amateur Championship in 1886 and 1887, but he is best known as a prolific author and proselytizer of the game. He became the first English-born captain of the Royal & Ancient (R&A) in 1908.

Foursomes were then more popular, and in 1849 a great match was played by Allan and Tom Morris against the brothers Dunn on the three links Musselburgh, St. Andrews, and North Berwick, success on each course to count a point. They scored victory on their respective greens, and at North Berwick the great deciding contest took place. After a most exciting match the Dunns were four holes ahead and eight to play. Yet the innate strength of character, marvelous training, and pure skill of Allan and Tom came to their aid just when needed. By an unequalled game of brilliancy Allan and Tom won the first and second, halved the third, won the fourth, halved the fifth, and won the sixth, making them all square and two to play. These two Allan and Tom won, and thereby came out victorious in one of the most extraordinary and brilliant matches in the whole annals of golfing.

Considering the narrow course, the bad state of the putting greens, the oppressively grassy hollows, the ever-threatening bunkers, the awe-striking whins [gorse], Allan's famous round of St. Andrew's links in 1859 in seventy-nine strokes is sufficient evidence of his exceptional powers as a golfer. This score will keep up his name for ever; it is probably equal to sixty-nine now.

These are mere specimens of Allan's consistently successful play. He had some most curious clubs, fitted for different situations. There was the Doctor, Sir Robert, the Thrawcruck, the Frying-pan, and others. He was not a long driver, but he never missed a shot, and he kept the line with undeviating accuracy. It was in his complete mastery of every club that his brilliant success lay. When within reach of the hole it mattered nothing to him whether the stroke required a driver or an iron, he made direct for it, with frequently a good chance of holing out in his next.

Allan Robertson, "The Prince of Golfers"

After the champion's sudden death, when only forty-four years of age, the Royal and Ancient Golf Club entered the following in their minutes, dictated by the late Principal Tulloch: "This meeting has heard with regret of the death of Allan Robertson, and they desire to record in their minutes the opinion universally entertained of the most unrivalled skill with which he played the game of golf, combining a ready and correct judgment with most accurate execution. They desire also to express the sense of the popularity of his whole conduct and unvarying civility with which he mingled with all classes of golfers, of his cordiality to those of his own, of his integrity, his happy temper, and the anxiety he always manifested to promote the comfort of all who frequented the links."

TOM'S EARLY DAYS

from *The Life of Tom Morris*, 1908*

This portrait of Old Tom Morris was painted by Sir George Reid, Scotland's leading portrait painter, when Tom was almost 81 years old. It hangs in the Royal & Ancient Clubhouse at St. Andrews

FACING PAGE
Old Tom Morris in front of the venerable stone clubhouse of the Royal & Ancient Golf Club of St. Andrews

TOM MORRIS WAS BORN, AS ALREADY MENTIONED, AT ST. ANDREWS ON THE 16TH OF JUNE 1821.
"You were born in St. Andrews, of course?"

"Ay, an' I've lived in it a' my days, except for the years when I was greenkeeper at Prestwick. I was born in the North Street. My father was a St. Andrews man, employed as a letter-carrier. He played golf in his spare time."

His father's name was John Morris, a much-respected man in St. Andrews in his day. His mother was Jean Bruce, but so far I have not been able to find out any particulars in regard to her parentage. She belonged to Anstruther. Tom was born in a house on the north side of the west end of North Street, which is still standing. . . .

He began to handle a club as soon as he could toddle, and very likely his first balls would be "chuckie stanes," with which the streets of St. Andrews abounded. By-and-by he would get as far as the links.

"I've played gowf close on eighty years, and that's longer than most folk get living. I began on the links doon there as soon as I could handle a club, and I have been doing little else ever since. My faither and mither lived in the North Street, and as soon as I could gang I and the other laddies would be doon on the links with any kind of a club we could get, and any old ball, or even a bit of one—balls werena sae cheap in thae days as they are the noo, though they're dearer again since the new rubber-core ball came in."

"You would be grown up before the old feather balls were displaced by the gutta?"

"That's true," he replied. "I began to play when I was six or seven, maybe younger. You ken a' St. Andrews bairns are born wi' web feet an' wi' a golf-club in their hands. I wad be driving the chuckie stanes wi' a bit stick about as sune's I could walk. When I left school I started how to learn to make golf balls. They werena much like the golf balls we have now, the old 'featheries,' but they could play fine afore the wind. I learnt to mak' clubs and balls wi' Allan Robertson. I was busy making 'featheries' when the gutta balls came into fashion, and a bonnie business he and I had owre the change. Allan couldna abide the sight of the new ball at first.

---

* **REVEREND W.W. TULLOCH** of Maxwell Church, Glasgow, wrote the classic biography of Old Tom Morris. Tulloch was elected a member of the Royal & Ancient on April 13, 1870. His father, Reverend John Tulloch, Principal of St. Mary's College, St. Andrews, served as Chaplain of the R & A and wrote the inscription that appears on Young Tom Morris's memorial in the churchyard of the St. Andrews Cathedral.

One day I was out playing with Mr. Campbell of Saddell, and I got stint of balls. Mr. Campbell gave me a gutta to try. Coming in, we met Allan, and somebody told him that I was playin' a grand game with one of the new balls. Allan said nothing at the time, but I saw he didna like it, and when we met in the shop we had some words about it; and this led to our parting company, and I took to making balls on my ain account."

DAVID OWEN

OLD TOM MORRIS

from *My Usual Game*, 1995*

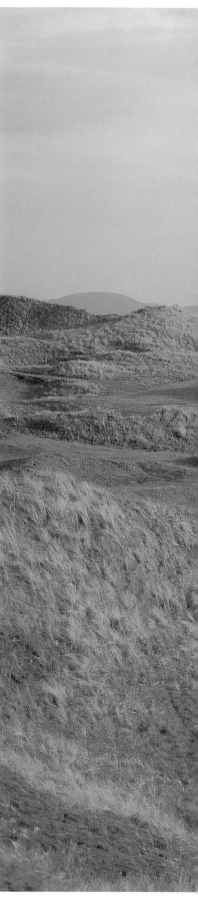

Rosapenna Golf Club, a beautiful and remote links that overlooks Sheephaven Bay in County Donegal, Ireland, was first laid out by Old Tom Morris in 1891

THE PREVAILING GHOST OF ST. ANDREWS IS THAT OF OLD TOM Morris, who served as the greenkeeper of the Old Course and the head professional of the Royal & Ancient for much of the second half of the nineteenth century. In photographs, Morris looks like a squat, grumpy Confederate general, with what appears to be a tobacco-juice spit trail down the center of his biblike white beard. He was a legendary clubmaker, course designer, and champion. He was the runner-up in the first Open Championship, in 1860, and he was the outright winner in four of the next seven—the last when he was forty-six years old. (His son, known as Young Tom, won the following four.) Old Tom didn't invent golf, but he might as well have. He made a huge impression on the game, not only at the Old Course, whose modern configuration he helped to shape, but also at the numerous courses he designed.

In Morris's youth, the Old Course was significantly different from the way it is today. When Morris, as a young boy, first began playing, there were just nine greens, each with a single hole. A golfer played to each of the nine holes heading out from the clubhouse, and then to each of the same nine on the way back in. Returning golfers had priority over those heading out. In 1832, when Morris was eleven, the greens were expanded, and a second hole was cut in each—a change necessitated by growing congestion on the course. Even with twice as many holes in the ground, traffic jams were common. Virtually no distinction was made in those days between greens and tees—or for that matter, between greens and tees and fairways and rough. The entire course was referred to as "the green"; the "putting ground" referred initially to the area within a club's length of the hole. Golfers teed up within a few paces of each hole,

---

* **DAVID OWEN** (b. 1955) is a frequent contributor to *The New Yorker* and a contributing editor of *Golf Digest.*

Old Tom Morris sitting in the first automobile in St. Andrews, circa 1902. The car, an Argyle, was owned by George Rusack, the son of the founder of Rusack's Hotel adjoining the Old Course. Posing in front of the car is Old Tom's granddaughter, who was married to George Rusack

originally using a pinch of sand extracted from the hole itself. Putting was a highly inexact art that had more in common with modern chipping. You didn't stroke your ball into the hole; you knocked it in the hole's general direction, over a surface that today would cause grumbling if it were presented as fairway.

At the age of eighteen, Morris was apprenticed to Allan Robertson, a renowned ballmaker and one of the dominant golfers of his time. A ball in those days consisted of a small leather pouch stuffed with a hatful of boiled goose feathers. Cramming in all those feathers—using a variety of wedges, pokers, and prods—was a difficult art. Finished balls were then hammered into roundness. Well-made ones were quite hard and durable, as long as they remained dry. They were also expensive, since a good ballmaker might manage to turn out just three or four in a day. Morris and his golfing partners spent a lot more time looking for stray balls than you or I do.

These early balls, later called featheries, didn't behave the way modern golf balls do. They didn't go as far (although a good golfer could still occasionally whack one two hundred yards), they curved prodigiously, and they were easily affected by the wind. These characteristics helped give rise to a golf swing that was longer, flatter, and looser than any good modern swing. The idea was to take a big, wide, below-the-shoulder turn and sweep the ball off the ground, launching it on a low, hooking trajectory that would minimize the effects of the wind and maximize the amount of roll (as well as reduce the likelihood of damaging the precious balls). Variants of this swing—which is often called the St. Andrews swing—dominated golf until the twentieth century, and they still linger in the Scottish gene pool.

Beginning around mid-century, the feathery was fairly rapidly displaced by the gutta-percha ball. Gutta-percha is a kind of resilient Malayan tree sap; like balata, which it resembles, it is a crude cousin of rubber. It was harvested with rapacious enthusiasm by forest-leveling nineteenth-century British colonials, and it found its way into a variety of products, including dental prostheses, doll parts, electrical insulation, and golf balls. Gutta-percha balls traveled farther and lasted longer than feather-filled balls, and they were easier and cheaper to manufacture. Feathery makers rightly saw gutta-percha as a threat to their livelihood. Allan Robertson made Tom Morris promise never to play with one; when he heard that Morris had betrayed him, Robertson sent his protégé packing. Morris became the green-keeper at Prestwick, on the opposite coast of Scotland. He did not return to St. Andrews until 1865, by which time the feathery was a thing of the past.

The gutta-percha golf ball underwent a rapid and complicated evolution, with many interesting dead ends. Ball makers discovered that balls with surfaces that had been scored, dented, dimpled, or otherwise scarified had aerodynamic advantages over the earliest, relatively smooth versions. They also discovered that solid balls were less satisfactory than balls with something other than gutta-percha in their middles. Over the years, the golf ball industry attracted its share of wacky inventors. There were balls with blobs of mercury or free-moving steel weights in their centers; there were balls whose surfaces were scored with curving grooves that were intended to produce a flight like that of a rifle bullet; there were balls with pits, and balls with bumps, and balls that appeared to have been covered with wicker. The most important innovation—the change that signaled the beginning of golf's true modern era—was that of Bertram Work and Coburn Haskell, two Ohioans who, in the late 1890s, made the first golf ball with a core made of tightly wound elastic. Their invention was significantly improved a couple of years later, when a man named John Gammeter (who, like Bertram Work, was an employee of the B.F. Goodrich Company) invented a machine to wind the cores, which had originally been wound by hand. Haskell golf balls (as they were known) worked so much better than other balls that they became the new standard within a very few years. No golf ball innovation since that time has instituted as big a change over what had been before.

Old Tom Morris lived long enough to play with Haskells. He died in 1908, at the age of eighty-seven, having competed in his last British Open just twelve years before. Tragically, Young Tom Morris died long before his father did. He died in 1875, at the age of twenty-four, after becoming deeply depressed following the death of his wife in childbirth. Golf pilgrims can visit the Morrises' graves, in the cemetery at the crumbling old St. Rule's Cathedral, on Sundays, when the Old Course is closed. (Old Tom used to say that golfers might not need a day of rest, but the course did.)

SANDY HERD

THE SOLLYBODKINS

from *My Golfing Life*, 1923*

I BEGAN GOLF IN THE WAY THAT IS BEST FOR THE LIKES OF ME.

As a man climbs a hill or a ladder, I started at the bottom. Even before being a caddie I was a "bare-fitted" golfer of the street, in the grey old city of St. Andrews, like "Andra" Kirkaldy before me, and others before us—and since our day.

Golf found me "daft aboot it," as my mother used to say when I could not afford to buy clubs or balls. But I was not kept from playing on that account. Shinty sticks, cut from

North Street, St. Andrews, facing the twin spires of the ruined Cathedral and the remains of the tower of St. Rule's Church, circa 1850. A double-masted ship is docked beside the pier

Strathtyrum Woods, where Mr. Blackwood of the famous Edinburgh firm of publishers lived, and champagne corks served well enough to begin with. The corks were gathered from a refuse heap behind the Royal and Ancient Golf Club, for in those days I suppose champagne flowed more freely than now.

In proof that we laddies had something in our noddles, let me tell you how we made these corks carry against the wind, of which St. Andrews gets more than its share. The matter troubled us a long time, till at last we hit on the plan of inserting screw-nails in the corks to give them weight. A local blacksmith put some in for us to start with.

Looking back on that boyish device now, I smile to think that we were the real pioneers of the cored ball. Great was our joy on discovering that it now became possible for us to drive nice long, low balls through the wind with our shinty sticks. Even today I rather think that is the best shot in my bag.

I remember that we gave the cork balls, with their screw-nail cores, the name of "sollybodkins." How we arrived at this name I cannot tell you now. Most likely it was just a name that came to our lips, a pure invention of boyhood. . . .

Our links was the cobbly streets of St. Andrews, with the lamp-posts for flags. My opponent and companion was Laurence Auchterlonie, destined, like myself, to be a champion

* **ALEXANDER "SANDY" HERD** (1868-1944), who writes about golfing on the streets of St. Andrews, was a colorful and popular St. Andrews professional who came up through the caddie ranks. Herd never achieved the success of the members of the Triumvirate, but he came close, winning the British Open in 1902 and finishing runner-up three times. He toured the United States with J.H. Taylor and for many years was the professional at Coombe Hill, outside London.

in his day. Laurie went to America afterwards, and won the Open Championship there. Returning to St. Andrews, he took to teaching the young idea, and the old idea, too, how to drive.

I have always held to the opinion that the real reason why the professional is able to more than hold his own against the amateur, who often plays quite as much and perhaps more, is that the professional has behind him the advantages of the caddie's upbringing.

This means much. Golf is a game with such possibilities that there is little chance of a championship for the player, professional or amateur, who does not begin in his teens. If earlier still, as in my case, all the better. It is never too soon to start golf, and, in another sense, it is never too late either.

"I suppose, Herd, you were reared with a 'spoon' in your cradle," said a well-known amateur to me at Coombe Hill, when I had a played a succession of my favourite shots to the green with the spoon. He was not far wrong, for I hardly remember anything earlier in my life than those "bare-fitted" golf matches with sticks and corks at the cathedral end of North Street.

Sandy Herd (far left) on the third hole at Coombe Hill Golf Club in 1921 with the Prince of Wales, who became Edward VII, and the Duke of York (far right), who became George VI when Edward abdicated. They both took lessons from Herd at Coombe Hill, a fashionable club in Surrey

A CADDIE
AT WESTWARD HO!

from *Golf: My Life's Work*, 1943*

Portrait of J.H. Taylor from the club-house of the Royal Mid-Surrey Golf Club, Richmond, England, where Taylor was the professional for many years. The original painting was destroyed when the clubhouse was consumed by fire in 2001

WHENEVER A GOLF COURSE IS LAID DOWN IT BRINGS IN ITS WAKE A CERTAIN AMOUNT of prosperity to the district, and especially to the younger members of the community. It can be imagined what it meant to Westward Ho! in the year 1857 in that remote corner of Devon. The establishment of a golf links there, at that early date, is in itself a romantic episode. The story has been told so many times—it has become almost legendary as part of English golfing history—that it requires no recapitulation by me. But that it was a most fortunate combination of circum-stances the history of Westward Ho! since that time bears eloquent testimony. Indeed, it may be also true to say that had the golf links not been made there, Westward Ho! would have remained a somewhat insignificant and remote spot well off the beaten track despite its safe bathing, glorious sands and unique Pebble Ridge. The coming of the links saved the place from possessing only these not inconsiderable attractions. I doubt whether Charles Kingsley's celebrated and romantic novel, *Westward Ho!*, would have done the trick of putting the place in the category it is today had not the links greatly helped its fame and probably enhanced its sales and well-deserved popularity. The novel gave it the name, but the links established its fame as one of the most natural and testing seaside golfing adventures in the country. With its delight-ful springy turf, sun kissed, and nurtured for centuries by the soft breezes off the Atlantic, and its natural hazards, it remained for many years unchallenged and unchallengeable in the problems that it set.

I have said that a golf course brings many advantages to the younger folks, affording them a diversion from the ordinary routine and outlook. This has proved true during the last

* **JOHN HENRY (J.H.) TAYLOR** (1871-1963) was born at Northam in North Devon. As a young boy he caddied at Westward Ho! and worked as a boot boy in the home of Colonel Hutchinson, the father of the illustrious golfing author Horace Hutchinson. Taylor left school when he was only eleven but wrote his very fine and lively autobiography on his own. He won five British Opens and was still good enough to finish fifth in the 1924 Open, when he was fifty-three years old.

The Quadrilateral: (left to right)
J.H. Taylor, James Braid, Harry Vardon,
and Sandy Herd

few decades, so it can be imagined how true it was in 1857. Here was something entirely new in thought and conception which inspired not only the young but the older folk as well, something that was gratuitous, adding very materially to the struggle for a livelihood that ordinary agricultural work could not furnish. Here was something beyond the ambition of driving a straight furrow, scaring birds or spreading muck, that gave the opportunity of earning occasionally some easy money and additional recreation. In short, the coming of golf changed the outlook for the very poor, and in the early Victorian years, how badly this was needed!

It will be seen that golf was established at Westward Ho! as a flourishing local amenity some years before I was born, so it is true to say that I grew up surrounded by its healthy atmosphere. I do not know how old I was before I became aware of the fact, but as soon as I became aware of anything, golf had entered into my life. At school I became dimly conscious that some of the older boys were known as "half-timers" and allowed the afternoon off to carry clubs if a job could be found. I envied the privilege, hoping in a year or so to join the ranks of the more fortunate, but, at the moment, had to be content with Saturdays and holidays, of which I made full use. Every hour of my spare time I scurried to the links in the hope that some accommodating golfer would take me on. I was a small delicate boy with almost snow-white hair, which gained for me the nickname of Wig. I was not very pushful

Hole 14 at Ganton Golf Club, Yorkshire, England, the course where Harry Vardon became famous

Three of his six championships were won after the introduction of the rubber-cored ball in 1902, but it was with the gutty, before his serious illness, that he was supreme. Had it not been for that breakdown in health his tally of victories would surely have been much longer; it was after his illness that his putting began to betray him. The modern golfer believes that Vardon was always a bad putter, but this is not so. He was not an outstanding putter, nor had he quite the same graceful ease on the green as elsewhere, but he was at least a very good approach putter and a competent holer-out. He could never otherwise have accomplished half of what he did.

Vardon's record is so long that it must be severely compressed. He was born on 9 May 1870, at Grouville in Jersey. He learnt the game there as a caddie and continued to play after starting work as a gardener at the age of thirteen. His younger brother, Tom, was the first to go out into the world, as assistant professional at St. Annes, and it was he who induced Harry to apply for a post at Ripon in 1890. In 1891 he moved to Bury in Lancashire and thence to Ganton in 1896. He had first played in the Open championship at Prestwick in 1893 (the year of Taylor's debut), but it was at Ganton that he became famous. In the spring of 1896 Taylor, who had been two years champion, came there to play Vardon a match and went home defeated by 8 and 6 and full of his conqueror's praises. A month or two later they tied for the Open championship at Muirfield and Vardon won the play-off by three strokes. In 1897 he fell away slightly, but won again at Prestwick in 1898 and the following year won with perfect ease at Sandwich. These were his two supreme years. It was in 1899 that he beat Taylor, who was playing well, by 11 and 10 in the final of the tournament at Newcastle, County Down, and also beat Willie Park in one of the outstanding matches of his life.

In 1900 Vardon set out on what was practically a year's tour of the United States, though he broke it to come home to defend his title in the championship and finished second to Taylor at St. Andrews. In America, where golf was still young, he traveled from end to end of the country playing an enormous number of matches and causing great enthusiasm; he hardly lost a match and won the American championship.

But the hard work of the tour took its toll, and it is doubtful if he was ever so brilliant again. After being twice runner-up in the championship to Braid and Herd respectively, he won at Prestwick in 1903 with a total of 300, and this he regarded as the best of all his achievements, since he was so unwell that he nearly fainted several times in his last round. Soon afterwards he had to spend some time in a sanatorium and made a more or less complete recovery. In 1905 came the second great match of his career, in which he and Taylor beat Braid and Herd over four greens by 11 and 10. Their play at Troon, where they won fourteen holes, was astonishingly fine, and so it was on the last links, Deal, though Vardon had had a haemorrhage the night before and was not really fit to play at all.

There followed a period of comparatively lean years and then, to the general joy, Vardon won again at Sandwich, in 1911, beating Massy so convincingly in playing off the tie that the great French player gave up at the 35th hole. The year 1913 saw Vardon tie for yet another Open championship, that of the United States, at The Country Club at Brookline. This was the historic occasion on which Mr. Francis Ouimet, then little older than a schoolboy, beat Vardon and Ray after a triple tie and may be said to have founded the American golfing empire. It was unquestionably a disappointing blow for Vardon; yet he won his sixth championship next year at Prestwick, beating Taylor by three shots. The two were drawn together on the last day and took the whole of a rather obstreperous crowd with them so that it was a marvel that they could play as they did.

When the war was over Vardon was almost fifty and his victorious days were of necessity nearly over. Yet in 1920 he tied for second place in the American championship, one stroke behind Ray. In all human probability he would have won had not a fierce wind come up as

he was playing the last few holes and was tiring fast. That was his final achievement, and during the later years of his life his health put golf to all intents and purposes out of the question. He bore the deprivation with philosophy and sweet temper, enjoying teaching when he could not play and always anxious to watch the younger players. This he did with an eye at once kindly and critical, being a staunch conservative and unshaken in his conviction that the greatest qualities of the game had departed with the gutty ball. From 1903 to the end of his life he was professional to the South Herts Golf Club at Totteridge, where he was an oracle and an institution. He has left a name affectionately regarded by everyone and an ineffaceable mark on the game of golf.

Harry Vardon teeing off at the U.S. Open at the Chicago Golf Club in 1900. Vardon won the tournament, finishing two strokes ahead of J.H. Taylor

HARRY VARDON

LEARNING THE
GAME ON THE ISLAND
OF JERSEY

from *My Golfing Life*, 1933[*]

I WAS BORN ON MAY 9TH, IN THE YEAR 1870, AT THE LITTLE town called Grouville, which is a few miles from St. Helier on the island of Jersey. My parents were both natives of Jersey, and my father was a gardener there all his life. We were a large family, consisting of seven boys and two girls. My brothers, George, Phil, and Edward, all came before me, Tom and Fred coming after in that order. . . .

Mr. Boomer, the father of those two fine golfers, Aubrey and Percy, was the schoolmaster at the village school in Gory which we all attended. I am sorry to say that learning had little attraction for me in those youthful days, and my old schoolmaster had certainly no reason to be proud of me at that time. Schooling was very different at this period from what it is today. Our parents paid the sum of twopence a week for each of us to attend the school, and both my brother Tom and myself were guilty on many occasions of playing truant. The one subject more than any other which I disliked was the lessons in French. Whenever it was possible to do so, we would spend the school fee on something more enjoyable than French. I particularly remember that at the arithmetic lessons Mr. Boomer, for some reason or other, always placed me at the head of the class. It was not long, however, before I was at the other end, and it was perhaps only right that I was considered the dunce of the school. I recall, on one occasion, when I had hastily passed from the top to the bottom of the class, that Mr. Boomer told me to go and clean out his rabbit hutch. To some boys this might have served as a punishment, but to me it

The 12th hole at Royal Jersey Golf Club, Grouville, Isle of Jersey, with medieval Mont Orgueil Castle in the background. Founded in 1878, it is where Harry Vardon was introduced to the game. A memorial marker next to the fairway reads: "Within Putting Distance of this Stone Harry Vardon (1870-1937) the Great Golfer Was Born"

[*] **HARRY VARDON** (1870-1937), the supreme golfer of his era, did much to popularize the game in America through his exhibition tours in 1900, 1913, and 1920. In 1920, when he was 50, Vardon finished one shot behind Ted Ray in the U.S. Open at Inverness. In addition to *My Golfing Life*, Vardon also produced another very fine autobiographical work called *The Complete Golfer*, written with Henry Leach.

was a happy release. Anything in the nature of activity appealed to me far more than the acquiring of knowledge. I was as enthusiastic as it was possible to be in any games that were played, and one of my first ambitions was to excel at cricket. I retained my liking for this fine sport all my life and played often in my later years.

It was when I was about seven years of age, in the year 1877, that the event which was eventually to map out my career for me came to pass. The people of Grouville lived a quiet, undisturbed life, and had, as is usual with those who live a somewhat uneventful existence, a whole-hearted respect for the sanctity of the Sabbath Day. It so happened, however, that this should be the very day which a small party of strange gentlemen selected to make their appearance on the common land. They brought with them instruments with which to survey and mark out places for tees and greens. The story that preparations were being made to play a game called golf was soon spread about the village. The indignation of the tenant farmers was quickly aroused, and they thought out and discussed every possible means by which they could expel these trespassers from the common land. Indignation spread through Grouville, and these golfers were regarded in anything but a friendly light. Having obtained the necessary authority and permission from the constable of the parish, their position was quickly made secure, and from that day a new feature entered into our lives. The natural state of the land was so perfect that little work needed to be done, and possibly no good golf course was ever so easily made. The grass was short and springy as it is on all good sea coast links. Sand was plentiful and natural hazards were everywhere. The grass was of such splendid texture that it was only necessary to put the mower and roller over the selected space and superior putting greens were made. I have, personally, supervised and laid out many golf courses during my career as a professional golfer, but never have I seen a first-class course so easily designed. A little inn close by was immediately renamed the Golf Inn. Thus the headquarters of the Jersey golfers was established. That in brief was the start of the Royal Jersey Golf Club.

The links when they were completed proved to be excellent, better in fact than they are today. One of the chief reasons for this is that most of the bunkers have since been filled with clay, which spoiled them. It was necessary to do this to prevent the sand from them being blown over the course by the strong winds which frequently sweep across the island. When everything was in readiness for play, many golfers came over from England to enjoy this, to us, new game.

I was first introduced to golf along with many other boys my age. We were enticed to carry the clubs of the visitors. As far as I can remember we did not think very much of this new game, but after carrying a few times we began to see possibilities in it. It was only natural that we should wish to try our hand at playing ourselves. This, however, was not so easily done. There were many difficulties to be overcome. Apart from not having any links on which to play, we had no clubs or balls. So keen, however, were we to play that these difficulties were eventually solved. As a start, we laid out our own course, consisting of four holes, each about fifty yards in length and for boys of our age quite good enough. When we had marked out and made out teeing grounds and smoothed out the greens, there next came the question of balls, and in the absence of real gutties we decided the most suitable article for us was the big white marble, which we call a taw, and which was about half the size of an ordinary golf ball. The question of clubs was a more difficult proposition, and caused a good deal of anxiety in our young minds. On reflection, I think great credit is due to us for the manner in which we solved this problem. As nothing would be really satisfactory except a club which resembled a real golf club, it was necessary to make many experiments before we were able to get the desired article. As a start, we decided that we must use as hard a wood as possible, and the wood from a tree which we called the "Lady Oak" was suitable for our purpose. First of all, we cut a thick

Harry Vardon's famous swing

branch from the tree, sawed off a few inches from it, trimming this piece as near as we possibly could to the shape of the heads of the drivers of those players for whom we had been carrying. As splicing was impossible, it was agreed that we must bore a hole in the center of the head. This we did with a red-hot poker. The shaft sticks were made of thorn, white or black, and when they had been trimmed and prepared, we proceeded to fit them into the holes. Then after tightening them with wedges, the operation was complete. All things considered, we were able to hit a long ball with this primitive driver. After a time, as we grew more accustomed to making these clubs, we became quite expert young club makers. The brassies seen on the links had made a big impression upon us, and as we had experienced some trouble with our oak heads—since they were green, they were rather inclined to crack—we eventually decided to sheathe the heads entirely with tin. This was not an easy thing to do, and we were further handicapped by the fact that our fathers declined to lend us their tools, and we had to "borrow" them when the proper occasion presented itself.

These tin-plated drivers, which we called our brassies, were an enormous improvement over our original clubs. So expert did we become at making them that occasionally one would stand out as far superior to the others. The reputation of the maker of this club was assured, and he did a good business in making clubs for others. A big price in marbles was demanded and paid to this expert club maker.

We played our elementary kind of golf whenever possible. I recall that most of our best games took place in the moonlight, which was exceedingly bright in Jersey, and enabled us to see quite well. We arranged competitions on the medal system by scores, and frequently got threes at our fifty-yard holes. With our home-made clubs and little white taws, coupled with our lack of knowledge and extreme youth, I can truthfully say that our efforts were very creditable. This was my introduction to the game of golf.

AL LANEY

SEPTEMBER 20, 1913

from *Following the Leaders*, published posthumously, 1991*

Francis Ouimet, painted by Thomas E. Stephens, wearing the red jacket of the captain of the Royal & Ancient Golf Club of St. Andrews. In 1954, Ouimet became the first American to be elected captain of the R & A

Thousands of dripping rubber-coated spectators massed about Ouimet, who was hoisted to shoulders while cheer after cheer rang out in his honor. Excited women tore bunches of flowers from their bodies and hurled them at the youthful winner; hundreds of men strove to pat him on the back or shake his hand.

—From the New York Times, *Sept. 21, 1913*

If I lived a thousand lives I should never again be spectator to such an amazing, thrilling and magnificent finish to a championship....You tell me that a child like this has beaten our Vardon and Ray for a real championship? When we can go for week-end golfing trips to Jupiter and Mars, I will perhaps believe that your little Ouimet has won today. There will never be another like it. When we are old men little golfing children will ask us to tell them again the romantic story of the 20th of September in 1913.

—Henry Leach, *English golf correspondent, writing in the* New York Times, *Sept. 21, 1913*

THERE HAD BEEN RAIN THAT SATURDAY IN BROOKLINE, MASS., BUT THE DAY WAS HOT AND humid 2,000 miles away in Pensacola, and a faint lazy breeze came in off the Gulf of Mexico. About the time the scenes described above were unfolding to astonish, delight, and dismay, I, a teenage lad, was making my slow way through the heat toward the office of the *Pensacola Journal*, to which I had been apprenticed for after-school and Saturday-night service.

I wore, more than likely, the common uniform of the teenager of the day—flat, peaked cap; straight, tapered pants ending just below the knees; home-made cotton blouse with tight neckband for collar; long, ribbed black stockings held up by elastic bands; and either high-laced shoes or white sneakers called easywalkers. Knickerbockers for boys were just coming in, and I stopped to admire a suit in the window of White and White's store. It was a beautiful gray suit with a belted Norfolk jacket, but the tag said $10, an enormous price that I knew was forever beyond me. Only a few of these suits with knickers had appeared in

* **AL LANEY** (1896-1988) traveled from New York to Paris in 1924, where he enlisted as a reader to James Joyce, who was nearly blind by that time. After Joyce dismissed him because he could not read Italian, Laney joined the staff of the *Paris Herald*, and later became a sportswriter for its parent paper, the *New York Herald Tribune*. Laney covered sports, particularly golf and tennis, for the *Herald Tribune* until it folded in 1966. He excelled in writing sensitive profiles of sports figures great and small. In this essay, written from his perspective as a teenager growing up in Pensacola, Florida, Laney recollects the impact of Ouimet's victory in the U.S. Open.

Francis Ouimet playing the 8th hole at Royal St. George's Golf Club in Sandwich, England, during the 1914 British Amateur Championship

the town or in school, and most boys of my acquaintance would jump right over knickers into long pants, the badge of manhood if not of maturity. I was, in fact, already saving up to buy my own first pair of long pants.

Under the overhanging balconies and upper stories of the building that shaded the sidewalks of the main street and gave an effect of a covered arcade, it was a little cooler, and my dawdling progress would have seemed aimless to an observer. There were few to observe, however. As I dawdled, I wrestled with a puzzle to which I was not to find the answer for many years. Why, I wondered, was I giving up a rare and precious free afternoon? Saturdays were grand, the only completely free time when I was really on my own, since all the news sources I usually checked after school were closed. The time could have been devoted to any number of pleasant schoolboy pursuits, such as sailing a boat, exploring any one of the many inlets and bayous off the harbour, or swimming at Bayview Park where many boys and girls gathered for fun and games. Actually, this particular Saturday afternoon had been set aside for a long, uninterrupted session of tennis that I had anticipated eagerly.

I could explain to myself no more than to my deserted companions why I had to disrupt our plans. They thought I'd suddenly gone strange, for they did not at all understand why I

Francis Ouimet with Harry Vardon
and Ted Ray after defeating them
in the 18-hole playoff

could be changed. This would not be the last golf story I would handle. I was dreaming the
sort of waking dreams that adolescents are forever dreaming.

Reality was the usual nightly stop at the Busy Bees Café where Angelo would just be
taking the buns and donuts from the oven and would respond as always to a tap on the side
door to the kitchen. The bun, all steaming from the oven, was fair exchange for the newspaper hot from the press, and both carried the thrill of things newly born. The smell of bread
fresh from the oven has still the power to bring back the approaching dawn of the
September day that was a prelude to golfing and newspaper adventures when, just lurching
out of boyhood, life was all anticipation, shimmering with the promise of wonderful things,
and when time was an invention of the elderly. An age was ending, the innocent period
before 1914. An affluent, confident, and, in a way, complacent era in American life was
about to turn into the hell of trench warfare, poison gas, and other horrors let loose.

BONNIE LINKS

CHAPTER THREE

BONNIE LINKS

Links golf is an affair of the heart, not of the mind. Like all matters of the heart, the allure of playing the great links courses is not always easy to define, and perhaps not completely rational, but the feelings they engender in the heart of the golfer — of sheer joy, indeed, of exaltation—are real.

Links courses are laid out on the land that literally links the sea to the mainland. These courses, which twist and tumble restlessly through windblown sand dunes, are common in the British Isles and Ireland but quite rare in the United States. There are some basic differences between playing links golf and the forested, inland courses more familiar to American golfers. In links golf, the vicissitudes of wind and weather play much more of a role and require us to shape our shots. The sandy soil produces very firm, fine turf, so our blows must be a bit crisper, and there is more emphasis on the ground game and running the ball up to the green instead of flying it to the pin. Everywhere we look we behold Serengetis of green and tawny sea grasses, emblazoned with outcroppings of canary yellow gorse, waiting to ensnare our stray shots.

The essence of links golf, though, is something of a more romantic and rarefied aspect. The inescapable sense of the sea and dunes, even if we seldom see the ocean, lends an air of adventure, the potential for the unexpected, and the desire for golfing conquest that is not found elsewhere. Links courses, because they present the type of terrain that inspired golf in the first place, and remains the best suited for it, are also the most natural and seemingly effortless in their design. In most cases, to describe these courses as designed is something of a misnomer, for they evolved over time in accordance with the peculiar physiognomies of the coastal landscape. These courses, each with its own proud personality, seem as if they have always been there and always will be. We are captivated by their tousled beauty, confounded by their fickle hazards, and comforted by their immutability.

H.N. WETHERED

THE PERFECT LINKS

from *The Perfect Golfer*, 1931*

WHEN ONE IS IN A REFLECTIVE MOOD ABOUT GOLF COURSES — AND IT IS SURPRISING
how vivid the memories can be—the mind is full of associations, each of them attached to
some particular links. To take only a few at random, starting from north to south, there is
Dornoch, the most northerly of any importance, with its blue seas competing with the rival
and modulated azures of the distant hills. One remembers, too, for some unknown reason,
that almost every green on the course is guarded by one defiant and exclusive seagull which
resents bitterly human intrusion as a personal affront and in the intervals when the green is
unoccupied stalks in solitary and indignant grandeur round its private domain. Let us hope
the majestic bird is intent upon finding, and devouring, leather-jackets.

Then there is Gleneagles, either wrapped in brilliant colour or else muffled in dripping
rain and heavy skies, while much of the immediate surroundings are reminiscent of a
Japanese garden with the little kiosks crowning the smaller hills and the quaint bridges
crossing pools fringed with bamboo which stirs and rustles in the breeze. St. Andrews is
remembered for its views over the estuary towards Dundee and the aerodrome, with the
planes circling like gnats against the dappled sky in the sunlight, unless by chance a
Turneresque effect of black clouds and lights glinting over the landscape heralds an
impending downpour. Taking a backward glance, the drifts of yellow gorse set off the grey
old town, "the town of the scarlet gown," against the opposing skyline.

In the West is Prestwick, impressive in quite a different way with its Cardinals,
Himalayas and Alps and the intimidating railway at the 1st hole. A friend once asked me to
guess the conundrum how he was twice out of bounds at that hole and still got a three.
Naturally I was at a loss. Then he explained that the first was a clear shot out of bounds
towards the signal box; the second took the same direction but struck a sleeper and carried on
to the green where a putt landed the ball in the hole. Such an elegant start against all regu-
lations resulted—rightly or wrongly according to the point of view—in winning the medal.

Turnberry I remember chiefly for the evening light over the sea, the lighthouse and the
conical island with its associations of a famous onion. Here, by the way, is a chance for the

Railway poster for St. Andrews
by Frank Mason, who was an accomplished painter of marine subjects

FOLLOWING PAGES
The 9th hole at the PGA
Centenary Course, Gleneagles,
Perthshire, Scotland

* In this passage from *The Perfect Golfer*, Wethered surveys golf courses from the Highlands of Scotland to Land's End
in Cornwall with a painter's eye. His other works include *From Giotto to John: The Development of Painting*, and a short
history of gardens that begins with the Garden of Eden.

GARDEN G. SMITH

THE LINKS OF EAST LOTHIAN

from *The World of Golf,* 1898*

THE COUNTRY LYING EAST OF EDINBURGH AND LEITH, WHICH IS BOUNDED ON THE south by the Pentlands and Lammermoors, and which stretches as far as Dunbar, along the southward shore of what Victor Hugo calls, in a moment of inexplicable aberration, "La cinquième de la quatrième," or Firth of Forth, is one of the most interesting parts of Scotland. From the agricultural point of view it is one of the richest, and the smiling and prosperous aspect of its well-tilled fields, its acres of waving grain or green-shawed turnips, its comfortable farm-houses, red-tiled, and encircled with sheltering trees and well-filled stackyards, amply justify its title to be called the "Garden of Scotland."

In the light of history, no Scottish district is richer in suggestion, or more stimulating to the imagination, and Scott and Stevenson, who knew and loved it well, have laid in it the scenes of some of their most enthralling romances.

Standing on Gullane hill, under one's eye lies the arena on which many of the most striking events of Scottish history were enacted, and the landscape seems peopled with the great actors who played their parts in it. The rock of Edinburgh, with Arthurseat for foreground, is visible on the western sky-line, and the strath between the Pentlands and the Forth was the channel, up and down which ebbed and flowed for many centuries, the tide of invasion and war. Along here, never to return, passed James the Fourth, with the flower of Scottish chivalry, to fatal Flodden Field. Close by also, in the '45, marched Bonnie Prince Charlie and his Highlanders, flushed with the victory of Prestonpans. From this hill one could have seen the smoke of battle. Tantallon, the stronghold of the Black Douglasses, is but a mile or two away, on the rocks beyond North Berwick, while many a ruined tower and "ancient fortalice," dotted over the plain, speaks eloquently of the stirring times of forays, and harryings, and Border warfare. Turning seawards the prospect is no less rich in romantic suggestion.

The Macdonald Boys, painted in the mid-eighteenth century by William Mosman. The brothers are Lord Macdonald of the Isles and Sir James Macdonald of Sleat (holding the driver)

* Described as a true Scot, whose father was the city architect of Aberdeen, **GARDEN GRANT SMITH** (1860-1913) was a landscape artist, who painted delicate golfing watercolors during his travels in Continental Europe. In addition to writing and illustrating *The World of Golf,* he and Harold Hilton edited and wrote sections of a magnificent magnum opus of the sport, *The Royal and Ancient Game of Golf.* Smith also edited the English publication *Golf Illustrated* from 1895 to 1913.

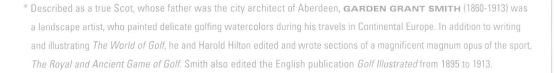

North Berwick Golf Club, East Lothian, Scotland, looking out at Bass Rock, a hump-backed volcanic mound over 300 feet high

The boat rocks at the pier o' Leith,
Fu' loud the wind blaws frae the Ferry,
The ship rides by the Berwick Law,
And I maun leave thee Bonnie Mary.

From Leith to the Berwick Law and the Bass, the waters of the Forth lie spread before the spectator. The Isle of May, Fidra, Craigleith, the Lamb, the Bass Rock, and other islands lie, gem-like, on its bosom, and in the far distance the shores of the kingdom of Fife, studded with villages, can be descried, backed by the Ochils and Lomonds and the Highlands of Perthshire.

Up and down this waterway what strange and ghostly pageants seem to pass! Along here, in the grey dawn of Western Civilisation, came the Roman galleys, with their strenuous crews, marveling greatly at the wildness of the land and the uncouthness of the barbarians who inhabited it. Little recked these bold Romans of a time coming, when those barbarians should bridge this wide water with iron, and when their own degenerate descendants would eke out a precarious livelihood amongst them as itinerant musicians and vendors of ice-cream!

So does the whirligig of time bring about its revenges.

Up here, too, passed Mary Stuart, fresh from the gaiety and light-heartedness of France, to take up, under Knox's stern and ascetic eye, the thread of her passionate and tragic reign. Here, for decades, passed to and fro all the statecraft, the learning and commerce of France and the Low Countries; and "furth of Scotland" from these sandy shores, sailed many a poor exile, either for his own or his country's good.

But the stirring and romantic memories of Scottish history which the scene inspires, though more than sufficient, in themselves, to attract and arrest the interest of the passer-by, are but a small part, after all, of the delights of this countryside. The climate is dry and bracing to a superlative degree. At North Berwick, Dunbar, Gullane, and indeed at almost any point along the coast, excellent sea-bathing is to be had, while the roads, either for walking, bicycling, or driving, are unsurpassed, both in quality and in the beauty of the scenery through which they pass.

The great attraction of the district, however, has yet to be named. It is Golf. All along the coast, untouched by the invading ploughshare, have been left stretches of the most beautiful golfing country in the world. Turf of exceptional closeness and elasticity, natural sand bunkers of endless shape and variety, sierras of benty dunes and saharas of sand, alternating with oases of verdure, make the place a veritable golfer's paradise. Here, surely, if anywhere, must have been the home of our first golfing parents, for nowhere else in the world is the golfing prospect so expansive and enticing, nowhere does the pursuit of the game seem so inevitable.

for home. Well, I shall be sorry to miss him, and yet my tears will have a certain crocodile's quality. Here is a precedent in point. In Italy there was, and doubtless there is still, a city, though for me it is a dream city, called Faenza. There was a rest camp there where the leave trains used to stop on the way from Taranto, and one had a bath and a Christian meal, and a band played "If you were the only girl in the world." As a rule, there was another leave party to be met there, a party that had been home and was going eastward again. I cannot honestly assert that its presence detracted from one's pleasure. On the contrary, I am afraid it added a poignancy to it. So it will be with that hypothetical gentleman at the station, who will be back in his black coat when we are daring the Burn for the first time.

Young women from St. Andrews College watching Abe Mitchell's drive in the British Amateur Championship at St. Andrews

I am afraid there is little that is new that I can think of to say about St. Andrews. I must borrow the words of a French author, quoted by the late Mr. Garden Smith in a pleasant book on golf, now hard on forty years old. It is doubtful whether this author had ever been there, because he thought it was in the neighbourhood of the powerful city of Glasgow, and his geography was otherwise a little vague. After mentioning the seat of learning, he went on—*"Et cependant a l'ouie du plus grand nombre, ce nom de Saint Andrews n'évoque ni une ville, ni une Université, ni un site ravissant couronné par la crête du Lochnagar, mais une étendue idéalement belle de Links verdoyants."*

He may have got it all out of somebody else's guide book, and he must have got Lochnagar out of his own head; he may not have had quite sufficient respect for Provosts and Professors and other well-known features of the town, but it is hard to deny that he had got to the root of the matter.

And now will the links be *verdoyant?* Observe, by the way, that our Frenchman made links plural and I make it, as I have been taught to do, singular. Or will it be, as are our southern courses, rather yellow and crumbling? I have no recent information and that makes the journey, if possible, more exciting. The Old Course was certainly verdant enough when it was reopened in spring and had retained enough of this good quality at the time of the Scottish Amateur Championship; but that was early in July, and even then the ball was travelling a long way with the wind at its tail. At the time of the Spring Medal I heard a distinguished golfer—and a Scotsman at that—make an almost blasphemous remark about the links. He said he had never enjoyed it so much because never before has he seen it playing so like an American course. That has an awful sound; one wondered for a moment that some frightful judgment did not descend on him; and, indeed, now that I come to think of it, I believe he did take a seven at the Road Hole in the Medal. Yet the poor man meant no harm. All he wanted to convey was that owing to the grass on the course it was playing at its proper length, and that people were not carrying straight over Hell with iron shots for their seconds at the Long Hole In and doing other ridiculous and irreverent things of that sort. Indeed, he meant entirely well, but his was one of the opinions that might have been expressed differently.

Green or brown, slow or fast, I am panting to be there, nor am I in the least depressed by the thought that my first day will be a Sunday, when no golf is. On the contrary, I shall thus have one more day to think about all those magnificent shots which I am assuredly not going to play. And then the first walk to the Burn and back. How heavenly—but I am forgetting Dr. Bonar's warning and had better say no more.

DAN JENKINS

THE OLDEST COURSE
from *The Dogged Victims of Inexorable Fate*, 1970*

THE MYSTIQUE OF MUIRFIELD LINGERS ON. SO DOES THE MEMORY OF CARNOUSTIE'S foreboding. So does the scenic wonder of Turnberry, and the haunting incredibility of Prestwick, and the pleasant deception of Troon. But put them all together and St. Andrews can play their low ball for atmosphere.

To begin with, St. Andrews is an old university town. Spires rise up over narrow streets littered with shops and cozy pubs. Students wearing red cloaks are bicycling around. Statues confront the stroller. An inn is here and there, and the North Sea just beyond.

There are four golf courses at St. Andrews: Old, New, Eton, and Jubilee, and they are all available to the public. The *new* course is over a hundred years old. Try that on for nostalgia. But no one, of course, is ever concerned about anything but the Old. The Old Course *is* St. Andrews, the R&A, all of those famed hazards. It is Jones, Vardon, Hagen, and old and young Tom Morris, and an R&A member standing on the balcony of his office in the R&A building just above the first tee surveying the entirety of the layout through a pair of mounted German submarine binoculars.

I was fortunate enough to secure lodging in the Old Course Hotel. Thus, I could walk out on my terrace and it was all there directly below me. To my left, the course stretching out to the eleventh green, and to my right, a matchless view of the eighteenth fairway leading up through the Valley of Sin with Rusacks Hotel standing there as it is supposed to be, and with the great gray edifice of the Royal & Ancient clubhouse forming a backdrop.

The Old Course has been called a lot of things because, at first glance, it looks like nothing more than a flat green city park. Some Americans have labeled it a "third-rate municipal course," and a "football field," but Bob Jones knew its subtleties better. It was, he said, the one course he would play forever if he could choose just one.

Two things strike the first-timer at St. Andrews immediately. First, the double greens. No fewer than fourteen holes share the enormous putting surfaces, the second also being the sixteenth, and that sort of thing. There are two flags, naturally, and often they will be as far apart as perhaps eighty yards, with many a dip and turn between them. The erring shotmaker is

---

* **DAN JENKINS** (b. 1929), who wrote for *Sports Illustrated* from 1962 through 1984, has had a long and celebrated career as one of the country's sagest and most sharp-witted writers about golf and football. His novels include *Semi Tough* and *Dead Solid Perfect*, which is about life on the pro tour. He is currently writer-at-large for *Golf Digest*.

apt to find the longest putts in golf at St. Andrews. Secondly, the Old Course is something of a paradise for one with a chronic hook. The first nine goes straight out, you see, with all of the heather and the sea on your right. And the back nine returns, parallel, giving the hooker all of those outgoing fairways to land on.

The difficulty of the Old Course lies in the wind and the putting, and the fantastically perfect location of such hazards as Hell Bunker, a deep and somewhat inescapable pit at the fourteenth, the Swilken Burn, a small brook which rushes right up against the green of the first hole and catches many a soft 9-iron, and the Valley of Sin, the cavernous lower level of the eighteenth green from which three-putts and even four-putts are commonplace.

I attacked the Old Course in the company of a caddie named Ginger who had merely been caddying there for forty-five years. For a few holes, he thought he had Henry Cotton again. The wind was behind and my shank, my top, my slice, and my putting jerk seemed to have disappeared. Through the tenth, I was only one over par, and I said to Ginger, "I don't know, but I think I'm bringing the Old Course to its knees."

And Ginger said, "Aye, ya made a putt or two, sir. But now we go home into the wind."

In rapid order, I was lost in the Elysian Fields, lost in the Beardies, trapped in Hell Bunker, gouged in the Principal's Nose, over the fence, smothered in heather, and even out of bounds on an overhang of the Old Course Hotel at the Road Hole. Finally, I limped up the eighteenth fairway en route to the Valley of Sin. Par for 86.

"You had a wee bit of hard luck," Ginger said. "But it can't spoil the fact that as we cum up the eighteenth, we sense a wee bit of tradition, don't we?"

The R&A member peered down from his balcony as I walked onto the green. I putted out. One final insult: a straight-in 4-footer which broke six inches. The secretary motioned me up for lunch in the R&A dining room. I toured the club and reread the letter that Isaac Grainger, then the president of the USGA, had written to the R&A on the occasion of its 200th birthday.

He had said, in part, "What golf has of honor, what it has of justice, of fair play, of good fellowship and sportsmanship—in a word, what is best in golf—is almost surely traceable to the inspiration of the Royal and Ancient."

I thought of those words again as I strolled back outside to stand and look at the sea, and at the town, and all across the gentle green sweep of the Old Course—the oldest course.

I had been there forever.

View of the 16th hole on the Old Course

H. N. WETHERED and T. SIMPSON

NORTH BERWICK

from *The Architectural Side of Golf,* 1929*

Unsolicited Advice. The 17th hole at North Berwick, Scotland

A STORY IS TOLD OF A LONDONER WHO, ON ARRIVAL AT NORTH BERWICK, GAZED OUT OF the window at a landscape blotted with rain and mist and in bitter accents exclaimed: "I don't call this East Lothian. I call it East Loathsome."

The story is not repeated in order to spread abroad a wicked libel on a romantic and beautiful country, but rather to admit that North Berwick can have, like every other place in the world, its unlucky days—sometimes as many as three in succession—when the islands off the shore disappear entirely from view, the scenery is wrapped in a heavy mantle of grey, and a piercing wind may be blowing to intensify the general depression. Under these distressing circumstances almost any epithet would be excusable. But this unhappy state of affairs is the exception rather than the rule, and is quickly forgotten. We remember only the inspired moments, the bright crystal quality of the air, the stimulating breezes, the wide prospect of the shores of Fife behind which St. Andrews lurks unseen, and, above all, we think of the friendly islands, Craigleith, the Lamb, Fidra, and Eyebrough—without which North Berwick is inconsolable—standing proudly and gaily like sentinels on guard. Undoubtedly full sunshine is needed to do justice to the scene. North Berwick must be able to spread her wings to be at her best, and then the most hardened critic might be tempted to call her East Lovely.

We could if we chose enumerate the attractions of the coast:

> *St. Abbs, the Bass, North Berwick Law,*
> *Tantallon's dour and duchty wa'—*
> *But stop! war I to name them a'—*

We need, in fact, only enlarge on two of them: the stately Bass Rock, where David Balfour spent a brief retirement in the company of Andie and the birds—"just the one crag

---

* One of the best books ever written about golf-course architecture, and certainly the most poetic, is *The Architectural Side of Golf* by **H.N. WETHERED** and **THOMAS SIMPSON** (1877-1964). Like Wethered, Simpson was independently wealthy and an intellectual, but he was also a highly accomplished golf-course architect. Simpson gravitated into course design, forming a partnership with Herbert Fowler, after studying law at Oxford and becoming a member of the Bar. He had strong views about course design, stressing a natural style and the importance of studying St. Andrews. Simpson did much of his best work in Continental Europe, including Chiberta in Biarritz, Morfontaine outside Paris, and Royal Antwerp in Belgium.

DAN JENKINS

THE SLEEPERS

from *The Dogged Victims of Inexorable Fate*, 1970*

THERE IS MUCH TO SEE IN THE NEIGHBORHOOD OF TURNBERRY, AND ALONG THE ROUTE TO either Prestwick or Troon, like a castle here and there, or a birthplace of Robert Burns, of which there must be a dozen, but never should a visitor miss that hill—that thing—called the Electric Brae. Years ago, bicyclists discovered it, one learns. They found themselves forced to pedal sweatily to get uphill when it obviously looked as if the road were going downward into the woods. It is an optical illusion, and you would lose your wallet betting on it. The proof is this: stop the car at a point where you are certain you are headed uphill. Put a golf ball on the road. It will roll uphill, that's all.

As mysterious as the Electric Brae is, it is no more mysterious than the course at Prestwick, the course where all of those early British Opens were staged beginning in 1860. Your first impression as you gaze out on a wasteland surrounded by an old stone fence is that this has to be the biggest practical joke in all of golf. I've got it, you say. You pay your green fee, put down a ball, and aim at the world, take four or five steps and are never heard from again.

Consider the first hole, only 339 yards. On your right, the stone fence, about ten feet away, separating you from a train that will come chugging by at intervals. On your left: mounds of heather and whin. Directly in front: waste. Sheer waste. Small and large clumps of it, sheltered by thin layers of fog. And the caddie hands you a driver. The fairway, presuming one is actually there, can't be more than twenty yards wide, but the caddie hands you a driver.

"Where is it?" I asked.

"Straightaway, sir," said Charles, who was distinguished from my caddie at Turnberry by two things. Charles wore a muffler and had his own cigarettes. "It's just there," he said. "Just to the left of the cemetery."

It is asking a lot, I know, to expect anyone to believe that you can bust a drive about 250 yards on a 339-yard hole, have a good lie in the fairway, and still not be able to see a green anywhere, but this is Prestwick.

The green was there, all right, as are all of the greens at Prestwick, but you never see them until you are on them, which is usually eight or ten strokes after leaving the tee. They sit behind little hills, or the terrain simply sinks ten or fifteen feet straight down to a mowed

---

* In this excerpt from an article titled "The Game of Golfe," **DAN JENKINS** brings his distinctively irreverent style to the eccentrically old-fashioned links of Prestwick.

J.H. Taylor taking a drop after hitting into the burn on the 4th hole at the British Open at Prestwick in 1914. The miscue cost Taylor the championship, losing to Vardon

surface or they are snuggled over behind tall wood fences over which you have nothing to aim at but a distant church steeple.

You would like to gather up several holes from Prestwick and mail them to your top ten enemies. I guess my all-time favorite love-hate golf hole must be the third hole on this course. Like most of the holes at Prestwick, it is unchanged from the day in 1860 when Willie Park, Sr., shot 174 to become the first Open champion.

First of all, without a caddie, it would take you a week and a half to find the third tee. It is a little patch of ground roughly three yards wide perched atop a stream, a burn, rather, with the cemetery to your back and nothing up ahead except fine mist. Well, dimly in the distance, you can see a rising dune with a fence crawling across it—"the Sleepers," the caddie says. But nothing more. Nothing.

"I'll be frank, Charles," I said. "I have no idea which way to go, or what with."

"Have a go with the spoon, sir," he said.

"The *spoon?*" I shrieked. "Where the hell am I going with a spoon?"

"A spoon'll get you across the burn, sir, but it'll na get you to the Sleepers," he said.

"Hold it," I said. "Just wait a minute." My body was sort of slumped over, and I was holding the bridge of my nose with my thumb and forefinger. "These, uh, Sleepers. They're out there somewhere?"

"Aye, the Sleepers," he said.

"And, uh, they just kind of hang around, right?"

"Aye," he said. "The Sleepers have took many a golfer."

The deep bunker with its wooden sleepers guarding the green of the Alps, hole 17 at Prestwick Golf Club, Ayrshire, Scotland

Somehow, I kept the 3-wood in play and when I reached the ball, Charles casually handed me the 4-wood. I took the club and addressed the ball, hoping to hit quickly and get on past the Sleepers, wherever they were. But Charles stopped me.

"Not that way, sir," he said.

"This *is* the way I was headed when we left the tee," I said.

"We go a bit right here, sir," he said. "The Sleepers is there just below the old fence. You want to go over the Sleepers and over the fence as well, but na too far right because of the burn. Just a nice stroke, sir, with the 4-wood."

Happily, I got the shot up and in the general direction Charles ordered, and walking toward the flight of the ball, I finally came to the Sleepers. They were a series of bunkers about as deep as the Grand Canyon. A driver off the tee would have found them, and so would any kind of second shot that didn't get up high enough to clear the fence on the dune. A worn path led through the Sleepers and then some ancient wooden steps led up the hill and around the fence to what was supposed to be more fairway on the other side.

It wasn't a fairway at all. It was a group of grass moguls going off into infinity. It looked like a carefully arranged assortment of tiny green Astrodomes. When Charles handed me the pitching wedge, I almost hit him with it because there was no green in sight.

I got the wedge onto the green that was, sure enough, nestled down in one of those dips, and two-putted for a five that I figured wasn't a par just because the hole was 505 yards long. Charles said I had played the hole perfectly, thanks to him, and that I could play it a thousand times and probably never play it as well.

I said, "Charles, do you know what this hole would be called in America?"

"Sir?" he said.

"This is one of those holes where your suitcase flies open and you don't know what's liable to come out," I said.

"Aye, 'tis that," he said.

"One bad shot and you're SOL on this matter," I said.

"Sir?" said Charles.

"Shit out of luck," I said.

"Aye," said Charles. "At Prestwick, we call it the Sleepers."

Royal Dornoch Golf Club,
Sutherland, Scotland, hole 3

burgh of Dornoch in 1628, his chief argument being that such recognition might speed up the lagging march of civilization in that part of the northern Highlands. (Dornoch, indeed, was the scene of the last witch-burning in Scotland, in 1722; the charge against the unfortunate woman, one Janet Horne, was that she had turned her daughter into a pony and had her shod by the Devil.) It was not until 1885, however, that the Royal Dornoch Golf Club was founded and Old Tom Morris was commissioned to come up from St. Andrews to lay out nine proper holes. A second nine was added shortly afterward, and then, in 1904, the wholesale changes that transformed Dornoch from just another course into a bona-fide championship layout were carried out under the direction of a remarkable all-round golf man, John Sutherland, who for over fifty years served as the club's secretary. . . . The leading golf pros of that period regularly took in Dornoch on their exhibition tours—J.H. Taylor, a five-time Open champion, also assisted in revamping a few of the more prosaic holes—but for the amateur cracks the course remained terra incognita until 1909, the year of the so-called "Dornoch invasion." That spring, the British Amateur was held at Muirfield, and two Dornoch players went down for it—T.E. Grant, a baker's apprentice who later became a successful professional, and Sutherland himself. These two unknown northerners proceeded to confound the golf world by eliminating the two greatest British amateurs of that era, Grant accounting for John Ball and Sutherland for Harold Hilton. Ball and Hilton were so taken with the delightful manners of their conquerors that they made a special trip to Dornoch after that season to play an exhibition match and see what the course was like. Soon everyone was "discovering" Dornoch. Immediately before the First World War, it became the place for well-to-do golf-oriented English families to rent summer homes. Ernest Holderness, who won the British Amateur in 1922 and 1924, developed his game during summer holidays there as a youngster, and so did Roger Wethered, the 1923 Amateur champion, and his sister Joyce, regarded by many as the finest woman player of all time. After the war, Dornoch enjoyed a second brief period of fashionableness, but by 1930 it was over. Like Machrihanish, it gradually became a place that avid golfers talked of visiting but few actually got to. When the course was remodeled once again, after the Second World War, and lengthened to its present 6,505 yards, the news of these changes created scarcely a ripple of interest south of Dornoch Firth.

What is there so special about Dornoch that it should nurture an exceptional architect like Donald Ross, exceptional players like Holderness and the Wethereds, an exceptional club secretary like John Sutherland, and, I am tempted to add, exceptional admirers like Sam

McKinlay, Dick Tufts, and Pete Dye? The answers came fast and clear the morning McKinlay and I played the course. The linksland that at first glance seems so commonplace and even unpromising reveals itself, once you have got two or three holes behind you and are into the heart of the course, to be beautiful golf country. Everything does look as if it had been there, untouched, for centuries. In its general topography—its billowing fairways, its deep and shaggy sand bunkers, the eccentric mounding around its greens—Dornoch probably resembles St. Andrews more closely than it does any other well-known course, but there are many basic differences. To begin with, Dornoch has far better turf than does the Old Course, which has been in spotty condition for twenty years. Unlike the Old Course, where a good deal of the trouble is hidden from view, Dornoch presents its hazards frankly, and there are few blind shots. Whereas the Old Course is famed for its huge double greens, which serve both an out-going and incoming hole, Dornoch's greens are comparatively small and sit atop mesalike rises with unusually steep banks. In the way they are sited and in the severe configurations of their surfaces, Dornoch's greens—and they are the course's most distinctive feature—are quite reminiscent of those at the Augusta National, although Augusta's are much larger. These Dornoch greens demand a good deal of finesse on the approach, for the pitch-and-run shot the Scots customarily play to their unwatered greens will as often as not kick awry off the contours and bounce on over one side or the back of the green. As Holderness has pointed out, the golfer who grows up at Dornoch is forced to learn how to "pitch a ball onto a slippery surface and stop it," and this is a skill that thereafter serves him handsomely wherever he plays. Furthermore, because he is so seldom confronted with a routine chip back to the flag when he misses a green, the Dornoch golfer learns how to improvise delicate little lob-and-run shots. In America, Donald Ross rarely found the kind of terrain that would permit him to reproduce the touchy subtleties of Dornoch's green areas, but their lasting influence on him is visible in the hilltop "crown greens" he built wherever he worked. When he revised the Pinehurst No. 2 course in the mid-thirties, he took special pains to create Dornoch-style mounds, slopes, and runoffs around the greens, and that course is generally acknowledged to offer the most exacting examination in chipping in this country.

Like St. Andrews and Nairn, Dornoch is a loop type course—in this instance, eight holes out, ten holes back—but the repetitiousness generally inherent in this kind of layout has been avoided with fine resourcefulness. On the eight outward holes, which are set along a shelf of high land, the tees have been placed so that the fairways do not swing quite the same way on any two holes, and as a result the wind hits the golfer from all directions. The incoming holes manage a similar diversity by rambling up and down between the crusty higher land and the duneland by the sea. The best hole on the course, to my mind, and one that nicely epitomizes Dornoch's originality and appeal, is the fourteenth, which is called Foxy. A complicated double-dogleg par 4, four hundred and fifty yards long, it has an outline resembling the Big Dipper as much as anything else. . . . McKinlay was around in even par, 72. I wasn't that low, but I played an exceedingly solid round, for me, and that was important to me. Dornoch was one course I wanted very much to like, and, say what you will, you cannot like a course unless you play it reasonably well. I should imagine that Dornoch usually elicits a golfer's best game. It doesn't overawe you with its length. It supplies plenty of gorseless *Lebensraum* to err in. It keeps you on your toes by making it clear from the outset that it rewards only shots that have been well thought out and well executed. And it encourages you to hit decisive shots by providing vigorous, close-cropped turf, on which the ball sits up beautifully, and very true greens, which are a joy to putt. In a word, I found Dornoch all I had hoped it would be—a thoroughly modern old links with that rare equipoise of charm and character that only the great courses possess.

JAMES W. FINEGAN

CRUDEN BAY

from *Blasted Heaths and Blessed Greens*, 1995*

THERE IS NO GRADUAL REVELATION OF THE GLORY OF CRUDEN BAY. YOU CLIMB OUT OF the car, walk over to the clubhouse on the heights, and look down. Below you, in all its turbulent splendor, lies one of the most awe-inspiring stretches of linksland in Scotland, indeed, in all of the British Isles. Against a backdrop of the gray-blue waters of the North Sea, the sandhills rise 40, 50, even 60 feet, their shaggy slopes covered with the long and strangling grasses that spell disaster to the off-target stroke. This is heroic ground, and if it is thrilling to contemplate, it is markedly more thrilling to play. From the medal tees the course measures 6,470 yards against a par of 70.

The first three holes are par fours—a very testing opener of 416 yards played from an elevated tee and calling for a gorse-skirting drive down the right to open up the angled green for the long approach; a 339-yarder, with the purest tabletop green waiting high above for a very carefully judged short pitch; and a blind 286-yarder over broken ground that, in high summer, the smiter just may reach with his drive. It is marvelous—and marvelously varied— but it scarcely prepares you for what is about to unfold: four consecutive great holes.

The 4th is simplicity itself, a 193-yarder played straight toward the sea (and often straight into the wind) from an elevated tee carved out of one imposing sandhill across a deep grassy hollow to an elevated green carved out of the facing hill. A bunker at the left front in the slope and a steep falloff on the right dictate the need for a pefect stroke. No other will suffice.

At the 5th, a daunting 454 yards, we begin with a blind drive from high and deep in the dunes, sighting on the wispy top of some vague hillock. This is followed by a full-blooded wood along the valley floor to a large but ill-defined green in a pleasant little dell. There is a cloistered quality to much of Cruden Bay, a feeling prompted by the high dunes that we have the course to ourselves.

The 6th—not for nothing it is called "Bluidy Burn"—is a dogleg left par five of 524 yards. Again the tee is cocked up in the sandhills, but this time the green, dramatically undulating, is tucked away beyond a dune and protected from the birdie-seeker's wood by a little burn, itself invisible, some 50 yards in front.

---

* JAMES W. FINEGAN (b. 1929) began in golf as a caddy at age 11. He graduated from LaSalle College, where he played No. 1 on the golf team, and spent his professional career in Philadelphia at the Gray & Rogers advertising agency, retiring as chairman in 1990. He has written for *GOLF Magazine*, *Golf Journal*, and *LINKS*.

One final hole in this sequence. The 390-yard 7th commences from another exquisitely sited tee high in the sandhills and, as at the mighty 5th, offers not a glimpse of the fairway. If we find it with our drive, we turn smartly left and face uphill, where the flag beckons from beyond two sandhills that guard the narrow green like the Pillars of Hercules.

Four great and unforgettable holes in succession—par 3, 4, 5, 4.

To whom are we indebted for this feast? Not, you may be surprised to learn, James Braid. At no point in Cruden Bay's near-hundred-year history did Braid have a hand in shaping it. No, it is the Englishman Tom Simpson, in partnership with Herbert Fowler, who deserves the

The tussocky sand hills of Cruden Bay Golf Club, Aberdeenshire, Scotland, and the view of Slains Castle in the distance. The castle inspired the imagination of Bram Stoker, author of *Dracula*

FRANK PENNINK

ROYAL COUNTY DOWN

from *Homes of Sport: Golf,* 1952*

The 9th hole at Royal County Down Golf Club, Newcastle, Northern Ireland, facing the green-and-purple panoply of the Mourne Mountains and the crescent of Dundrum Bay

THOSE OF US WHO APPRECIATE TO THE FULL THE NATURAL BEAUTIES OF THE WORLD have an irresistible longing to return to those which have entranced us most. It is so with me for the panorama of the Jungfrau, roselit by the setting sun, the views from the Corniche roads on the Cote d'Azur, and those along the twisting Moselle and Rhine. When my mind turns to the comparatively prosaic subject of golf, I long first and foremost to be among the sandhills of the Royal County Down Golf Club at Newcastle, under the shadow of Slieve Donard, the highest of the Mourne Mountains. The sight from the hill over which we drive at the ninth hole is surely the most beautiful that can be obtained from any course in the British Isles. Looking south, the peaks of those majestic mountains drop 3,000 feet, steep and sheer to the sea itself, towering in ever-changing colours from pale silver greys and shades of yellow ochre to every tint of blue. Turning to the sea, there is the wide expanse of Dundrum Bay before you, with its fine beach of firm golden sands stretching as far as the lighthouse at St. John's Point: turning inland you may see the beautiful country-side extending to the Ballynahinch Mountains many miles to the north.

In this setting of enchanting loveliness lies the links of the Royal County Down Golf Club, where golfers complain that the breath-taking vistas of mountain and sea distract and divert them from the task on hand. It would indeed be an anti-climax if this were a links made entirely by the hand of man and full of human ingenuities: but happily it is not so, for the golf is wonderfully natural. It could hardly be otherwise amongst sandhills which run so conveniently; nor could Tom Morris have managed to complete his plans and map out the course, on the meagre allowance of £4 granted him in 1889, as a result of a meeting held in the hall of Mr. Lawrence's Dining Rooms, Newcastle. . . .

When it is remembered that the golfer, leaving London at 7 p.m. can be on the first tee at Newcastle for a comfortable round before lunch, it does not really seem so far to this loveliest of British courses "Where the Mountains of Mourne Sweep Down to the Sea."

---

* **FRANK PENNINK** (1913-1983) was a golfing triple threat. A topnotch player, he captained the Oxford University team and won the English Amateur Championship in 1937 and 1938. For several years, he covered golf for the *Daily Mail*. Pennink really made his name, though, as a golf-course architect, designing several outstanding courses in Europe, including Vilamoura in Portugal, Noordwijk in the Netherlands, and Halmstad in Sweden.

ROYAL PORTRUSH

from *A Round of Courses*, 1952*

"White Rocks," the 5th hole at Royal Portrush Golf Club, cascades down to the chalky cliffs and caverns of Northern Ireland's Antrim Coast

PORTRUSH IS H.S. COLT'S MASTERPIECE (THOUGH HE MAY NOT AGREE WITH ME). Certainly the ground is worthy of a great links; there is spaciousness and grandeur; these ranges of sandhills are, to ordinary sandhills, what the Alps are to the Grampians. Out to sea lie the rocky ridges of the Skerries—originally, I imagine, the coastline, for either side of the links the cliffs soon rise again dour and grey: but within the Skerries the Atlantic has swelled and broken, and piled in rollers of sand, creating a stretch of country on the grand scale. The sandhills rise shelf upon shelf and it is upon the most landward shelf that the links is set. One has the curious feeling of playing along a cliff top—high above the sea, but the whole *cliff* is made of sandhills. I have never seen a links which so invites adjectives of nobility and size; of space and height. Sometimes in dreams one has the sensation of flying or gliding gently and easily as a gull from the cliff-side. Portrush is flying golf—one longs to take off after the ball, and indeed the air from the Atlantic is so fresh that such levitation does not seem impossible. The rough is composed of wild briar rose, thick, long claggy grasses and (if there is a wet season) moss; the whole compound has the consistency of porridge and is entirely hellish; a kind of Sargasso. I speak first of the rough because Portrush is proud—and rightly proud—of the fact that it has very few bunkers. (You may remember that another giant, Carnoustie, is busy removing its surplus.)

You will not be impressed by the first hole, though you may be irritated. How wide the fairway, which slopes gently down and away with a rather meadowy inland look; how well to the left that boundary fence; how far to the right that other fence; yet in the days of stroke and distance a scratch player has been known to play 13 from the tee—that means six consecutive shots out of bounds! It is so unlike the first drive at Hoylake, so charmingly obvious and avoidable, and yet. . . . A straight long drive and all is well. I think Portrush is particularly a driver's links. There is trouble in front of most tees, real ghastly give-it-up-at-once kind of trouble; but the carries—even from the back tees—are not fierce. Anything crooked goes into the porridge—there's no chance of landing on another fairway and getting away with a long, wild wicked one. No, the ball from the tee must be hit straight and true. That, I know,

---

* **PATRIC DICKINSON** (1914-1994), born in Nasirabad, India, was an English poet, playwright, translator, and a broadcaster for the BBC's radio program *Time for Verse*, which aired in the late 1940s. Dickinson's *A Round of Courses* consists of beautifully crafted and unerringly accurate portraits of his eighteen favorite courses.

is one of the oldest clichés of the game; at Portrush you'd better forget it's a cliché and come freshly upon it as a great Discovery: the one magical secret of golf! Note that I have just put the adjectives "straight" and "long" in that order. Second shots are a joy, there are plenty of opportunities to use wood; and where that is so, you are given that special kind of do-or-dare shot which may reach the green—yet, if hit correctly, gives you entire pleasure even if you do not. Such a heavenly swoop is the second shot at No. 2. Away goes the ball downhill (so to speak) through a curving pass, or defile, just out of sight, to reappear at rest across a further gully and on the edge of the green. There are lots of chances for the pitch-and-run from twenty yards—owing to this lack of bunkers—for Colt has placed his greens brilliantly, achieving here, I think, the perfect mating of the old-fashioned cup-in-a-hollow and the new-fashioned mushroom-on-a-hill style of green. Owing to the largesse of Nature he has been able to place his greens up and still to have them among hills whose shoulders and slopes diminish their size to pinheads. This makes the long second, or the short third, always an exciting and exhilarating shot.

From the second green you climb steeply up to the third tee and from it you have one of the most marvelous views: landscape and seascape and golfscape. There is something quite ravishing to the golfer in these winding viridian ways towards the emeralds with the bright flags stiff in the wind; the "silence and slow time" of it and the pacing, intent figures. And on the third tee, here, the tract of sandhills appears so vast, the human figures so small that one looks with a hawk's or an airman's eye, and having spent this lyrical moment, like stout Cortez and all his men, the wonder gives place to wild surmise: how long this shaft is! how small this club-head, how minute this ball! How far the green! How can I do this at all? Luckily for you the 3rd is a short hole, and not a very difficult one. It is called "Islay" and there is Islay out on the horizon. But on, to the fourth hole—a beautiful two-and-a-half shotter like the word "every," which you can give three or two syllables to, as you choose. There is an out-of-bounds fence along the right and a well-placed fairway bunker nudging you over towards it, and another of those long hopeful seconds taking you to the mouth of a green beautifully placed in among dunes.

The greens are, on the whole, easy to putt on. They are not over-large and not too full of burrows. One should never get the horrors on them. They are greens for the attacking putter.

Now for the 5th: one of the most romantic holes in the world. (And this is a great romantic links.) Standing on the highest point of the dunes inland (and we have come east all along the inside perimeter between dunes and wild hill-side), you turn at right angles and face directly seaward. The ground collapses down towards the sea in a huge series of lumpy mounds, a steeply sloping field of giant molehills; the gradient is violent and away below and to the right, on the edge above the sea, is the green. It looks miles away. But as the ball flies it is only a drive and a No. 3 or 4. This drive is really enchanting. You must hit well to the left of where you'd like to—for over the hills and less far away, there is a fairway which you can't quite see from the tee. The more you bite off on the direct line the more likely you are to land among the briary hills and to take 3 more (the 1st backwards and the 3rd sideways) to reach the fairway. I cannot begin to describe the fantasy of this awesome and beautiful golf hole. It is like playing down a long doglegged waterfall with the green a still, deep, green pool below the rapids. And if you go over that, you go down, down into the sea. It is well that one turns inland to the next hole and that it is a long one-shot hole of a reasonably tame nature: but only one generation from wildness, like a tiger-cub born in a zoo. The talons on its green paws know what to do. . . .

The 12th has a very small seductive tortoiseshell of a green from which second shots retreat rejected in a thwarted way. I must admit that I do not admire this hole as much as I am told I should. I feel it has somehow had its sting removed, it feels bowdlerised. But for the next two holes my admiration is unbounded. The 13th, like the 5th, points seaward, but this time you drive up a steady slope to the crest of a ridge. Across a small valley lies the green, again on the sea-edge with a deep rushy chasm to its left and a steep convex slope to its right—in fact it is placed exactly on the top of a large dune, and it needs a nice straight, high No. 5 into the wind or through it. This is a beautifully proportioned hole and gives no hint of what is to come.

Stepping off the green westwards, a marvelous view presents itself: you are on the end of a striding-edge with an almost sheer drop to the right. Down below is a great hidden valley containing another whole golf links! You can have no real conception of this small grandeur till you see it. I must emphasise again the scale of these ranges of dunes at Portrush—they are Alpine, Apennine, foreign. On this fourteenth tee you are standing upon the point of a V, the right-hand arm goes out guarding the coast; in the middle is the valley, and along the left-hand arm, exactly along its edge, is this next hole called with tactful under-statement "Calamity Corner." It is two hundred yards long and there is no room on the left, which is the wild rushy crest of the ridge. A yard to the right and over you go, sheer down this grass cliff whose gradient must be 1 in 1. It is a romantic chasm, an opening of hell, and to escape from it it is necessary to defy gravity, taking your stance almost like a fly on a wall, and striking a rocket-shot up to the zenith of heaven. You can do this any number of times, for I almost dare not say that the lies on this cold hill's side are not, well, exactly favourable to pyrotechnics. Having encompassed this, we play "Purgatory" which swoops all the way down the landward side of the ridge in a superb toboggan-run to a green at the bottom—another less-feathery bed. The drive at Purgatory is very thrilling, for the tee is just below the horizon-line and you hit madly into thin air—the ball disappears away down almost like dropping a penny into a well. These three holes 13–14–15 should be done in 4, 3, 4!

The 16th is a very fine long two-shot hole, notable for its tee, which is sixty-five yards long. If one is at the back end, it is rather like the runway of an aircraft-carrier. The hole doglegs to the right and your second must carry some diagonal traps before reaching safety. There's a grass gully to the left of the green, and a bank on the right.

The finish is a little disappointing after the adventures and explorations we have had. True, the drive at the 17th ought to disappear over the end of a long hog's-back or steer exactly between it and a great rearing sandhill whose near face is all bunker; but once through this Scylla and Charybdis you come out on to the flat, on to almost a field, an inland-looking stretch of harmless grass-and-bunkers. These last two holes are both long, and two steady 5's are not beyond the bounds of probability. But left with two 5's to win, I can see them dwindling into 6's without one's quite knowing how or why. If Portrush can be said to have any bad holes, I must record that I think the 18th is at any rate not a good hole! It is, so to speak, comforting, but officially comforting and without affection, like an income-tax rebate or the kiss of a strange aunt.

The Championship Committee was right as can be to choose this links for the first Open Championship to be held beyond the sea.

both the U.S. Open and the PGA Championship in 1922, but he went through some lean years before capturing both the U.S. and British Opens in 1932, and catapulting to victory in the Masters in 1935 with his famous double eagle on the 15th hole.

Sarazen remained incredibly spry, with a razor sharp mind, well into his nineties. He made a hole-in-one on the Postage Stamp hole while playing the British Open at Troon in 1973, fifty years after he first competed there in 1923. Even more remarkable was watching Sarazen trot out with his characteristically brisk strut at the medal ceremony after Greg Norman won the Open at Royal St. George's in 1993. Sarazen delivered a moving, unscripted speech in which he explained the significance of Norman's victory, and how it had come sixty years after Sarazen's own victory at the neighboring course of Prince's in the 1933 Open.

The Twenties also marked a newfound independence and greater cultural role for women. In the era of flappers and jazz, women golfers were in the vanguard of defining society's new attitudes toward women and were also shaped by the shifting expectations of what women could achieve in sports.

The young and stylish golfers who emerged in the Twenties included Glenna Collett, Edith Cummings, Virginia Van Wie, Bobby Jones's childhood friend Alexa Stirling, and Joyce Wethered in Britain. These women, like their fictional counterpart Jordan Baker in *The Great Gatsby,* played modern golf and were liberated from the constricting long skirts and corsets of the pre-War generation. Collett and Wethered were the two transcendent players of the era, trans-Atlantic rivals who established the popular image of the woman golfer.

Glenna Collett Vare, the "Great Glenna," learned the game at Metacomet, a Donald Ross-designed course in Rhode Island, and went on to win the U.S. Women's Amateur in 1922, '25, '28, '29, '30 and '35. Like Jones, her personality, intelligence, and achievements on the course captured the public imagination and helped propel the women's game in America into the modern era, just as Jones had done for men's golf.

Wethered, who came from a well-to-do and cultivated English family, was shy and unassuming, but the power of her golf astonished all those who witnessed it. Jones, who understood the golf swing better than anyone and had a natural predisposition to understatement, described Wethered as the finest golfer he had ever seen, man or woman. In their great battle in the 36-hole final of the 1929 British Ladies' Amateur, Wethered, who subsequently became Lady Heathcoat-Amory, came from five holes down to beat Collett 3 and 1.

Henry Cotton turned professional in 1924, when he was seventeen years old, but did not really break through until the 1930s, winning the British Open in 1934, 1937, and 1948. He was undoubtedly the greatest English player of his generation and a peerless striker of the ball. Cotton in his personal style and attitude was very much a figure of the Twenties. He was a man of parts, who moved in fashionable circles and elevated the status of the British professional. Cotton retired to Portugal, where he designed Penina, the first great golf course in the Algarve, a region that he helped to make into the major golf destination that it is today.

TOMMY ARMOUR

PEN SHOTS
OF THE MASTERS—
WALTER HAGEN

from *The American Golfer*, May 1935*

IF THE SPORT HISTORIANS ARE CORRECT, AND THE SCOTCH TOOK OVER GOLF FROM THE Dutch, Hagen evened the score for his progenitors. Walter, the Rochester (N.Y.) Dutch boy, took the game back from the Scots.

He did all right by the Scots. He released the pros from bondage to the old caste system.

He can do almost anything to anybody—and have them like it because he makes no excuses.

Making a million—or having the return of his laundry delayed by fiscal factors— nothing bothers Hagen. If it's a money matter; money is no matter to Walter. If it's a time element; after all, time will continue and Hagen knows the futility of standing like King Canute on time's shores and trying to sweep a tide of seconds back to the moment when he was due on the first tee.

He never gives a damn—and doesn't even admit that.

I'd rate him the greatest shotmaker who ever lived, although only with one club—the mashie niblick—has he been generally rated as a master operator and there are plenty who are convinced others are Hagen's superior with that club. BUT. . . . When any shot HAS to be made, Hagen can make it, and has made it repeatedly with utterly amazing precision.

He is one of the most profound, authoritative and nonchalant students of the game. What he says is gospel, even if you try to argue against it. I have debated with him and finished convinced he was right.

His natural touch is as sensitive as a jeweler's scale. He can grade balls from lightest to heaviest, arranging them in order, when there is only a pennyweight or so difference between half a dozen balls being judged. If he estimates a club's weight and the scales don't check with Walter's estimate, the scales are wrong.

He could relax sitting on a hot stove.

He's the most generous of mortals. He will do anything for you—if it's no trouble to

---

* **TOMMY ARMOUR** (1895-1968) was born in Edinburgh, the son of a confectioner. He served in the Black Watch Highland Regiment during World War I as a machine gunner, and was gassed at the Battle of Ypres, losing the sight in his left eye. In 1921, the "Silver Scot" emigrated to the United States and went on to win the U.S. Open in 1927, the PGA in 1930, and the British Open in 1931. Later in his career, Armour became a fabled teacher and wrote the classic and still popular *How to Play Your Best Golf All the Time*.

him. You can have the shirt off his back—if you can unbutton it and slide it off while he's sinking back in an easy chair like a contented and grinning Buddha and sipping a pleasing beverage. Take it. What of it? He has a trunkful in the next room.

He will stay up later than anyone in the room. He will sleep later than anyone in the same room, too. He concentrates on whatever he really *wants* to do. That's why he has been the master marvel of golf—and may again demonstrate it because Walter's far from through if he happens to get stirred up to conquest again.

Walter's a great marksman with firearms. From his speeding automobile en tour he will bang off pheasants and other game. At any time he will interrupt a lucrative exhibition tour to go fishing.

He needs no press agent but for ten years had the greatest one in golf, Bob Harlow. With Hagen's casual attitude on most matters he could have become either extreme—a tramp or a tradition. With Harlow's adroit, canny handling Walter became advance man for all professional athletes in society.

Hagen broke down the age-old barriers that had corralled athletes out of polite society and plutocracy. After Walter came Ruth and $100,000 a year; Rockne and a sideline fortune; Tunney and big business; Richards and Tilden into tennis capitalism; Rickard and the million-dollar gates and dinner-coated ringsiders; Jim Londos and the Midas touch on the wrestling burlesque.

OPPOSITE PAGE
Walter Hagen teeing off

There's the blaze of Robin Hood in the fellow. Automobile dealers offered him town cars and chauffeurs in livery to cart him to and from golf tournaments. Walter accepted. Most of the cars' use was in carrying young sports who had drunk up their taxi money the first night they arrived. A great sacrifice, or thoughtfulness on Walter's part? No. Some fascinating female with a flashy car longer than the Ile de France always turned up to drive Walter. Everyone was happy. That's what Walter wanted, as long as it was no trouble to him.

If Hagen would ever make up his mind to really go to work at this golf game, it would be too bad for the rest of the hopeful stars. But all the rest of us, old and young, are safe. Walter languidly turns his head toward Leningrad whence comes that fierce call, "Workers of the world, arise," and inquires, "Why?"

Hagen has the answer to making the world kind to him. He is kind to himself.

THE CADDIE

from *The Walter Hagen Story,* 1956*

The young Haig

LATE IN THE SPRING WHEN I WAS TWELVE YEARS OLD, I WAS IN THE SEVENTH GRADE and sitting looking out the window, feeling the nice warm air and the sunshine on my face. I could see the golfers out on the course at the Country Club of Rochester. Suddenly I couldn't take it any longer. When Mrs. Cullen, the teacher, wasn't looking I jumped out the window. I never went back to school regularly again.

Throughout that summer I spent every weekday caddying, and on Sundays I played baseball. I was a good caddie, conscientious about my job, and soon members of the Thistle Club asked me to caddie for them. This was a big step up for me. The Thistle Club, composed of charter members of the club which had preceded the Country Club of Rochester, was a sort of inner group whose word carried a lot of weight. I picked up a lot of pointers on the game and played around on my own cow-pasture course when I had the free time.

That fall when golfing was over I decided to learn a trade to support myself until I was ready for the big leagues. It seemed natural that anything I'd learn to do would involve skill with my hands. I came from that kind of family. My father was not a large man physically—he stood about five feet eight inches—but he had big powerful hands, perfect for a blacksmith. I was built more like my mother and, like her, I soon towered a good three inches over my dad. Sports writers have often written about *my big hands* but actually my hands are about average for a man of my size. I wear a size nine and a half glove. However, my fingers, even when I was a youngster, were unusually long and tapering.

Harry's Garage in Rochester was taking apprentices in car repairing for a fee of twenty-seven dollars a month. In order to make the payments, I got a part-time job with the Foster-Armstrong Piano Company as a wood finisher. I also went to school three nights a week taking a course supplementary to the car repair work. As a sideline, I enrolled in a correspondence course in taxidermy. A little later, with the piano company job as background experience, I landed a job as a paid apprentice to a mandolin maker. These two jobs gave me a good basic knowledge of woods and woodworking as well as appreciation of fine grains and finishing.

---

* The irrepressible **WALTER HAGEN** (1892-1969) learned the game as a caddie at the Country Club of Rochester. In typical Hagen style, his autobiography is captioned, "By The Haig, Himself as told to Margaret Seaton Heck."

When I became a professional golfer my clubs were always bright and polished. As a fellow pro once remarked, "You can shave in Hagen's clubs."

I continued to caddie at the Country Club of Rochester through the summer and the Thistle Club members fixed it so I could play the club course. By the time I was fifteen Andrew Christy, the club pro, needed an assistant and it had to be me.

My pal George Christ and I had been saving our caddie fees for some time and we got the idea we'd be smart and buy motorcycles. He found a secondhand Harley-Davidson and I bought a bright red Indian in a similar need-of-repair condition. We finally got them in running shape and there wasn't a foot of road around Rochester that we didn't cover. We hadn't thought it wise to tell our folks we'd spent all our savings on the machines and I'll never forget shutting off the motor at the top of the hill near home and coasting down. Then I hid the motorcycle in a clump of trees.

The deception didn't last long, however, for I confessed to my mother and asked her to come out and see me ride it. Instead of scolding me, she said, "I've been wishing you could have one of those things. Now you and George can have a lot of fun."

I was playing the Country Club of Rochester course with Mr. Christy when I broke 80. He played with me quite often when we were through work in the pro shop at the end of the day. But we played *with* each other, not *against*. In my own mind, though, I always played him a match on the q.t.

One day, with forced nonchalance, I said, "It's a fine evening, Mr. Christy, and all the members are in. I'll just take you on for nine holes."

His answer set me back on my heels. His eyes covered me slowly for a few seconds, then he said, "Young man, when I want to play golf, *I'll* ask you." Then he turned and walked away.

Was my face red! What a lesson he taught me. I never forgot that. Afterwards when I wanted to play with him I was always careful to ask politely, "Would you play a few holes with me, Mr. Christy, and give me some pointers on my game?"

I could beat him and he knew it, too. But he had carried that incident off big. He made himself and his position important and dignified. Win or lose, he let me know he was still the pro, the big guy. I was just a kid and I could beat him, but he still looked and acted the role of the champion on that course. In later years I took some clobbering defeats and wore many a championship crown, yet it was the lesson he taught me that kept me in the groove through all walks of life.

Walter Hagen in a characterisic pose

WHO'S GOING
TO BE SECOND

from *It Was Good While It Lasted,* 1941*

IF I WERE CAST UP ON A DESERT ISLAND, WHICH THE LORD DEFER, AND WERE PERMITTED to choose one man as my companion in exile, I sometimes think I should call for that great philosopher and good companion, Walter Hagen.

The prospect of being cast upon a desert island with a golfer is one to fill the mind with a horrid anticipation. But to Hagen, third greatest golf player of all time, golf was only a means to an end. He used it as Gene Tunney used prize-fighting, and as Henry Cotton, as I think you will find, will turn out to have used golf.

Hagen was bigger than the game by which he rose to fame. In any walk of life into which he might have drifted he'd have been a success. He probably stuck to golf because it brought him with the least trouble the things he most desired from life—wealth, luxury, travel, the limelight, and the company of famous men—and women—on level terms.

That he made a million dollars from golf is certain. It is equally certain that he will not die a rich man. "Easy come, easy go," was Hagen's motto with money, and maybe he was right.

My own affection for Hagen, whose name, incidentally, rhymes with "pagan," not with "jargon," bordered almost on hero-worship. What a character! Staggering self-assurance; wit and good humour; a bronzed, impudent countenance with a wide-open smile; inexhaustible zest for life; and a unique ability to combine wine, women, and song with the serious business of winning golf championships—that was Hagen. A fellow whose like you meet once in a lifetime.

His golf exactly matched his personality. Often brilliant; never, never dull. He won the open championship of this country four times and of his own United States twice, and he made more bad shots in doing so than the man who finished second would make in a month. He finished at the top because his powers of recovery were almost superhuman. When he won his first championship at Sandwich, he went through six rounds without taking a six, yet four times he was still in a bunker beside the green in three.

It was only natural that such a man should capture the imagination of the crowd. At first they resented his swagger and his multi-hued attire. On one regrettable occasion in the

---

* **HENRY LONGHURST** (1909-1978) was for many years the peripatetic golf columnist for *The Sunday Times* in London, contributing essays on every facet of the game. He was a fine amateur golfer, who captained the Cambridge University team in 1930, and for a brief time served as a Member of Parliament. Longhurst is remembered by American golfers as the authoritative and decidedly English voice of televised golf broadcasts during the 1960s and early 1970s.

early days they even clapped when he missed a shot. But that soon passed when they came to understand the real Hagen, and long after he was past his prime they flocked round with him like sheep.

He took them through all the emotions. He would play a succession of holes as though divinely inspired, while they marvelled at his skill. Then from a clear sky would come a stroke of unbelievable inaccuracy—a wild slice, or a "top," or a quick, semicircular hook—and the heart of the duffer warmed to the god that could descend to the level of man. And then, when all was apparently lost, he would extricate himself with a recovery which to the faithful seemed nothing less than a miracle.

Where other men strove vainly for consistent perfection, it was part of Hagen's philosophy, typically enough, to expect his quota of downright bad shots in every round he played. He expected them—so they did not upset him, as they did the others, when they came.

He was, of course, the showman *par excellence*—the master golfer-entertainer. No matinee idol ever had a stronger hold on his audience. I recall a tournament at Porthcawl, when his days of winning championships were already over. Hagen, still in London, was informed that he was to be partnered next day with a certain British Ryder Cup player and that they were to start at 10:30 a.m.

Walter Hagen gets a kiss from his wife after winning the British Open at Royal Liverpool Golf Club (Hoylake) in 1924. It was the second of his four British Open victories during the 1920s

"I'll start at three," said Walter.

He is the only man in the game who would not have been disqualified. Instead, they meekly replied: "Very well, you shall start at three."

Word went round the little town, and no one bothered to watch the morning play. They stored their energy for the afternoon. The master arrived in a huge Daimler saloon—I can see him now—seated in the small space left by a number of cabin trunks. He had his feet up, and genially waved a large cigar. In the front seat sat his sixteen-year-old son, Junior.

Hagen knew he had not the remotest chance of winning the tournament. So did every one else. But did that make any difference? Not a bit. Every spectator on the course was there at three to see him drive off. They followed him eagerly to the end. He took eighty-one.

Next day they were there again. Hagen by this time had no chance of even qualifying for the final day's play, but who cared? He played deplorably and again took eighty-one. Every one was happy. They had seen Hagen play golf. . . .

Hagen had—and I suppose I must use the past tense, for though he's only forty-eight now, the days of his glory are past—an overwhelming confidence in his own powers. "Waal, who's gonna be second?" he would drawl as he strolled out to the first tee. Then he would win—and win against the best competition the world could offer. His imitators cried: "Who's going to be second?" and then finished twentieth.

Innumerable tales, some of them true, are told of his irrepressible self-assurance. Perhaps the most characteristic concerns the finish of his Hoylake championship. He frittered the shots away in his last round and was out in 40 or 41. At any rate, he had to come home in 36, and knew it, to beat Ernest Whitcombe's total of 302—and there is no tougher finish in the world than the last five holes at Hoylake.

He got by the tenth with a four and drove into a bunker at the Alps (the short eleventh). He blasted it out and holed the putt. Bunkered again at the twelfth, he holed a whopper for his four. Then his tee shot to the short thirteenth floated away into the sand, and that, surely, was the end. There were no strokes to be picked up on the last fives holes, even by Hagen, and a four at the thirteenth must cost him the championship. He flipped the ball neatly out to within a few feet and got his three.

And so he came to the seventeenth needing two fours to win the Open. At the seventeenth he played what must stand as one of the greatest iron shots of all time, a long, low shot that ran nimbly through the narrow opening and lay eight feet from the hole. A three there would clinch it—but he rolled the ball casually along and missed it. Four to win! Every man in Hoylake, and half Liverpool, as it seemed, crowded round the last green. Watchers craned their necks from every window.

Hagen hit his second shot right over the back into the long grass. His approach, not bad in the circumstances, ran within eight or nine feet of the hole. One putt to win!

Where most men would have spent an age in preparation, Hagen strolled up to his putt and with scarcely a preliminary glance ran it into the hole.

As he walked from the green, having duly been embraced by his wife, a colleague of mine said to him: "You seemed to treat that putt very casually, Hagen. Did you know you had it to win?"

"Sure, I knew I had it to win," drawled Walter, "but no man ever beat *me* in a play-off!" . . .

Life has been very much the richer for having known Hagen. He was the most colourful, spectacular personality cast up by the game of golf, and will take his place in sporting history with the giants—with "W.G.," Jack Dempsey, Babe Ruth. Their statistical records may have been surpassed, but they stay on their pedestals, men who became legends in their own lifetime.

ROBERT TYRE JONES, JR.

from *The New Yorker*, April 1972*

THE 1972 MASTERS, BESIDES LACKING THE DRAMA AND EXCITEMENT THAT USUALLY accompany the event, was different from its predecessors in another way. The tournament is inextricably bound up with Robert Tyre Jones, Jr.—Bobby to sports historians, Bob to his friends—who, after his retirement from competition, in 1930, helped to found the Augusta National Golf Club, became its one and only president, designed its superb course in conjunction with Alister MacKenzie, the Scottish golf architect, and served as host of the Masters from its beginnings, in 1934, as an informal spring get-together, until 1969, when the severe illness he had borne quietly for twenty years became so incapacitating that he couldn't make the journey to Augusta from his home in Atlanta. Jones died last December 18th, at the age of sixty-nine, and at Augusta this April everyone felt his absence sharply and continually. I think this was to be expected. What was surprising was the sense of shock and grief that so many people in golf experienced when word came of his death. After all, we had been prepared for this news for years, and, in addition, in a corner of our hearts we knew it would be a blessing, since the spinal disease that Jones was afflicted with—syringomyelia—was inordinately cruel and crippling. And yet, how hard the news hit when it came! In another corner of our hearts we had been nursing the faint hope that somehow or other Jones would make it back to Augusta one of these springs and we would be seeing him again and talking with him again, and now we knew we wouldn't.

Of the people I have met in sports—or out—Jones came the closest to being what we call a great man. Like Winston Churchill, he had the quality of being at the same time much larger than life and exceedingly human. Jones had a remarkably fine mind, with an astonishing range. As a young man, he first thought that he would like to become a mechanical engineer, and he earned a B.S. degree at Georgia Tech, completing the four-year course of study in three years. During his last semester at Tech, however, he decided that he didn't want to be an engineer after all. He enrolled at Harvard, where he took a variety of courses, mainly in English literature, and received another B.S. degree, at the end of two years. (In one of his literature courses, he was introduced to Henry Fielding, who remained his favorite author; he

Bobby Jones portrayed by Anthony Ravielli. Ravielli, who drew the golf swing with meticulous accuracy, etched the swing sequence illustrations for *Ben Hogan's Five Lessons: The Modern Fundamentals of Golf*, an instructional classic

---

* **HERBERT WARREN WIND'S** essays in *The New Yorker* about the major tournaments were eagerly awaited by generations of golf fans. He did not simply recap the action but wove together three or four different themes in his detailed, leisurely style. Some of Wind's finest essays from *The New Yorker* are collected in *Following Through*.

was very fond of *Tom Jones* but thought that *Joseph Andrews* was a touch better.) Then Jones, who was the son of a lawyer, went to Emory University Law School, in Atlanta. Halfway through his second year, he passed the Georgia State bar exams and entered practice. There was very little he couldn't do if he set his mind to it. His first book, *Down the Fairway,* which was published by Minton, Balch in 1927, was written in collaboration with O.B. Keeler, the celebrated sports chronicler of the Atlanta *Journal,* but Jones loved good writing, and the desire to be a competent writer was strong in him, and from that time on he personally wrote everything that appeared under his name—one of the few sports figures of whom this can be said. I really wonder if anyone has ever written about the business of playing golf better than Jones. . . .

Jones had other exceptional gifts. He had a sense of proportion uncommon in a man with a vigorously perfectionist side to his nature. His family—his wife, Mary, and their three children—came first; his work as a member of his Atlanta law firm came second; his golf came third. He had incredible strength of character. As a young man, he was able to stand up to just about the best that life can offer, which is not easy, and later he stood up with equal grace to just about the worst. On top of everything else, he had tremendous personal magnetism. In the nineteen-twenties, golf, though very much on the rise, had not become the major game it is today in this country, yet no other hero of the Golden Age of Sport had quite the hold on the affections of the American public that Jones had. Everybody adored him—not just dyed-in-the-wool golfers but people who had never struck a golf ball or had the least desire to. They admired the ingrained modesty, the humor, and the generosity of spirit that were evident in Jones's remarks and deportment. They liked the way he looked, this handsome, clean-cut young man whose eyes gleamed with both a frank boyishness and a perceptiveness far beyond his years. (This was one time when a person's appearance perfectly matched his substance and charm.) Jones, in short, was the model American athlete come to life, and it is to the credit of the American public that they recognized this almost instantly. His presence was enough to guarantee the success of any tournament. More than eighteen thousand spectators wedged themselves onto Merion's famous East Course, outside Philadelphia, for the final of the 1930 United States Amateur to see their hero complete his Grand Slam of the four major championships—the British Amateur, the British Open, the United States Open, and the United States Amateur. Jones's appeal crossed oceans. For the Scots, he was the dream golfer they had been waiting for all their lives. This was particularly true of the natives of St. Andrews, and on several occasions when Jones was involved in a match on the Old Course, or was just playing an informal round, the whole town poured onto the links to watch him. (The Royal and Ancient Golf Club of St. Andrews, of which Jones was an honorary member, will hold a memorial service for him on May 4th, at the end of the club's spring meeting.) To protect himself from his frenzied idolaters during a championship, Jones at times took the precaution of having two friends convoy him down the fairways, one walking on each side of him, but inevitably tournament play—trying to live up to everything that was expected of him, trying to maintain his concentration and timing under prolonged pressure—took a great deal out of him. Many peopled missed this, for he somehow managed to appear unfrazzled, and when he spoke, even under stress, his words still oozed out in that slow, thick Georgia drawl, like Karo syrup. But Jones felt the strain, all right. During one Open championship, he lost eighteen pounds. During another, he was so exhausted and numbed at the finish that he couldn't get his fingers to unknot his sweat-soaked tie, and his friend Keeler had to cut it off with a pocketknife. Jones loved to compete—beneath the controlled exterior beat a heart every bit as fiery and determined as Ben Hogan's—but there was no way he could escape the punishment that the championships brought on, and this, as much as any other single factor, prompted his decision to retire from competitive golf in 1930 following his Grand Slam.

This portrait of Bobby Jones, painted by Margaret Fitzhugh Browne in 1928, is in the collection of the High Museum of Art, Atlanta

There was something that touched his arm in the big swing, and diverted his short putts off line as he worked about the course that I think he loves best of all in this country. And I knew what it was. Bobby may have been puzzled, but what rode with him at Merion was the Fourth Horseman of the Apocalypse of Championship.

Had this been just another amateur championship? If Bobby had not won the other three, it would have been a breeze in the field in which he found himself after his first match with Ross Somerville. But just behind him every step of the way, there was riding a horseman he could not see; the white horseman of the fourth championship. And I am very sure that the thunder of his pursuit would have broken any other golfer in the world.

The significance of Jones' victory furnished more interest than the final match. That he would win was accepted as a foregone conclusion from the beginning. He won the qualifying medal with a record-equalling 142, and he was never down to his five opponents in match play. Homans in the final round, through his courageous finish, extended the match farther than it seemed possible after Bobby was 7 up at noon. Bobby's golf was not always Jones' golf in the machine-like perfection it is usually considered, but it was much too good for his opponents to match. Like Alexander the Great, Bobby had no more worlds to conquer. And he was only twenty-eight years old.

Bobby and Jess Sweetser had played in a dozen championships but had met only once, so the match at Merion was a sort of return bout. Bobby with a card of 72 was 4 up on Jess at noon, and in the afternoon he was fully as innocuous as Hamdryas or King Cobra, the match ending on the tenth green. Jess said:

"I did not want to take the match to the eleventh green, and let it end 8–7. Then I could have said we were still square. That was where our match ended at Brookline, you remember."

Bobby blushed or might have blushed had it not been for several layers of sunburn.

"I felt sort of mean at that tenth green, the way that pitch stuck up there," he said, "like a stab in the back or a shot in the dark."

"It was no shot in the dark," said Sweetser.

On a September day eight years before in the semi-final round of another national amateur championship, it was Jess who spanked a pitch of 90 yards into a hole for an eagle, and went on to give Bobby the greatest defeat he ever absorbed in a tournament, 8–7. History has a curious way of repeating itself, sometimes in reverse.

Among the telegrams Bobby received as the great test got under way was a brief one, in Greek, from Johnny Boutsies, proprietor of a restaurant in Atlanta. It must have been a struggle to get the telegram transmitted, Greek words in English letters, but it came through. It read:

"E TON E EPITAS."

You remember what the Spartan mothers of old said to their Spartan sons, as they buckled on their shields, setting out for battle. The English equivalent is rather difficult but the meaning is clear, about the shield and the warrior's return:

"With it, or on it."

Bobby came back with it.

The match of the tournament was the ferocious battle of twenty-eight holes between George Von Elm and Maurice McCarthy, the black Irishman and the blond Prussian, that set a record for stubborn bouts in the U.S. amateur championship. Von Elm, playing by his own declaration in his last amateur championship, was not shooting as good golf as McCarthy, but Maurice was giving the holes to him by taking three putts. He did this four times when he had the Uhlan in his grasp. So it came to the home hole all square. A half there and they were off on the most amazing struggle in all the annals of golf. At the end of nine holes, they were still square the last six holes being halved in pars. Then came the break. At the tenth extra

hole. After good drives, Von Elm was on a dozen feet from the pin, safe for a par. McCarthy's pitch ran closer—it ran still closer. It touched the cup, rolled around and stopped a few inches away. That was the winning stroke, the coup-de-grace, a birdie 3 at the tenth extra hole. McCarthy had also set another record by scoring an ace in the qualifying round, the only ace ever shot in qualifying for the amateur championship.

So it was goodbye at Merion, as, long ago, it had been good-morning there. It was at Merion in 1916 that Bobby had played in his first national championship; it was there in 1924, he had won his first amateur championship; and there he finished. The chunky schoolboy had grown into the calm and poised young man, whom the world called the master of golf—and who was not less truly master of himself.

"There is a destiny that shapes our ends."

The long, par-4 16th hole at Merion Cricket Club, Ardmore, Pennsylvania, the famous Quarry Hole

clubhouse with 289's. He won the P.G.A. at Pittsburgh's famous Oakmont course.

Half a century has worn a hole in the slicked-down haircut, but otherwise the years have left few traces. The Piping Rock tan is as deep as ever. The Mr. Kleen grin still starts under this ear and stretches clear to that one, crinkling the face so that wrinkles of merriment fan out from squinty eyes. The half-column britches are still de rigueur on the course, and he moves with the same purposeful strut that could get him through a whole round in the Masters championship in an hour and 56 minutes.

Even from demigods, however, age exacts a toll. When Gene shot a 69 at Marco Island last week it took him more than two hours.

Sometimes it bugs him that fans seem to remember only one shot out of all the brilliant rounds he has played. That's the wood he holed out for a double-eagle 2 on the 15th at the Augusta National Club. With one swing he gained three strokes to tie Craig Wood, who was in the clubhouse accepting congratulations on winning the Masters; Sarazen won the playoff.

"Show me the plaque marking the spot," said a guy at a later Masters.

"Plaque hell," Gene said. "They just threw a handful of Italian rye in the divot."

He made a face. "You know, I won the U.S. Open and the British Open and the P.G.A. and I don't know what all, and yet wherever I go you'd think I'd made only one shot in my life. Even in Japan they ask me, 'How about the dubber eager?' "

A few months ago Gene went to Boston to play for the Francis Ouimet Caddie Fund at Charles River Country Club. On the par 5 seventh hole he sank his second shot for a double eagle. He used a No. 3 wood.

Gene Sarazen on his way to winning the British Open at Prince's Golf Club, Sandwich Bay, Kent, England in 1932

"What did you hit at Augusta?" he was asked.

"A 4-wood," he said, "but 35 years later I needed more club."

Gene will celebrate the golden anniversary of his first British Open when the tournament returns to Troon in Scotland. Barely able to hold his feet in a gale off the Firth of Clyde, the 21-year-old shot 89 in 1923 and failed to qualify.

"Impossible," Alan Gould, sports editor of the Associated Press, cabled when the score came in. "You mean 69." The answer was prompt: "Sarazen's score 45–44. You add it."

Champion golfers don't celebrate 89's. "But I'll be there if I'm walking," Gene has told the Scots.

He is a world figure with a strong peasant strain, an inborn love of the soil. When he first got into the big money he bought a Connecticut farm.

"It was stone walls and fruit trees and I sold it," he said. "After I did, I felt lost, like I had no rights in this country because I didn't have a piece of ground. Driving up the Hudson one day, I stopped and bought two farms at Germantown, N.Y."

That was home for him and Mary until they sold out last year. Now they live in Florida and summer in New Hampshire, and they have rights everywhere.

ROBERT T. JONES, JR.

JOYCE WETHERED:
THE GREATEST OF GOLFERS

from *The American Golfer*, 1930*

ORDINARILY I WOULD NEVER TAKE ADVANTAGE OF A FRIENDLY ROUND OF GOLF BY MAKING the play of a person, kind enough to go around with me, the subject of an article. I realize that everyone likes to play occasionally a round of golf when reputations can be forgotten, with nothing more at stake than the outcome of the match and a little friendly bantering afterwards.

Just before the British Amateur Championship at St. Andrews, Miss Joyce Wethered allowed herself to be led away from her favorite trout stream in order to play eighteen holes of golf over the Old Course in company with her brother, Roger, Dale Bourne, then recently crowned English Champion, and myself. At the time, I fully appreciated that Miss Wethered had not had a golf club in her hand for over a fortnight, and I certainly should have made no mention of the game had she not played so superbly.

We started out by arranging a four-ball match—Roger and Dale against Miss Wethered and myself—on a best and worst ball basis. I don't know why we didn't play an ordinary four-ball match, unless we fancied that the lady would be the weakest member of the four, and that in a best-ball match her ball would not count for very much. If any of us had any such idea at the start of the match, it is now quite immaterial, for there is not the slightest chance that we should admit it.

We played the Old Course from the very back, or the championship tees, and with a slight breeze blowing off the sea. Miss Wethered holed only one putt of more than five feet, took three putts rather half-heartedly from four yards at the seventeenth after the match was over, and yet she went round St. Andrews in 75. She did not miss one shot; she did not even half miss one shot; and when we finished, I could not help saying that I had never played golf with anyone, man or woman, amateur or professional, who made me feel so utterly outclassed.

It was not so much the score she made as the way she made it. Diegel, Hagen, Smith, Von Elm and several other male experts would likely have made a better score, but one would all the while have been expecting them to miss shots. It was impossible to expect that Miss Wethered would ever miss a shot—and she never did.

To describe her manner of playing is almost impossible. She stands quite close to the ball, she places the club once behind, takes one look toward the objective, and strikes. Her swing is not long—surprisingly short, indeed, when one considers the power she develops—

Joyce Wethered with her great
admirer, Bobby Jones

---

* **BOBBY JONES** was a regular contributor to *The American Golfer*, which was edited by his friend Grantland Rice.

Joyce Wethered's perfectly
balanced swing

but it is rhythmic in the last degree. She makes ample use of her wrists, and her left arm within the hitting area is firm and active. This, I think, distinguishes her swing from that of any other woman golfer, and it is the one thing that makes her the player she is.

Men are always interested in the distance which a first-class woman player can attain. Miss Wethered, of course, is not as long with any club as the good male player. Throughout the round, I found that when I hit a good one I was out in front by about twenty yards—by not so much when I failed to connect. It was surprising, though, how often on a fine championship course fine iron play by the lady could make up the difference. I kept no actual count, but I am certain that her ball was the nearest to the hole more often than any of the other three.

I have no hesitancy in saying that, accounting for the unavoidable handicap of a woman's lesser physical strength, she is the finest golfer I have ever seen.

PAGES 160, 161

Cypress Point Golf Club, Monterey, California, hole 15, par 3

Charles Blair Macdonald, patriarch of American golf, shown at the National Golf Links of America, Southhampton, New York, the course he designed based on the ideals of Scottish links golf. This portrait by Julius Garibaldi Melchers hangs in the Links Club in New York City

coming on the scene are creating new American classics like Sand Hills in Nebraska, designed by the duo of Ben Crenshaw and Bill Coore, and Tom Doak's wondrously beautiful Pacific Dunes along the remote Oregon coastline.

Of all the great American courses, Pine Valley is the archetype of the American school of penal golf course design. The unlikely Torquemada behind Pine Valley was George Crump, a Philadelphia hotelier who succeeded in creating a dazzling and diabolically difficult melange of golf holes in the sandy pine barrens of southern New Jersey. Crump consulted experts, including the great English architect Harry Colt, but he designed the course himself, literally camping out on the site for five years. He died in 1918, one year before the course was completed. Pine Valley remains unsurpassed, perennially ranked as the number one course in the world by *GOLF Magazine*.

California's Monterey Peninsula offered the opportunity for creating cliff-side golf above the Pacific on a grand scale never imagined before. The potential for magnificent golf in a uniquely American setting was brilliantly realized at both Pebble Beach, a public resort course that opened in 1918, and Cypress Point, an extremely private enclave. The man who fulfilled this golfing manifest destiny at Pebble Beach was Samuel Morse, the developer of the Monterey Peninsula. He was a grand-nephew of Samuel F.B. Morse, the artist and inventor of the telegraph and Morse Code. After graduating from Yale, where he had been captain of the 1906 football team, Morse went West, and in 1914 he bought 8,400 acres in Monterey with a group of businessmen. Morse commissioned two relatively unknown California State Amateur

champions, Douglas Grant and Jack Neville, to design the course.

Cypress Point, which O.B. Keeler unforgettably described as "the crystallization of the dream of an artist who has been drinking gin and sobering up on absinthe," is the masterpiece of Alister MacKenzie. A Scottish-born physician, MacKenzie designed courses of exceptional artistry in far-flung places around the world, ranging from Royal Melbourne in Australia to the Jockey Club in Buenos Aires.

Pinehurst was founded in the Carolina sandhills by the Boston soda fountain sultan James Tufts. Tufts and his friends were partial to a game similar to croquet, called roque, but in 1898 a golf course was introduced, and Pinehurst was on its way to becoming the golfing mecca that it is today. Much of Pinehurst's success as a golf resort stems from the quiet genius of its original resident golf course architect, Donald Ross. As a young man in the 1890s, Ross emigrated to Boston from Dornoch, where he had been the pro and greenskeeper. Ross came to Boston at the urging of Robert Wilson, an astronomy professor at Harvard, who had spent summers in

Dornoch. Wilson found Ross a position as a golf professional in Waterville and he was eventually introduced to Tufts. Ross's grand achievement is Pinehurst No. 2, which he used as a kind of outdoor laboratory to concoct the crowned greens and scalloped chipping areas that are hallmarks of his work. He designed and built hundreds of fine courses throughout the United States, employing a staff of experienced and loyal construction superintendents who did much of the work on site.

A.W. Tillinghast, like MacKenzie and Ross, was a pioneering golf course architect and authentic genius, designing courses with a boldness and flair that has never been outdone. Tillinghast, who came from a well-off Philadelphia family, became entranced with golf during a summer visit to St. Andrews, where he took lessons from Old Tom Morris. After a more or less misspent youth, he designed his first course at Shawnee-on-Delaware, Pennsylvania, in 1907, and found his true calling. His designs are a roll call of American classics, including San Francisco Golf Club, Winged Foot, Baltusrol, Somerset Hills, and Philadelphia Cricket Club.

Tillinghast, who lived in high style and had a theatrical personality, lost his money in the Depression, abandoned golf course architecture, and moved to Hollywood, where he opened an antique store. He continued to do some consulting work for the PGA in the 1930s, and had a major role in the design of the courses at Bethpage State Park on Long Island. In preparation for the 2002 U.S. Open at Bethpage, Rees Jones did a splendid job of restoring the Black Course in keeping with Tillinghast's original design, using the cavernous, flashed-up faces of the bunkers at Winged Foot as the prototype for

Bethpage. The Black Course lived up to its reputation as a "Man Killer" at the Open, in which it took one Tiger to tame another.

As exemplified by Pine Valley and Bethpage Black, Americans developed an obsession, bordering on compulsion, with building punishing golf courses. Oakmont, outside Pittsburgh, is the paragon of the penal school of architecture, a beautiful brute with its church pew bunkers and glimmerglass greens. Oakmont reflects the very powerful and punitive vision of its founder, the steel magnate Henry Fownes, and his equally resolute son, William Fownes.

Augusta National was conceived and designed by Bobby Jones and Alister MacKenzie in reaction to and as a movement away from the penal school of design. Jones set out to design an ideal course based on the strategic principles of the great Scottish golf courses, particularly St. Andrews. Jones had the foresight to enlist MacKenzie, who had studied the art of camouflage as a surgeon in the English army during the Boer War. Augusta National, built on a former nursery that bursts into flower every Spring with barrages of purple and pink azaleas, looks nothing like a Scottish course, but its constant demand for proper position makes it the ultimate test of strategic golf that Jones and MacKenzie intended.

Shinnecock Hills was founded in 1891 and first hosted the U.S. Open in 1896. The tournament did not return again until 1986, revealing the glory of this American links on the East End of Long Island for all the world to see. That event proved so successful that the Open returned to Shinnecock in 1995, when Corey Pavin was the gritty winner, and Shinnecock hosts the Open again in 2004. The course in its current configuration was designed in 1931 by

Cassique Golf Club, Kiawah Island, South Carolina. Although the course is named after a chief of the Kiawah Indians, it has a distinctly Scottish flavor

the Philadephia-based architectural team of Howard Toomey and William Flynn. Of all the great old American courses, Shinnecock comes closest to being a true links, and like all the great links courses it appears altogether natural as it soars and swoops through the sand hills above Shinnecock Bay, with its shingled Stanford White–designed clubhouse on the highest crest.

The National Golf Links of America was the first great golf course in the United States. Completed in 1911, the National was the brainchild and personal fiefdom of Charles Blair Macdonald. Macdonald became completely enamored of golf as a visiting student at St. Andrew's University and was a prime mover and shaker in the establishment of golf in the United States, winning the inaugural U.S. Amateur at Newport in 1895.

Macdonald searched the East Coast for a suitable site on which to create his ideal golf course, which would be modeled after the best holes found in Scotland. He found an idyllic property just north of Shinnecock Hills, overlooking Peconic Bay. Working with Seth Raynor, a local surveyor who went on to design a trove of great courses on his own, Macdonald created an enduring classic that is true in spirit to the Scottish models but with a swirling pageantry that is completely original.

The courses of Macdonald and Raynor, whose work together set the standard for American golf course architecture, are personal favorites of Pete Dye, a truly visionary course designer who first came on the scene in the 1960s. Dye recognized early in his career that modern earth-moving equipment would allow him to re-create the dunelike features and sharply etched hazards that he admired in the classic Scottish courses. Dye proceeded to apply these techniques to different types of landscapes, creating a portfolio of stunningly sculpted courses that includes the Ocean Course at Kiawah Island and the Pete Dye Golf Club in West Virginia. There is no place where Dye's design wizardry is more on display than at the Kohler Resort in Wisconsin, which features Blackwolf Run and Whistling Straits. Whistling Straits, Dye's interpretation of Scottish links golf in a Wisconsin hamlet overlooking Lake Michigan, hosts the PGA Championship in 2004.

Jack Nicklaus, who has established himself as an outstanding contemporary golf-course architect, began his career as a designer working with Pete Dye on the Harbour Town course in Hilton Head, South Carolina. Today's golf-course architects must run a gauntlet of environmental challenges and constraints that their predecessors could never have imagined. Nicklaus faced the ultimate environmental challenge when he was called upon to design a course at a Superfund clean-up site in Anaconda, Montana, which had once been one of the world's largest copper smelting facilities. Nicklaus's design at Old Works is an example of modern American ingenuity, creating a golfing oasis along Warm Springs Creek that incorporates the old foundry equipment and a Sahara of black slag into the completed course.

ROBERT GREEN

PINE VALLEY

from *Golf World* (U.K.), August 1985*

George Crump, who carved Pine Valley from wilderness in southern New Jersey

WHILE IT'S CERTAINLY NOT TRUE THAT ALL GREAT GOLF COURSES ARE LOCATED IN grotesque surroundings, the thesis is not without foundation. Ballybunion is beside a caravan camp in an unsalubrious seaside resort, Augusta National is opposite a Piggly Wiggly store and a succession of filling stations along Washington Road, and Pine Valley is to be found in Clementon, New Jersey, a billboard-strewn and burger-bar infested town some 45 minutes across the Delaware River from Philadelphia.

Finding a jewel like Pine Valley in such a neighbourhood is as incongruous as it would be to see the Taj Mahal in the middle of Spaghetti Junction. Its name is apt—the 6,765-yard course is lined with pines (as well as oaks, firs and birches) and most holes run through a valley of trees and the fairways run a terrifying gauntlet of sand. There's more sand than on Copacabana Beach. One disheartened professional called it "a 184-acre bunker."

At Pine Valley there are tees, fairways and greens. There is almost no rough. Instead, there is perdition. The course is theoretically fair—the fairways are generous and the greens large where appropriate—but the penalty for missing either target is so severe that one is intimidated into doing just that. Many holes demand a long carry from the tee and the punishment for being short, left or right is frightening. Miss a green and your score can move into double figures well before you start to negotiate its fierce contours with your putter.

But though the course is so unremittingly tough and remorselessly unforgiving that even the Light Brigade might have been inclined to retreat, this is no valley of Death. Pine Valley is beautiful. The trees and the magnificent terrain, the splendid isolation of each hole, the quietness without contrasted to the turmoil within as one seeks to conquer the mental and physical examination set by each shot—all these facets and more produce an awesome combination, a mixture of thrill and fear. Confronted by the stupendous 2nd hole, one English visitor asked: "Do you play this hole or do you photograph it?"

It is also a privilege to play there. Not only does the course have a worldwide reputation unmatched by any other unexposed to regular public scrutiny via television, it is as exclusive a golf club as exists. Perhaps those with the best deal in this respect are the overseas members, who pay a nominal sum having been selected for membership because of their material

* **ROBERT GREEN** is currently the editor of *Golf International*, which is published in England. His article on Pine Valley appeared in connection with the Walker Cup Match held there in 1985.

contributions to the good of the game. Among them are professional Gary Player, actor Sean Connery, R&A secretary Michael Bonallack, journalist Donald Steel and Gerald Micklem. But the name of Pine Valley is not primarily known because it may be the hardest course in the world to get on. It's because it is the hardest to get round.

The Machiavelli who designed the course was George Crump, a Philadelphia hotelier and fine amateur golfer who proved himself the world's greatest amateur golf architect. He vanished into the wilderness of the pineclad New Jersey sandhills in 1913 and by the time of his death in 1918 he had produced a masterpiece.

The criteria he laid down were followed religiously, although he received assistance from the renowned British architect, Harry Colt, and after Crump's death in 1918 Hugh Wilson, the creator of Merion, and the British firm of Colt, Mackenzie and Alison completed holes 12 to 15 on the principles Crump had enunciated.

The diabolical par-3 10th hole at Pine Valley Golf Club, Clementon, New Jersey

THE CARDIAC CLIFFS

from *Strokes of Genius*, 1989*

Ask every professional on tour what his five favorite golf courses
are in the world, and the one name that will be on everybody's list
is Pebble Beach.

Tom Watson, practicing for the U.S. Open

Jack Nicklaus on the fairway of hole 9 at Pebble Beach Golf Links, Pebble Beach, California, in the 2000 U.S. Open

FACING PAGE
The short but treacherous par-3 7th hole at Pebble Beach, where the wind plays havoc with the tee shot

PEBBLE BEACH, CALIFORNIA, JUNE 16, 1982 —
As he walked to the tee of the tiny, precipitous, sand-locked, surf-rocked, wind-wracked 110-yard seventh at the Pebble Beach Golf Links, Jack Nicklaus paused to look at the vista before him. Standing at the top of the tip of this peninsula, Nicklaus, playing a practice round before the U.S. Open, had the full panoramic sweep of Pebble Beach around him.

To his right was a sheer cliff drop down to Stillwater Cove, and, in the distance, the cypress-wooded promontory of Pescadero Point. To his left was blue-black, kelp-clogged Carmel Bay lapping on a mile of white Monastery Beach and, beyond that, the long rocky reach of Point Lobos. Around the tee was impenetrable barranca, full of wildflowers, Scotch broom and sea grasses. On those huge ocean rocks not washed with waves were perched hundreds of sea birds. Behind Nicklaus, the foothills of the Gabilan Range began their climb, their heights covered with fog. Straight ahead lay the Pacific.

"This sure is beautiful," was all he said.

Like many who come here, Nicklaus has learned the foolishness of trying to hem in Pebble Beach with words. Robert Louis Stevenson called this Monterey Peninsula "the greatest meeting of land and water" anywhere on earth—and Stevenson got around some.

Even photographs are inadequate to the sight. They catch only a narrow arc of the place's 360-degree impact. And, inevitably, they tend to flatten what is, in reality, a wild and craggy place. Take two steps off the right side of the eighth fairway and it's two hundred feet straight down to the rocks and driftwood.

Occasionally, something in the world of sport actually surpasses expectations. Once in a while, Peggy Lee's wrong; that isn't all there is. Pebble Beach is natural, wild, stark and capricious. That's why it is, perhaps, the ideal U.S. Open venue. In February, at the annual Bing Crosby Pro-Am, Pebble Beach is wet, green, close-cropped and pretty, even if the weather is raw. But, in summer, with high rough and the general brownish tinge of longer grasses, Pebble Beach has the mean look it deserves. "It reminds you of a lot of British Open and Scottish courses. Yup, lotta Scottish golf in this course," said Watson. "From the seventeenth tee, for example, all you see is sky and ocean and flat grasses. It's a beautiful blue-gray setting."

* **THOMAS BOSWELL** (b. 1947) began writing sports for *The Washington Post* in 1969, shortly after graduating from Amherst. His essays about golf are collected in *Strokes of Genius*.

The 17th is a straightaway par 3 that typifies the subtle challenge of Pinehurst No. 2

about golf by going to the source of all information and had spent several summers at Dornoch. Naturally he became acquainted with Donald and, recognizing his abilities, urged him to seek his fortune in America. In 1899 Donald reached the new country, having spent practically his entire fortune for the trip and without any idea whatever of where he might find a position. However, Professor Wilson did not fail the immigrant and quickly located him as the professional at the Oakley Country Club in Watertown, Mass.

In the summer of 1900 James W. Tufts, seeking a professional for his new golf course in Pinehurst, asked Donald to come to his home in Medford for an interview. At this meeting a verbal understanding was reached on the terms of employment. This agreement, covering Donald's arrangements at the club, was to be carried on for 48 years under the management of Pinehurst by three generations of the Tufts family.

At first Donald served only as professional at Pinehurst during the winter and at Watertown and later Essex during the summers. As the demand for golf in Pinehurst grew, new holes were built by Donald and Frank Maples, the Pinehurst superintendent of courses. The architectural features developed by these two men proved to be popular, and as a result Donald was asked to build courses being developed by those who had visited Pinehurst and who had there developed their love for the game. Gradually Donald Ross's fame as an architect spread with the result that by 1910 he had terminated all his professional connections, except for Pinehurst, and was devoting a large part of his time to golf course architecture. Donald Ross not only designed golf courses, he also built courses and often had as many as six or eight construction projects in progress at the same time. During his life time he did work on a grand total of some six hundred odd courses.

One of Donald's greatest services was the establishment of early golf at Pinehurst on the very highest standards. He never forgot his early training under Tom Morris and in all his work lived up to the traditions learned in the old gray town under the old master.

Donald Ross established his home in Pinehurst and in his later years became a director in the company which now operates the resort. He died there in 1948 after years of fruitful contribution to the game of golf in America.

The massive, chockablock bunkering of the par-5 4th hole at Bethpage Black

FACING PAGE
Hole 18 at the Bethpage State Park Black Course, Long Island, New York, another Tillinghast marvel

5 of course. When this is played from the full length of the teeing-ground it should prove one of the most exacting three-shotters I know of anywhere. In locating and designing the green, which can only be gained by a most precise approach from the right, I must confess that I was a trifle scared myself, when I looked back and regarded the hazardous route that must be taken by a stinging second shot to get into position to attack this green.

Without doubt were the other courses at Bethpage as severe as Black the place would not have enjoyed the great popularity it has known since it was thrown open to the public. Yet thousands of "weak sisters" undoubtedly will flock there insisting on at least one tussle with the Black Leopard, just to show that they can "take it." This at least has been the situation at Pine Valley since the day it was noised through the land that this man eater was loose. From all quarters the underdogs of golfdom travel to take maybe just one snap at the old killer. If they had to play under such punishing conditions, week in and out, they probably would chuck their clubs in the lake and take to pitching horseshoes for recreation.

But for the more exalted par-shooters, and there are a great many of these lads, too, who want to know exactly how good they are, there are Pine Valley, Old Black and a few others to humble them, and the country may well stand a few, just a few, for this humblin' operation, which, after all, will make greater golfers of them.

Since this writer was honored by being selected as the consultant in the planning of these courses by the Long Island State Park Commission, it seems entirely proper that some observations may be made at this time. Certainly any conception of the true golf importance of this work is limited to comparatively few.

The three courses (Black, Red and Blue) are of great excellence and charm. This could not well be otherwise, for the large tract of land offered unusual opportunities for the creation of golf holes. As a matter of fact it must be regarded as one of the most truly great golf properties in the world. This statement is inspired by no other sentiment than admiration and appreciation after many years of observation. The Bethpage tract is superb.

Fownes's revisions went well beyond bunkering. Holes were lengthened. In order to improve drainage—and, as it happened, to beleaguer the hapless golfer—he had ditches dug in the rough. Better drainage was also nominated as the reason for canting the greens, which, in the bargain, were clipped extremely short, to about 3/32nds of an inch, day in and day out. And for an important tournament, Fownes and Loeffler made sure that the greens would be all but unmanageable, "firming them up" (some would say "packing them down") by means of a 1,500-pound roller pushed by eight men.

Oakmont—perhaps even more so than Pine Valley—had become the nonpareil of penal golf course design. And if it prompted little in the way of affection (at least from those who confronted it only when their careers depended on it), it did earn universal respect. It was impregnable. It was implacable. . . .

If the early '60s saw the demise of the infamous furrows, by the close of that decade another change was getting underway, though the fruits of it would not be apparent for quite some time. Over the years, observers tended to label Oakmont "plain." *The Encyclopedia of Golf* (published in 1975 and with Herbert Warren Wind in all likelihood providing the commentary on Oakmont) characterized it thusly: "Oakmont is not a pretty course. The visitor will not be distracted by flowering bushes, stately trees, or shimmering water hazards. . . . But then, a pretty Oakmont would be incongruous. It is not intended to arouse feelings of warmth and affection. . . ."

Except for the continued absence of water, the worthy *Encyclopedia* has been outdated. Today Oakmont is very pretty. Indeed, it is an exquisite parkland course in the tradition of Winged Foot and Baltusrol, both outside New York City, with an assortment of handsome hardwoods—maple, oak, sycamore—to say nothing of silver birch and flowering cherry and dogwood and the deep forest green of pine and fir. It is a veritable arboretum. And it is not at all what either Fownes had in mind. As a matter of fact, it is not necessarily what all of its members today have in mind. . . .

There are three truths about the Oakmont greens that suggest the danger inherent in virtually every putt.

First, Oakmont is perhaps the only great course where, under normal weather and playing conditions, a putt missed can be a putt made. This writer has seen, on the second green, an uphill left-to-right putt of about nine feet ghost toward the hole on the high side, slip cleanly past the cup some six or seven inches as it belatedly took the break, pause almost indiscernibly, then, seeking a place to stop, retreat down the short slope and tumble into the hole. A bit of patience is all that's required.

Second, on the long lag putt (say, on the 602-yard 12th) you can literally stroll alongside your ball after you've struck it and even read the fine print on its cover as it creeps across the silken surface before coming to rest, usually a good 12 feet beyond the cup.

Third, Oakmont greens generally have to be slowed down a tad for the Open. Banks Smith, 62-year-old chairman of the club's Grounds Committee, says, "We keep them somewhere between 11 and 12 on the Stimpmeter—maybe closer to 12—for everyday play. The USGA wants them at 11 for the Open. Years ago our greens were brown and fast. Today they're green and fast. We use very little water—none at all if we can get away with it. We want them as fast as they can be without stressing them. That's the way the majority of our members like it. Matter of fact, for one of our member-member tournaments, we try to get them to 13, maybe a little higher. Now *that* is fast!"

When asked how visitors feel about these putting surfaces, Smith laughs, "Most people seem to have fun here, even when they're lining up their fourth putt."

Sounds very much like the Oakmont of Henry and William Fownes. Oh, admittedly,

the furrows are long gone now and the aesthetes have had their day in court (and the courtroom may never look the same again), but the original design of the holes has remained solidly intact, the bunkering continues to intimidate as on no other site of American major championships, and the greens have not lost their power to make strong men tremble—and twitch. The course has, in truth, never been revamped, though it has frequently been refined.

Bobby Jones, who won the 1925 U.S. Amateur here, wrote, "It was, and is, a severe golf course, Oakmont. I think it's the best test of championship golf in this country."

That judgment may, almost 70 years later, still be valid. Eternal Oakmont.

The famous "Church Pews" on the 3rd hole at Oakmont Country Club, outside Pittsburgh. The bunkers were originally filled with river sand and furrowed with heavy iron rakes

AUGUSTA NATIONAL

from *A Golf Story: Bobby Jones, Augusta National, and the Masters Tournament,* 1986*

Detail of a first-day cover for the opening of Augusta National

IN 1857, A BELGIAN BARON NAMED LOUIS MATHIEU EDOUARD BERCKMANS, WHO WAS AN amateur horticulturist, purchased nearly four hundred acres on the western border of Augusta, Georgia, that had once been an indigo plantation, indigo having been one of the South's chief exports, along with cotton and rice, until the Civil War. The plantation was said to have been the site where General James Edward Oglethorpe had sat about a cheery fire of pine knots and smoked the pipe of peace with the Cherokee Indians, thereby opening the way for Georgia to become a colony and, eventually, a state.

Berckmans's son, Prosper Julius Alphonse, was also a horticulturist, and a professional one at that, as well as an agronomist. Forming a partnership under the trade name of Fruitlands Nurseries, the two Berckmanses started what may have been the first commercial nursery in the South. It was certainly the largest. A catalogue they issued a few years after opening the nursery listed thirteen hundred varieties of pear and nine hundred varieties of apple. Additionally, they imported a number of trees and plants from all over the world, the progeny of which, nurtured at Fruitlands, ended up decorating the exterior of some of the South's grandest homes and plantations for the next half century. Chief among their decorative plants was the azalea, which Prosper Berckmans popularized and which remains to this day the floral signature of everything below Mason and Dixon's Line.

Fruitlands Nurseries lay on the south side of what is now known as Washington Road in an area just beyond the city limits of Augusta. Baron Berckmans died in 1883, and not long afterward Prosper Berckmans lost his wife, who had borne him three sons, two of whom became horticulturists in their own rights.

In time, Prosper remarried, on this occasion to a woman thirty years younger than he. They lived together in Prosper's home, a beautiful manor house entered from Washington Road along a carriage path, three hundred yards long, lined on both sides in sentry straightness by magnolias.

The Manor, as Prosper called the house simply enough, was not old by Augusta standards, having been built in 1854, when the property had still been an indigo plantation. But it had a

* **CHARLES PRICE** (1925-1994) was a leading American golf writer, who started out as a reporter for *Golf World* in the late 1940s and became the first editor of *GOLF Magazine* in 1958. His books include *The World of Golf: A Panorama of Six Centuries of the Game's History*. Price was a close friend of Bobby Jones.

gallery in attendance, usually in the hundreds, often in the thousands. Additionally, he wanted to have a hand in helping design a course that would express a lot of his architectural ideas and that would be championship in every sense of the word, something that was sorely lacking anywhere in the South. Roberts filed Jones's ambitions in the tidy warehouse of his mind.

During one of his many golf junkets to Augusta, Roberts met Thomas Barrett, probably at the Bon Air Vanderbilt and possibly over a bridge game. Barrett had never played golf in his life, although he was active in other sports, having engaged the support of the Chamber of Commerce behind a number of athletic events in Augusta. Like so many millions of non-golfers in the country, he admired Jones immensely, an admiration that was increased all the more by having met him.

Just after Jones had made the public announcement of his retirement, he and Roberts had a short conversation in Atlanta about the idea of his private club. It was agreed that Augusta was a more logical place than Atlanta for it. To begin with, Jones was interested in a club where golf could be played primarily in the winter. Secondly, Augusta had a number of winter residents whose wealth had survived the stock market crash. The nucleus of a national membership could be built about them. In Atlanta, that seemed unlikely.

It was agreed that Roberts would handle the financing. Jones at that time was nearly broke, having spent most of his earnings playing in championships on both sides of the Atlantic. He had yet to select, let alone make money, from the avalanche of commercial propositions that was now overflowing his office. With the inestimable stature of Bobby Jones behind him, Roberts had few misgivings about the project. The Depression couldn't last forever.

Back in Augusta, Roberts felt that the most logical man to consult with first was Tom Barrett, active as he was in the Chamber of Commerce. Barrett immediately recalled the hullabaloo about Commodore Stoltz and the Augusta Fleetwood. He recommended that Roberts look into the property held by the Washington Heights Development company—Baron Berckmans's old Fruitlands Nurseries.

By now, it was the spring of 1931. Roberts telephoned Jones to come to Augusta as soon as possible so the two of them could look over the property. To be sure, Jones had seen the run-down nursery before. Having played so often at the Augusta Country Club, which adjoins it, he couldn't have helped but see it. But that view had been at the lowest point on the property, where Rae's Creek cuts across the southeast corner of the old nursery and disappears to the south. (Herbert Warren Wind would label it "Amen Corner" years later.) Now, for the first time, Jones was to drive through that honor guard of magnolias that leads to the Manor and then to look down on the flowering expanses from the lawn behind the house.

"I shall never forget my first visit to the property," Jones would write years later.

> The long lane of magnolias through which we approached was beautiful. The old manor house with its cupola and walls of masonry two feet thick was charming. The rare trees and shrubs of the old nursery were enchanting. But when I walked out on the grass terrace under the big trees behind the house and looked down over the property, the experience was unforgettable. It seemed that this land had been lying here for years just waiting for someone to lay a golf course upon it. Indeed, it even looked as though it were already a golf course, and I am sure that one standing today where I stood on this first visit, on the terrace overlooking the practice putting green, sees the property almost exactly as I saw it then. The grass of the fairways and greens is greener, of course, and some of the pines are a bit larger, but the broad expanse of the main body of the property lay at my feet then just as it does now.

For the rest of Jones's life, some of the most serene hours of that not very serene future were spent just gazing at that view.

JAMES P. LEE

SHINNECOCK

from *Golf in America*, 1895*

The First Clubhouse in America, by Leland Gustavson. The clubhouse at Shinnecock, completed in 1892, was designed by Stanford White, the leading American architect of the Gilded Age

FACING PAGE

The soaring 9th fairway at Shinnecock Hills Golf Club in Southampton, New York, climbing up to the white porticoes of the clubhouse. This is one of the great vistas in American golf

THESE DETAILS ARE JOTTED DOWN HERE WITH REGARD TO THE various clubs which are mentioned, because it is pleasant as time goes on to be able to look back at the beginning of things, and because these times form a starting-point in the history of golf in this country.

For natural fitness and suitability, no links in the country can be said to excel those of the Shinnecock Hills Golf Club. It has already been said that the ground which one finds upon links by the sea is always apt to be more favorable for the game than that upon an inland course. Not only does the sandy soil drink in water with great rapidity, but the formation of the country is more likely to be that of low, rolling hills, admirably adapted to the game. The course at Shinnecock Hills extends over some two or three miles of excellent turf, affording fine lies for the ball and abounding in hazards and bunkers. The game of golf can hardly be played to the greatest advantage upon a course entirely devoid of sand bunkers, and it is here that these exist in abundance. The clubhouse is built upon the summit of one of the hills, and from the piazzas on either side are seen Peconic Bay to the north, and to the south, Shinnecock Bay, cut off from the ocean merely by a narrow strip of sand dunes. On either side are the rolling hills and valleys which make the formation of this particular part of the island so unique. No trees exist to break the graceful outlines of the hills, and in the fall of the year they assume that fine purple coloring which is characteristic of the country similarly situated in Scotland.

---

* **JAMES PARRISH LEE** wrote the first book about golf in America, and it is a surprisingly sweet and perceptive work. Lee, who was a descendant of General Robert E. Lee, graduated from Harvard and was a good all-around athlete, but, alas, not a good golfer. Lee was a member of Shinnecock and knew the course well. His uncle, Samuel L. Parrish, was one of the founders of Shinnecock, as well as the first Treasurer of the USGA.

PAT WARD-THOMAS

PILGRIMAGE TO THE
BIRTHPLACE
OF THE WALKER CUP

from *The Long Green Fairway*, 1966*

Hole 17 at the National Golf Links,
overlooking Peconic Bay

ALMOST FORTY YEARS HAVE PASSED SINCE BATTLE FIRST WAS JOINED FOR THE WALKER Cup between golfers of the United States and Britain. The encounter was on the National Golf Links of America, and at the outset of the present pilgrimage it seemed fitting to visit an enchanting place.

The streets were still heavy with the night's clinging warmth as we crossed town to the Pennsylvania station and took train for Southampton on the maligned Long Island Railroad. The hideous sprawl of Brooklyn sped by more swiftly than we had dared to hope, and after a glimpse of the cool lawns and creepered walls of Forest Hills, there was all change in Jamaica. This sounded more romantic than it was, but soon the great surge of people, the most cosmopolitan of all, urgently seeking the island's beaches, was gone; there was a parlour car, still and comfortable, and the soft voice of a Negro attendant offering Danish and coffee. Now there was no need to envy the big cars gliding along the expressways, and Southampton no longer was a hundred miles away. The suburbs were thinning, the pine and sand country might have been that of Surrey running down to Hampshire, and an affection for the Long Island Railroad was growing.

The National is not far from Southampton, a charming little town of white timbered houses, spacious and peaceful amid trees, that has been in existence since the eighteenth century, but until one is almost upon the Links there is little suggestion of the beauty to come. Then abruptly the road sweeps round a curve in the woods and a tiny bay, and there on the crest of a gentle green hill stands the National. The prospect on that breathless summer morning was almost overwhelming in its suddenness. The whole perfect expanse of Peconic Bay, a vast inlet of Long Island Sound, lay before us; there was a wonderful feeling of detachment and peace, and Manhattan might have been on the other side of the earth.

There are more than six thousand courses in the United States, but few bear any resemblance to a links. The National is not one in the sense that it lies amid sandhills on low ground by the sea, but it has several things in common. Always one is aware of the presence of the sea,

---

* **PAT WARD-THOMAS** (1913-1982) was a luminary of British golf writing, following in the august tradition of Bernard Darwin. Ward-Thomas was the golf correspondent for the *Manchester Guardian* from 1950 through 1977 and began writing the golf column for *Country Life* in 1957, alternating with Darwin. Many of his lyrical essays from *The Guardian* and *Country Life* are collected in *The Long Green Fairway*. This article originally appeared in *The Guardian* in 1961.

COLOSSI OF MID-CENTURY

CHAPTER SIX

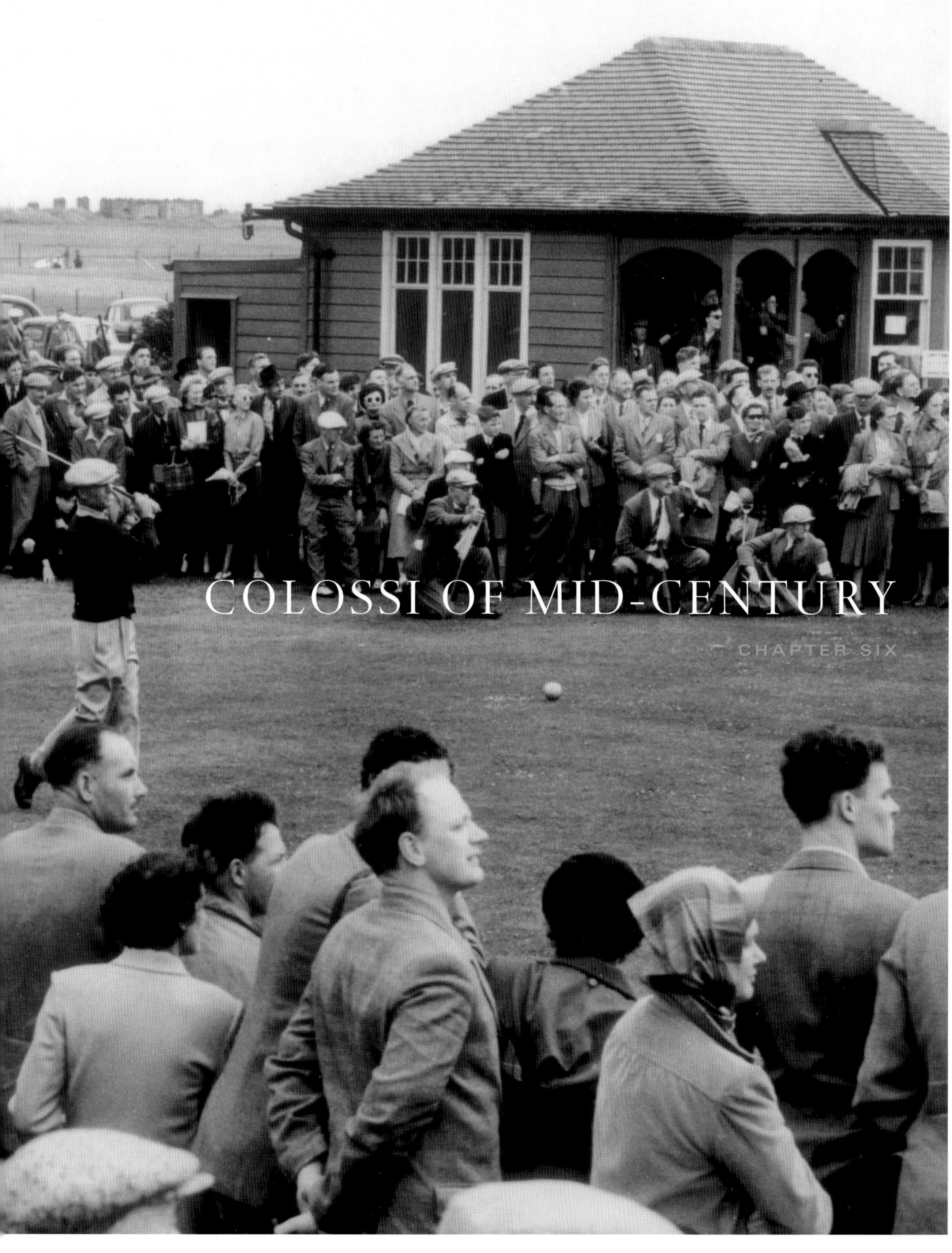

COLOSSI OF MID-CENTURY

Four American originals dominated golf in the 1940s and 1950s. Three of these golfing legends were born in 1912, each a uniquely authentic American personality. Ben Hogan and Byron Nelson were both born in Fort Worth, while Sam Snead came from the hollows of Hot Springs, Virginia. Babe Didrikson was born in 1914 in Port Arthur, Texas, and grew up in Beaumont, the daughter of Norwegian immigrants.

Hogan, Nelson, and Snead played a long time ago but we feel we know them very well. Their careers took markedly different paths, but each left such a strong and distinct golfing legacy that every golfer understands who they were and what they stand for.

Of the three, most of us have the clearest image of Snead because he played so well for so long. Here was a golfing Methuselah who retained his wonderfully natural gift right up to the end, serving as honorary starter at the Masters until 2002, just a few weeks before his death.

Slammin' Sammy Snead must surely have had the sweetest swing of any golfer who ever lived. He was a tremendous natural athlete, with a naïve quality out of an American picaresque novel—but he also shrewdly cultivated his hillbilly image when he came to national prominence in the late 1930s. It was an image that stuck with the public. Snead won a record 84 PGA tournaments, including the 1965 Greater Greensboro Open when he was fifty-two years old. But he was also a star-crossed golfer, a man who while blessed with enormous talent, never won the U.S. Open. He came close many times, the closest of all in 1947, losing in an 18-hole play-off by one stroke to Lew Worsham.

What strikes us most about Snead, though, is how clearly he loved playing golf. He continued to play, always for a wager, right up until he died. For Snead, golf was life.

Byron Nelson's career stands in sharp contrast with Snead's in many respects. Nelson

PAGES 202, 203

Ben Hogan hitting his opening drive in the British Open at Carnoustie Golf Club, Tayside, Scotland. He went on to win his third straight major championship in his epic 1953 season

The Babe lines up a long putt

actually had a brief playing career but it was meteoric and memorable while it lasted. In 1945, he won a record eleven consecutive tournaments. With the passage of time, Nelson's feat, like Joe DiMaggio's 56-game hitting streak, appears to be a record that will never be broken. Nor was Nelson simply beating up on weak fields. His scoring average in the 30 tournaments he played in that year was a phenomenal 68.33. Nelson retired from competitive golf in 1946, when he was still young, so that he could fulfill his dream of owning his own ranch in Texas. Yet we feel we also know Nelson very well, mainly because for many years he was a commentator on television golfing broadcasts and continues to host his own popular tournament in Dallas, the Byron Nelson Classic. We have seen Nelson for so many years on television and listened to him being interviewed enough times to have no doubt that, in the words of Dan Jenkins, he is "the nicest, warmest, friendliest immortal ever to come down a fairway."

Of these three Olympian figures, the one held in the most awe is Ben Hogan. Hogan, like Nelson, learned golf in the hardscrabble caddy shacks of Fort Worth, but his personality was as saturnine as Nelson's was sunny. He became the greatest golfer of the 1940s and 1950s, and a figure of such intense and obsessive dedication to perfecting the golf swing that he continues to inspire fascination among golfers young and old fifty years after his heyday.

Hogan and his wife Valerie, as all followers of golf well know, were nearly killed in a head-on car collision with a bus in 1949. But Hogan came back more determined than ever, winning the 1950 U.S. Open at Merion. His landmark year was 1953, when he won all three majors he entered—the Masters,

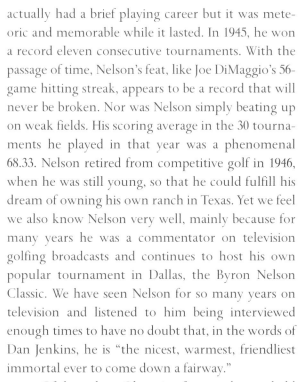

the U.S. Open at Oakmont, and the British Open at Carnoustie (the British Open conflicted with the PGA that year).

We feel we know Hogan, not in the familiar sense that we know Snead and Nelson, through watching and listening to them on television, but in that we understand the mythical Hogan. We understand that what made Hogan great was his relentless will to conquer the game.

Mildred "Babe" Didrikson Zaharias, generally regarded as the greatest all-around woman athlete who ever lived, set records in the hurdles, javelin, and high jump during the 1932 Olympics. Unlike Nelson, Hogan, and Snead, Babe Didrikson was introduced to golf later in life and quickly became the supreme woman golfer of her generation. She was a driving force in the founding of the Ladies Professional Golf Association in 1950 and became the LPGA's marquee player. The Babe won 31 events in her eight years as a professional, including the U.S. Women's Open in 1948, 1950, and 1954. Yet for all her accomplishments and zest for the game, Didrikson remains a more elusive figure than her great male counterparts because she died so tragically young.

DAN JENKINS

THE MOTHER OF ALL STREAKS

from *Fairways and Greens*, 1994*

The flowing swing of Byron Nelson

SOME OF MY CHUMS IN THE GOLF WRITING SOCIETY HAD A MERRY OLD TIME ONE recent spring when they made a big thing out of a "streak" that Fred Couples went on, a two-month journey in which the popular fellow bagged three firsts and two seconds on the PGA Tour. Let me say that I wasn't embarrassed at the time by the flood of adjectives in which my brethren almost drowned poor Fred—I knew how starved they were for a new American hero—so I hope they weren't too disturbed by my yawns.

Not that I wasn't happy to see the boyishly handsome Couples become better known, to see his lazybones swing become more familiar to the masses, to have him endear himself to us all with his famous statement: "I never answer the phone at home—somebody may want to talk to me." That was a nice spree Couples enjoyed, a fine binge, but you wouldn't call it a "streak."

It was nothing you would carve in marble or sew on a pillow. It was hardly a performance of historic significance. It wouldn't live in infamy, or even a neighboring town, and I might add that it would die of hunger in Fort Worth, Texas, where Byron Nelson and Ben Hogan come from, not to forget me, your dogged statistician.

As an old streak watcher, I know a streak when I see one. A streak is when the Oklahoma Sooners win 47 football games in a row. A streak is when Joe DiMaggio hits safely in 56 straight games. A streak is when Joe Louis passes through my entire childhood knocking out Bums of the Month. Real streaks don't eat quiche.

In golf, I also know that streaks were defined once and for all by Byron Nelson.

Most grown-ups of the golf persuasion are aware of the grandest streak in the history of the game. I speak of 1945, when Byron won 11 tournaments in a row and 18 for the year. What most grown-ups of the golf persuasion do not realize, however, is that Nelson's streak started in 1944 and ran through much of 1946.

Before I get to that, I think I should point out that Byron is probably the nicest, warmest, friendliest immortal that ever came down a fairway. As a kid, I was lucky to see

* **DAN JENKINS,** like Byron Nelson and Ben Hogan, is a golfing legend from Fort Worth, only Jenkins blazed his trail as a writer. Jenkins started covering golf for the *Fort Worth Press* at the same time that he enrolled in Texas Christian University, where he was captain of the golf team. Like Hogan and Nelson, Jenkins has the distinction of finishing runner-up in the Fort Worth City Championship. He is a member of the Texas Golf Hall of Fame.

This portrait of "Lord Byron" by Everett Raymond Kinstler hangs in the USGA Museum

him in his prime. We became friendly later and enjoyed a lot of discussions, at my prodding, about how it was back then.

Golf's grandest streak couldn't have happened to a better person. Now then.

Not a lot has ever been said about 1944 because it gets confused with 1943, which was the dreariest and most inactive year in the annals of American sport. World War II brought an end to everything in '43 except for Notre Dame football and Stan Musial's bat with the St. Louis Cardinals.

But things began to look up in '44. Italy had surrendered—it was one down and two to go where the war was concerned. So the PGA Tour made a comeback with 22 tournaments. That was when a tall, fast-playing Texan began to be known to newspaper poets as "Lord Byron Nelson, golf's mechanical man."

Nelson won eight of those 22 events, four in a row at one point, and was either first, second, or third in 17 out of the 22. His worst finish in '44 was a tie for sixth at Oakland. Horrors.

Suddenly, he was a familiar figure in sport, a presence. As Bobby Jones had become familiar in his knickers and necktie, Nelson was an idol in a white visor, white golf shirt, brown slacks, brown shoes, a shotmaker deluxe with a gloveless grip, upright swing, a straight hitter, a fire-at-the-pin type of player.

Incredibly, he was not a great putter. He used an old blade putter, one with loft.

"You needed some loft on the putter in those days," he would remark later. "Some of the greens we putted on weren't in the best condition." To put it mildly.

Anyhow, then came 1945. Nelson started off by finishing either first or second in the first eight tournaments, three of which were won by Sam Snead. The illustrious streak began on March 11 when Byron teamed up with Jug McSpaden to win the Miami Four-Ball. Next came a tough victory in the Charlotte Open, where he had to go 36 holes to beat Snead in a playoff. After that, it was magic time. Nelson won the Greensboro Open by eight strokes, the Durham Open by five, the Atlanta Open by nine, the Montreal Open by ten, the Philadelphia Invitational by two, the Chicago Victory Open by seven, the PGA Championship in Dayton, Ohio, at match play where he defeated Gene Sarazen, Mike Turnesa, Denny Shute, Claude Harmon, and Sam Byrd in that order, the Tam O'Shanter back in Chicago by eleven, and the Canadian Open by four.

The streak didn't end until August 19, when he wound up in a tie for fourth at Memphis. Thus, Nelson went five months—*five* months, pardon my shouting—without losing a golf tournament.

It's a footnote to the streak that Byron came back the week after Memphis to win the Knoxville Invitational by ten strokes in a field that included, among others, Ben Hogan and Sam Snead. In those days, the others often included Jimmy Demaret, Craig Wood, Henry Picard, Vic Ghezzi, Dick Metz, Jug McSpaden, Johnny Revolta, Porky Oliver, Dutch Harrison, Lloyd Mangrum, Lawson Little, Ralph Guldahl, Toney Penna, Ky Laffoon, Clayton Heafner, George Fazio, Herman Barron, and Frank Stranahan. Which is to say that Byron wasn't exactly whipping up on dog meat.

And what of 1946? Well, after all of the aforementioned, Nelson started off in '46 by winning the first two tournaments of the year, the L.A. Open at Riviera by five and the San Francisco Open at Olympic by nine. Considering that he had captured the last two events he entered in '45, the Seattle Open by a mere thirteen shots and the Glen Garden Invitational in Fort Worth by eight, this gave him four in a row again, or one of those minor streaks that's been overlooked.

He then took some time off and began to think seriously about retirement. The constant pressure of trying to live up to everyone's expectations was burning a hole in what had always been a weak and unruly stomach anyhow. He went ahead and competed sporadically through the rest of '46, entering twenty-one tournaments in all. Guess what. He won six of them and even tied for the U.S. Open at Canterbury in Cleveland but lost by a slim one stroke to Lloyd Mangrum in what became a grueling 36-hole playoff.

He did retire at the end of '46, at the astonishingly tender age of thirty-four. Among the game's immortals, only Bobby Jones, at twenty-eight, quit competitive golf at a younger age than Nelson.

The arithmetic for this amazing three-year period shows that Byron won 32 of the 72 tournaments he entered. That's very nearly half of them, folks. The arithmetic also shows that he was either first, second, or third in 57 out of the 72.

If I were an exclamation point user, there wouldn't be any left by now. In today's world, he would have earned a different nickname—Lord Barbarian Nelson, golf's Terminator Predator.

Through all of this mischief, Nelson's lone finish *out* of the top 10 was a tie for thirteenth place at Pensacola one February week of 1946, which prompted the wise-cracking Jimmy Demaret to observe, "I've been telling you all along he's overrated."

53

from *Hogan*, 1996*

THE UNITED STATES OPEN, JUNE 11-13, OAKMONT, PENNSYLVANIA

Ben Hogan had won three of the five previous Opens, but the USGA required everybody (except defending champion Julius Boros) to participate in a thirty-six-hole qualifying tournament on the two days before the main event. Making Hogan qualify for the U.S. Open was like running a credit check on John D. Rockefeller, an insult and a waste of time. And although Hogan made the field without much trouble with a 77 at Pittsburgh Field Club and a 73 at Oakmont, the extra rounds cost him some of his limited supply of energy and a pulled muscle in his back.

Monumental and forbidding, Oakmont was the Mount Everest of golf courses. A river ran through it, the Allegheny; as did a turnpike, the Pennsylvania. Some of Oakmont's huge trees met at the top to form canopies, breaking the light into kaleidoscopes of sunshine and shadow. The shifting patterns were pleasant to contemplate even when your ball was hunkered down in the too-tall grass near a too-big tree or buried in a bunker with *furrows* in it for godsakes, like a freshly plowed field. The first, tenth, and twelfth greens tilted *away* from the fairway, a difficulty almost as maddening as the unplayable sand pits. Architect Henry Clay Fownes designed Oakmont in 1903 to be the toughest course in the world and he succeeded. Shots that strayed from the straight and narrow indicated an evil heart, Fownes seemed to say from across the years. Suffering was called for.

Salvation lay not on the greens, which undulated like a belly dancer. Although they were less steep than those at Augusta National, Oakmont's carpets were even quicker. Golf writers searched for similes involving hockey rinks and pond ice. Snead joked that the dime he used to mark his ball slid off one green. Grantland Rice wrote of seeing quite a number of the world's best players take five putts on some greens during the 1935 Open at Oakmont. He even witnessed a *six*-putt—from *ten* feet.

Hogan began memorizing and analyzing the old course nine days before the tournament started. "I have no practice system," he told a *Pittsburgh Press* writer, then described his practice system. "I go over the course a couple of times to decide what type of golf I'll have to

* **CURT SAMPSON** (b. 1952) lives in Texas and was a professional golfer. In this excerpt from *Hogan*, he describes in vivid reportorial style Hogan's win at Oakmont in his record-breaking season of 1953. Sampson's other books include *Royal & Ancient: Blood, Sweat and Fear at the British Open*, a very entertaining history of the British Open, and *Chasing Tiger*.

BEN HOGAN

from *Masters of Golf,* 1961*

Hogan teeing off at Carnoustie
(detail of photograph on pages
202, 203)

THE WIND STOOD STRONG FROM THE WEST; THE FLAGS STRAINED AT THEIR MASTS AND a great multitude was gathered about the first hole at Carnoustie. There was tension and expectancy abroad and a sense of history such as I have never known at the outset of any championship. On the tee, awaiting his call from the starter, stood the slight grey figure of Hogan, the man who had become a legend in the minds of golfers all over the world. For years we had hoped, even prayed, that he would play in Britain. It would have been so wrong if he alone of the great golfers in history had never competed on a British course, and now, on that first hole at Carnoustie, the moment was at hand. There is no particular distinction about the hole; there are many finer beginnings. It had no significance in the play of that championship, but for thousands it meant that a longing had been realized. Here in the flesh was Hogan. Not only was there a compulsion to watch him and examine a remarkable technique, but also to set eyes on a man who had achieved so much in the face of an awful adversity.

All the world knows of the accident that foggy morning in Texas which almost killed him and then threatened to prevent his ever playing golf again; and all the world knows that within eighteen months he had won his second American Open Championship. Now, in the year of 1953, when a queen was crowned and Everest conquered, there came a summer that will remain indelible in my memory of golf, as I am sure it will in Hogan's and many others.

In the spring of that year at Augusta he had won the Masters with a total of 279, five strokes lower than any other total in the history of the event, and as many in front of Porky Oliver, his nearest challenger. The American Open was a similar procession, with Hogan six strokes ahead of the field; and then it was that people, Gene Sarazen not least among them, began to urge that he should play in the British Open. Hogan needed persuading for he limited his tournaments strictly after the accident; he did not like traveling and in a way stood to lose more than he would gain, even by winning. In the end he yielded and I think there was an awareness of destiny behind his decision. Hogan is a modest man; he speaks almost humbly of his golf but I am sure he knew, as we felt, that if posterity was to acclaim him as the supreme golfer of his generation, he must compete in Britain. This would preserve the fitness of things for evermore.

---

* In *Masters of Golf*, **PAT WARD-THOMAS** profiles each of the great golfers of the 1950s, but it is in Hogan and his invincibility at Carnoustie that he finds his most awe-inspiring subject.

Carnoustie was a fearsome challenge for Hogan. He had never been to Scotland; he had never played with the small ball; the condition of the turf was quite alien to him, because I doubt whether he had ever played on a real links before. There were none of the comforts standard in American clubs, and, lastly, there were strange people. I believe that Hogan was astonished at the numbers who plainly were anxious for him to win, even in a country which normally is as passionately preoccupied, to the exclusion of all else, with the deeds of its own. This knowledge must have been an increased burden to him. His temperament had thrived on a sense of opposition, nearly all his life, and now almost everyone, except of course the other competitors, was on his side. This was a new challenge to his spirit; the great old course a new one to his technique.

Hogan arrived two weeks before the championship and spent days analyzing and dissecting the course with the cold detachment of a surgeon. Every line, the position of every bunker, the effect of the winds, the falls of the ground and the greens were scrutinized with extreme care. The playing of the course was planned with the exactness of a modern military operation. Then came the farce of the first qualifying round when hordes stampeded, in his pursuit, careless of the fate of W.J. Branch, his partner, who often had to play over the heads of the crowd. But none of this mattered very much, save to poor Branch, for the great moment was at hand.

The 1st hole at Carnoustie Golf Club, Tayside, Scotland

WATCHING AND SUFFERING

from *The Glasgow Herald*, 1969*

Ben Hogan steadying himself before blasting from the water at the 17th hole in the final round of the U.S. Open at Cherry Hills Country Club, Denver, Colorado, in 1960. Hogan lost to Arnold Palmer

ONE OF THE GREAT AND MOVING STORIES OF GOLF CONCERNS THE SEVENTEENTH HOLE at Prestwick as it was played in the final of the 1899 Amateur championship by John Ball and Freddie Tait.

The big Alps bunker was flooded and Tait played a miraculous shot out of a deep puddle onto the green, to be followed there by Ball, who played an equally great shot from hard, wet sand close under the face of the black wooden sleepers.

Tait's ball was a gutty, and floated, and it rocked on the little waves he made in the puddle as he waded in, like Agag, who, as every student of the Bible knows, walked delicately.

It was while the ball was rocking and Tait was taking his stance that a Scottish supporter of the gallant Black Watch officer was heard to cry out in agony, "Wait till it settles, Freddie, wait till it settles."

There are moments in every sport and in many spectacles when one's emotions are over-wrung.

Take, for example, the old gentleman F. L. Lucas describes in his essay on Tragedy who, in the middle of "Othello," stood up and thundered, "You great fool, can't you see it's all right?" There could be no truer tribute to Shakespeare and the actors.

It is the onlooker, not the participant, who suffers most, and who enjoys the most exquisite joy from a superb *coup de main* or *coup de theatre.* Thus, one of the most moving moments I have seen on a golf course was while Hogan was playing the last hole at Carnoustie in that memorable 1953 Open championship.

He was, humanly speaking, home and dry after his drive, which was immensely long and plumb in the middle of the fairway. No doubt he was seething with emotion, but he looked like the little ice man as he stalked stiff-legged down the deserted fairway from which all but the players and their attendants had been banished.

* The late **SAMUEL LIVINGSTONE (S.L.) McKINLAY,** born in 1907, wrote about golf for the *Glasgow Herald* with a great deal of lightly worn literacy. In this excerpt, he provides a poignant insight into the Wee Ice Mon's final march down the 18th hole at Carnoustie. McKinlay started out at the *Herald* as a junior copy editor in 1929 and wrote 345 golf columns from 1956 through 1980. A leading Scottish amateur, he played on the British Walker Cup team in 1934, when the match was held at St. Andrews. In 1950, McKinlay became a member of St. Andrews, but his favorite course always remained Millport, on the small island of Great Cumbrae in the Firth of Clyde, where he learned to play golf as a boy.

There was a vast crowd all willing him on to victory, but no one, I swear, was more involved and more interested than some of his fellow-competitors playing behind him. They paid him the greatest tribute any golfer can win, for they postponed playing their own shots at the adjacent sixteenth and seventeenth holes and stood, almost reverentially, watching as he settled down to the shot and then drilled a perfect medium iron into the heart of the green. And they clapped, too, like the rest of us.

The gallant Freddie Tait gets ready to hit out of the Alps bunker filled with water to the 17th green in the final of the British Amateur at Prestwick in 1899. Tait would lose the match to John Ball on the 37th hole

JIM MURRAY

AN AMERICAN LEGEND

from The Jim Murray Collection, 1988*

*Legend—That which is characterized as something wonderful that occurred in the past, a series
of remarkable events occurring to an individual or group believed to have historical basis in fact.*
—Webster's New 20th Century Dictionary

EVER REGRET THAT YOU DIDN'T SEE DIMAGGIO HIT? GEHRIG HOMER? HUBBELL PITCH?

Feel cheated you never got to see Dempsey punch, Grange run, Jesse Owens jump,
Nagurski block? Like to have seen Jones putt, Luisetti shoot, Sande ride or Seabiscuit race?
Maybe you wish you could have seen Nijinsky dance, Barrymore act, Tilden volley?

All those are yesterday's roses. Faded dance cards in the attic. The memories of old men
nodding in the sun over cobwebbed chess pieces. Heirlooms of the mind.

The old-timers watch the moderns, shrug, shake their heads and say, "Yeah, but you
should have seen Cobb." Or Pie Traynor.

Sam Snead belongs to that past. Sam Snead came up when DiMaggio did. Gehrig and
Ruth were still around. So were Jones, Sande, Hubbell, Grange and Owens. None of them was
a bigger legend than Snead.

No one ever swung at a golf ball with the purity, the poetry Sam Snead did. Snead on
a tee was a thrilling thing to watch.

It was pure Americana. The barefoot boy with the trap lines and the fishing pole
with a cork on the line came walking out of the Blue Ridge Mountains of Virginia, the trail
of the lonesome pine, to shock the sports world. He came from a long line of people who
slept with their hats on and their rifles by the bed. His first golf club was a swamp maple
limb with a knot in the end and the bark left on for a grip. He didn't have boxes of new
Titleists to hit—he had round rocks.

Sam could have been anything—soda jerk, farmer, prize-fighter. Or moonshiner. The
sky was the limit down there in that army of North Virginia country where, Sam says, the
hollows were so narrow "the dogs had to wag their tails up and down."

* **JIM MURRAY** (1920-1998) is a sports writing legend. He joined the *Los Angeles Times* in 1961, after helping to found
Sports Illustrated, and before that he served as the Hollywood correspondent for *Time.* Murray's sports columns are
free-flowing streams of one-liners with cascades of metaphors. In this 1981 article, he pulls out all the stops for Sam Snead.
Murray received the Pulitzer Prize in 1990.

No one ever taught him how to hit a golf ball. He was double-jointed, rhythmical, had wrists like wagon tongues and could coil like a spring. No one had ever hit the ball as straight as Samuel Jackson Snead. He drove into the president of the Chesapeake & Ohio Railroad on a green one day and the man was apoplectic.

"Son, don't you know better than to hit a fairway shot into an occupied green?" he shrieked. "Mr. Bradley, that wasn't no fairway shot, that was my tee shot," Snead said. Since Alva Bradley had never seen a 345-yard tee shot, he made him do it again. Snead did.

What is so remarkable about Samuel Jackson Snead is, he's not in a wax museum someplace with his porkpie hat and Popeye arms. He's on a golf course, where he's been for over 50 years. He's 68 years old, and he shot a 69 in the opening round of the Vintage Invitational here the other day in a field that should be a patsy for Samuel Jackson—everyone in it is over fifty. Sam is more used to shooting 69s in fields that include people 48 years younger.

Sam won the L.A. Open in 1945—and finished second in the same tournament on the same course in 1974. He won the Greensboro Open for the first time in 1938—and for the 12th

Sam Snead shows off to Seve Ballesteros at the Greenbrier Hotel in White Sulphur Springs, West Virginia, before the 1979 Ryder Cup Match. Snead was the host professional at the Greenbrier for many years

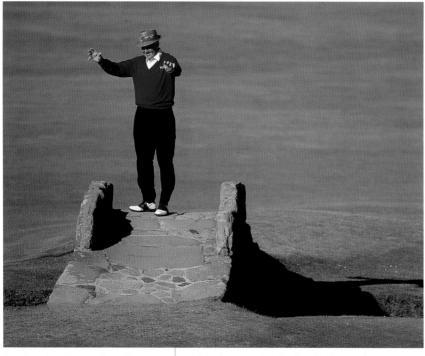

Sam Snead performs a jig on the Swilcan Bridge at St. Andrews during the 2000 British Open

and last in 1965. At age 52 years 10 months, he was the oldest ever to win a tournament.

They never got Sam out of the hills—or the hills out of Sam. He'd still rather hunt squirrels than tour Europe. He came to Hollywood periodically but it didn't take. Sam made the film, and then went home to soak his feet, and then back to Virginia to shoot ducks. His pleasures are biblical and simple. Once, when he went to a nightclub, he ordered soft drinks all night—then took the bottles home in his pocket to claim the deposit.

He played in a hat to cover his bald head and, today, only about 11 people in the word know he is bald. He won't wear a wig, just a hat. His humor runs heavily to barnyard, but his vocabulary has the "oot" and "aboot" of the Old Dominion. His handwriting, in Elizabethan script, would gladden the heart of the oldest schoolmarm in the land. But, otherwise, not the social graces for Sam Snead.

You might think you would find this legend of golf in fading old movie clips, or on the yellowed pages of a scrapbook. After all, he did win his first tournament the year DiMaggio broke in with the Yankees. But Snead, through the miracle of his own remarkable genes, is present, in person and intact in a palmetto hat and a 1-iron at the Vintage golf course this weekend.

He won 84 PGA tournaments, 22 more than anyone else, and 135 tournaments worldwide. He shot a 66 when he was 67 and a 68 when he was 69. It was figured out that, had he been able to shoot 69 in the last day, he would have won six U.S. Opens and tied four more. He never won any. But that was Snead.

No one was more exciting to watch on the golf course, with the possible exception of Arnold Palmer. No one had the trouble shots Snead had. Once, playing the Masters, on the third hole, a well-wisher, Freddy Corcoran, his manager, wondered where he was.

"He's over in the trees in the middle of all the squirrels and pine cones and needles and rocks," someone advised. "Good," nodded Corcoran, "he knows how to play that shot. I was afraid he was in the middle of the fairway."

He's an athletic marvel you might want to see before one of you dies. He's not gonna drive the ball into railroad barons 345 yards away anymore, but the singing swing is still there. He can still kick a doorsill 7-feet up, he still crabs about photographers clicking on his backswing, he hasn't mellowed and he still won't give you strokes. "Every time a guy tells me he's 'between a 12 and a 14 handicap,' I say 'Oh-oh, here I go again.' "

If you missed DiMaggio and Hubbell and Gehrig and Owens and Grange and Barrymore and Garbo and Tilden, catch Snead. And stand when he enters the room. He's a genuine, dyed-in-the-wool-hat American legend, Dan'l Boone with a 1-iron, Huck Finn in a hat. Mark Twain would have loved him. Sam Snead, coonskin golfer. We shall not see his like again. A legend past his time.

RHONDA GLENN

A FRIEND REMEMBERS
BABE ZAHARIAS
from *Golf Journal*, July 1984*

IN 1950, BABE DIDRIKSON ZAHARIAS HELPED ORGANIZE THE LADIES PROFESSIONAL Golf Association, gave it a kick in the pants and a poke in the funnybone and sent it on its way. In 1954, in one of the most inspiring victories in sport, she won the U.S. Women's Open Championship a year after a section of her colon was removed because of cancer.

By the end of 1956 she was dead.

She won that 1954 Women's Open—her third—at the Salem Country Club, in Salem, Massachusetts, where it returns this month.

Now, nearly 30 years later, we still talk of her and think of her and write of her, for she was a curiously complex woman. Depending on the source, she was remarkably generous, or petulant and spoiled; she was boastful and a braggart, or she was painfully shy. It's possible that, controversial in the way that brilliant people sometimes are, she was all of those things.

It is not arguable, however, that she was the greatest female athlete ever, and that, for all her flaws, she was my first female hero.

This story begins rather pitiably not long after her remarkable triumphs in the 1932 Olympic Games, in Los Angeles. She had qualified for eight events, but she was allowed to enter only three. She won two of them—the javelin throw, setting both world and Olympic records, and the 80-meter hurdles, with an Olympic record. She lost the final of the high jump.

Earlier she had won the AAU Women's track and field team championship by herself.

Because of the times and some unwritten rules, however, the road ahead was rough.

Pictures of her from those early days show a lithe girl in a track suit, with a boyish figure, a shock of short, straight hair, and a square jaw and prominent chin. Her smile is generous, if a bit lopsided in that self-conscious half-grin peculiar to some women athletes, and her eyes, in all pictures, are remarkable—lightly tinted, crinkled at the corners, full of fun. The eyes of the Babe are alert and joyous and, well, kind.

"You bet I liked her," said Barbara Romack, herself a flamboyant player. Miss Romack, the 1954 Women's Amateur Champion, was paired with the Babe several times.

"She was a great competitor, but she was also great to her friends, great to the galleries, great to kids."

---

* **RHONDA GLENN** (b. 1946) is an author and commentator on women's golf. Her books include *The Illustrated History of Women's Golf*. She was runner-up in the 1965 NCAA Championship and has played in two U.S. Women's Opens.

At the time of her death, Byron Nelson said, "She was the toughest competitor and the most gracious lady I ever met on a golf course."

Nevertheless, she was not universally admired. Those who didn't like her said she added no dignity to the game, that she was a foul-mouthed huckster who bullied her way to the top. She could be a charmer, they said, but there was a darker side, too, an almost childish demand to be the center of attention.

The darker side, the side we'd rather ignore in our search for true heroes, could have developed from the early assaults on the character and integrity of young Mildred Ella Didrikson.

Perhaps the person who knew her best during those lean early years is Bertha Bowen, of Fort Worth, Texas. In her autobiography, *This Life I've Led,* Babe wrote of Bertha and R.L. Bowen, "They were like my godmother and godfather."

"I still miss her like sixty!" Mrs. Bowen said during a visit. . . .

Babe Zaharias's career resumed when, in 1943, after eight years, she was reinstated an amateur.

She won 17 tournaments in rapid succession in the mid-40s, including the 1946 U.S. Women's Amateur and the 1947 British Women's Amateur; she was the first American to win them both. After winning the Broadmoor Invitational, in Colorado Springs, Colorado, she was offered $300,000 to make a series of ten movie shorts.

"I really hated to give up my amateur status; I worked hard to regain it," she said then, "but that money looked too good."

Bertha Bowen remembers the days before Babe married George. During that time Babe had saved enough money, she thought, to work on her game for three years. She naively underestimated.

"At first she wore my clothes, not that I had that many, but we wore the same size and she didn't have any," said Bertha. "But she was a good person who was generous with her time when she didn't have the money. She had a hard life. I mean her life was really hard and rough."

In 1950, with Patty Berg, Fred Corcoran, and the Wilson Sporting Goods Company, the Babe helped reorganize the Women's Professional Golfers' Association into the Ladies Professional Golf Association. This was a rollicking and happy time. The players rolled along the back roads, building what would one day be a multimillion-dollar business, but in 1950, it was Tobacco Road. Patty Berg usually kicked her winnings back into the pot to help other players make a go of it. There were very few tournaments in the beginning, and the Babe spent a lot of time on the telephone calling friends.

"Hey Joe," she'd say, "we got some time off and we need a tournament. How about putting up some money and I'll bring the girls." And then they would put up prize money and Babe would bring the girls to play golf and the LPGA Tour began.

There are, of course, stories about Babe as a prima donna, and they are probably true. She was the star and she knew it, reveled in it, and sometimes exploited it.

"Babe, you better be nice to these girls. To be a star you gotta have a chorus line," said her good friend Patty Berg.

Most of the stories come from this era, of the early 50s. How she knew the Rules so well, but seldom paid much attention to the players grouped with her. The Tour was more loosely structured then—Babe usually made her own pairings. Some players liked to be paired with her since she played in her own little world.

One memorable day her playing companion hit a tee shot into the rough, far to the right.

"Hey Babe, that's casual water isn't it?" asked the hopeful player. "I get a free drop, don't I?"

Babe Didrikson Zaharias (on right) and Patty Berg, the first two women to be inducted into the World Golf Hall of Fame, at Sunningdale Golf Club outside London in 1951

"Honey," said the Babe, "I don't care if you send it out and have it dry cleaned!"

But Babe knew the Rules, perhaps better than anyone on the Tour, and she tried to use them to her advantage. Another story concerns a tournament in Florida. The course had two landmarks, two huge cement statues of lions. When Babe hit her ball up against one of the stone lions, she called George. A big man, George was a famous wrestler. With Babe's encouragement, he huffed and puffed as he tried to hoist the lions as "movable obstructions."

There are lots of happy stories like that, but it was only a short period of bliss. In April, 1953, Babe and George were spending time with the Bowens, in Fort Worth. There had been aches and pains already, and the Babe spent a lot of time soaking in the tub.

"We bought her all sorts of medicine, but she wouldn't see a doctor," Mrs. Bowen said. "She was rough in spots, but she was modest, too, and she didn't like to have physical examinations. She waited too long; that was the big trouble."

Mrs. Bowen walked into the guest room that had belonged to Babe and George.

"I'll never forget it," she said. "They came in from the doctor's and George was white-faced. Babe threw her purse on the chair and flopped down on the bed. 'Well B.B., I've got it and it's the worst kind. Grade three,' she said."

It was cancer and Babe Zaharias began the battle that would eventually claim her life. But not quite yet.

The colostomy and the long recuperation period drew national attention. The Babe Zaharias Cancer Fund began and letters and contributions poured in. The beautifully coordinated body was beginning to give way, but one of its greatest tests was still to come. With the help of friends, fans, family, and a crack medical team, Babe Zaharias began to come back.

"She had many low moments," Mrs. Bowen said. "When she began to try to play, sometimes her strength would fail and she would just break down and cry on the golf course. It was just pure spirit that got her through it."

Unseen qualities make us what we are, and, as one friend said, "That's when Babe really showed her stuff."

The 1954 Women's Open was played at Salem. Crucial to the championship was the final 36 holes, all played on Saturday. The double round made the Open more than a test of a player's golf game; it was a test of her endurance.

After playing a practice round with Babe, Lionel MacDuff, the club president, decided that none of the other entrants could approach her in hitting greens in regulation. He laughed at suggestions that she would tire.

Fifteen months after she was stricken, Babe shot an amazing first two rounds of 72 and 71. Her closest rival was Betsy Rawls, who was seven strokes behind. Saturday was to be the turning point. Prior to the Open, Babe had faded toward the end of a tournament. Tiring, she had blown to high scores.

Saturday morning, paired with Mickey Wright, the 1952 Girls' Junior Champion, Babe shot a fine 73. The real test came in the afternoon. Babe took a nap in the clubhouse after lunch.

That afternoon, in one of the most climactic finishes in sports, Babe Zaharias swept to an emotional victory, shooting a final round 75, winning by 12 strokes. It was not a suffering sort of finish; she didn't cripple in—she won proudly and well, with all of the old Zaharias verve and dash. She wore a broad-brimmed straw hat that she doffed with a flourish on every good shot, and she quipped with her fans as she marched in.

It was a grand victory.

"I feel good for 20 more years," she said later. "If I've ever had any doubts that I might be able to go on—and let me tell you I've had plenty, they are gone now. For the first time

since the operation, I feel like the same old Babe again. My prayers have been answered. I wanted to show thousands of cancer sufferers that the operation I had will enable a person to return to normal life. I've received 15,000 inquiries from those who have undergone the operation. This is my answer to them."

That year she was given the Ben Hogan Award for overcoming her illness and returning to golf. Of course, she had not overcome it completely and she did not have the "20 more years." She would win a few more tournaments, but the disease recurred. Her last tournament was the old Titleholders, in Augusta, Georgia, in the spring.

"That was the last time I saw her," Barbara Romack recalls. "She was just kind of there. But you could kind of feel her around. I'd see her around the practice tee or sitting on the patio. The light had gone out of her eyes."

In July, 1955, Babe re-entered John Sealy Hospital, in Galveston. Physicians said the condition was incurable. She was in and out of John Sealy. In March, 1956, doctors severed spinal nerves to ease her unbearable pain. Early in the morning of September 27, 1956, Babe Zaharias died. Her ashes were lowered into a grave in Forest Lawn Park, in Beaumont.

In December, 1955, just nine months before she was to die, Babe and George came to the Bowens' home in Fort Worth for their last Christmas. Babe asked to see a golf course one more time. Mrs. Bowen recalls:

"I took her over to Colonial, where you could drive up to the second green. She got out of the car in her pajamas and robe. She could barely walk. She just went over and knelt down and put her palm flat on the green. Then she got in the car, and we went home."

GOLF DREAMS *and* DREAMY GOLF

H. B. FARNIE

OUR OLD ACCUSTOMED LINKS

from *The Golfer's Manual; being an historical and descriptive account
of the national game of Scotland,* by "A Keen Hand", 1857[*]

WE CANNOT REFRAIN FOR THE LIFE OF US FROM CLOSING OUR REMARKS ON GOLFING
with some expression of our intense attachment to it. Nor is this attachment a passing fancy,
or the offspring of national prejudice. In the alembic of experience many youthful pleasures
have been tested and found dross; — following back on the trail of our life, we have marked
many erring steps; and maturity shakes its head at the wayward fancies of younger days. But
thou gentle sprite! whose empire is the dark green links, and whose votaries wield the bending
club and speed the whizzing ball, are as dear to us now in the sere and yellow leaf as when first
we flew to share in thy health-inspiring rites with the flush and ardour of boyhood.

Vividly do we recollect our step initiatory in the game; —the unleaded club, bedaubed
with gay red paint, —the patched-up feather ball purchased (malgre the seductive influence
of the neighbouring pastry cook) with diverse copper relievi of royalty carefully hoarded for
the purpose from week to week; then, the strong inclination to practice the game indoors,
strenuously resisted by the powers that happened to be; and the convenient but erroneous
idea, when alas! our ball was numbered amongst the things that were, that stones were quite
as good and certainly more available.

Then, years passing away, we can well remember, the stolen holiday for a quiet match at
our beloved pastime; indeed, we shrewdly suspect, if memory be not a treacherous warder, that
it was quite our custom of an afternoon (more especially on those fainting days in June which
breed dark thoughts of revolt in the breasts of imprisoned school-boys) to rush frantically from
Syntax to Prosody — our goal, the links — our purpose, golf. That a perusal of these our
delinquencies may not have a baneful effect on our youthful reader, leading him away from
the narrow path of duty and . . . , we may add by way of moral, that on the mornings following these impromptu holidays, the whole *foursome* were soundly birched, and returned for
the time being to those paths of learning which did not wind over the links.

It would warm an old golfer's heart to have seen our enthusiastic efforts to mimic the
champion player's style; the reverence with which we would listen for hours together to mar-

---

[*] **HENRY BROUGHAM (H.B.) FARNIE** (1836-1889) was the "Keen Hand" who wrote *The Golfer's Manual,* one of the earliest
books about golf. *The Golfer's Manual* was reprinted in 1947 by the Dropmore Press with an introduction by Bernard Darwin.
Farnie was a Scottish-born librettist who also translated popular French operettas, including Gounod's opera *Romeo et
Juliette,* into English.

Golfing watercolor, nineteenth century
Scottish School

vellous incidents of the game; and our passing anxiety to possess a brace of clubs, which in casual talking we alluded to in a general way as "our set." A malison on those whins! we never could enjoy a match without an interlude of hide-and-seek for our only, our cherished ball; and alas! to lose it, and our pocket money at low ebb was equivalent, in those days of feathers, to an involuntary exile from the course.

HAEC OLIM MEMINISSE JUVABIT
[IN DAYS TO COME IT WILL PLEASE US TO REMEMBER]

And, still later in years, after sojourning in strange lands, or in brick-built towns wherein is no green thing, but jealousy and Venetian blinds, we can recall the ecstatic pleasure of again tasting the enjoyment of a round over the breezy expanse of our old accustomed links.

LAMBERHURST

from *The Weald of Youth*, 1942*

SQUIRE MORLAND'S PARK, WHICH I MENTIONED NOT FAR BACK, PROVIDES YET ANOTHER excuse for dawdling a bit longer in the vicinity of the River Teise.... Let me add that although the course wasn't at all a good one I must have played many more rounds there than on any other. The worst thing about Lamberhurst golf was that it provided very poor practice for playing anywhere else. In fact one could almost say that it was "a game of its own." For one thing, you were perpetually hoicking the ball out of tussocky lies; and for another, the greens had justifiably been compared to the proverbial postage-stamp. If you pitched adroitly on to a green, it was more than likely that you wouldn't remain there. If, on the other hand, your ball fell short, you stopped where you were, which was in the rough grass. And the otherwise almost hazardless charm of our local links didn't always atone for these disadvantages, especially when one happened to be playing a medal-round at the Spring or Autumn Meeting. During the summer months the course got completely out of control and nobody bothered to play there except Squire Morland himself, and he had seldom done the nine holes in under fifty at the best of times. Go there on a fine April day, however, and there was nothing to complain of, provided that one gave the idyllic pastoral surroundings their due and didn't worry about the quality of the golf. I say "pastoral" because the place was much frequented by sheep, and I cannot visualize it without an accompaniment of bells and baa-ings.

Standing near the quiet-flowing tree-shaded river at the foot of the park, one watches a pottering little group of golfers moving deliberately down the south-westerly slope. It is one of those after-luncheon foursomes in which the Squire delighted; and there he is; playing an approach-shot to the third hole in that cautious, angular, and automatic style of his. The surly black retriever is at his heels, and his golf-bag has a prop to it, so as to save him stooping to pick it up, and also to keep his clubs dry. The clock on the village school strikes three, and one is aware of the odour of beer-making from the Brewery. The long hole to the farthest

---

* **SIEGFRIED SASSOON** (1886-1967) was one of the celebrated War Poets, whose poems vividly decry the horror of trench warfare. Sassoon was wounded in action and wrote a letter of protest about the conduct of the War that was read aloud in the House of Commons. *The Weald of Youth* describes Sassoon's life in Kent prior to 1914, when his primary pursuits were writing poetry and fox-hunting, plus the occasional round of golf at Lamberhurst Golf Club. Lamberhurst celebrated its centenary in 1990 and is much better maintained these days than in Sassoon's time. The members included Denis Thatcher, the famous golfing husband of the former Prime Minister.

Lamberhurst Golf Club, Kent, England. Golfers teeing off in 2002 below the steeple of Saxon Church

corner of the park is known as "the Brewery Hole." And now they are all on the green, and gallant old General Fitzhugh, who had conspicuously distinguished himself in the Afghanistan campaign some thirty years before, is taking tremendous pains over his putt. The General has quite lately acquired one of those new Schenectady putters, mallet-shaped and made of aluminum, and popularized by Walter Travis, the first American who ever reached and won the Final of the Amateur Championship in England; and the non-success of his stroke is duly notified when he brandishes the weapon distractedly above his head. I now identify the stocky upright figure of my old friend Captain Ruxton, who evidently has "that for it," and sinks the ball with airy unconcern; whereupon the Squire, I can safely assume, ejaculates "My word, that's a hot 'un, Farmer!" in his customary clipped and idiomatic manner.

The fourth member of the party, I observe—unless one includes a diminutive boy from the village who staggers under the General's bristling armoury of clubs—is Mr. Watson, a tall, spectacled Scotsman, still in the prime of life, whose game is a good deal above Lamberhurst standards. Watson is a man well liked by everyone—without his ever saying much, possibly because he can't think of anything to say. My mother once remarked that when Mr. Watson ran out of small talk at a tea-party he told her that he always gave his hens salad-oil for the good of their health. But his favourite conversational opening was "Have you been to Macrihanish?"—Macrihanish being an admirable but rather un-get-at-able golf course within easy reach of the Mull of Kintyre. A person of strict principles, he had never been heard to utter the mildest of expletives, even when he found one of his finest drives reposing in the footprint of a sheep. After making a bad shot he used to relieve his feelings, while marching briskly toward his ball, with a snatch of cheerful song. "Trol-de-rol-de-rol" went Mr. Watson. But one had to have been to Macrihanish if one wanted to get much out of him in the way of conversation.

The friendly foursome is now well on toward the fourth green, where—in my mind's eye—I am standing by the tin flag, which requires repainting and has been there ever since the Club was founded. Following the flight of their tee-shots, I have remembered with amusement that Squire Morland occupies what might be called a duplicated position in the realms of print. His name appears, of course, in Burke's *Landed Gentry* and similar publications of lesser importance. But it also figures in *The Golfing Annual* as "green-keeper to the Lamberhurst Golf Club." (Nine holes. Subscription 21/- per annum.) The Squire's assumption of this sinecure appointment is due to the fact that by so doing he cannily obtains for himself and his cronies all the golf balls that he needs, at wholesale price. It is just conceivable that he does pull the light roller up and down about once a year; but I never heard of him doing so, though I myself had put in an hour's voluntary worm-cast sweeping now and again—the green-man being rather apt to neglect his duties.

In the meantime the foursome has another fourteen holes to play before it adjourns to the House for tea and a stroll in the garden to admire the daffodils. And while those kindly ghosts gather round me on the green I can do no more than wish that I could be greeting them there again, on some warm April afternoon, with the sheep munching unconcernedly and the course—as the Squire used to say—"in awful good condition." But as the scene withdraws and grows dim I hear a blackbird warbling from the orchard on the other side of the river; and I know that his song on the springtime air is making even elderly country gentlemen say to themselves that one is only as old as one feels, especially when there is nothing forbidding about the foreground of the future—into which they are now, with leisurely solemnity, making ready to smite the ball.

PATRIC DICKINSON

HAGEN AT SANDWICH

from *The Good Minute*, 1965*

GREEN IS THE COLOUR OF MAGIC—FOR ME IT IS ESPECIALLY THE LONG SOFTLY UNDULATING expanse of the first hole, its enchantment almost audible.

> *There, where the grass takes on a shade*
> *Of paradisal green, sun-clear . . .*

Soon Mr. Jeston gave me an afternoon of a different and thrilling delight. He took me to the last afternoon of the Open Championship which was being played at Sandwich. He gave me a large bag of mixed fruit drops (how did he know they were my favourite sweet?) and told me to meet him at the clubhouse at six. I was alone to go where I pleased among the crowds and watch whom I liked. I knew all the great professionals by photographs; I pored over every golfing magazine. I had read much about their feelings, their triumphs and disasters when the pressure was on. Now I saw them. I was there at the black moment one of my heroes, Archie Compston, took three putts—*three* putts—from quite close. I saw his face suffuse, I knew how he felt and I longed to rush up to him and comfort him. I saw and felt for the first time the callousness of golf-spectators. They sidled and melted away. No use watching him any more, he's cracked. I stayed loyally for a while but the virtue *had* gone out of him and soon I too sidled off. Being small and nippy I got easily to the front of any crowd (it is always best to watch golf alone). I kept my ears open, too, picking up the rumours that whiz supersonically round any links while the battle is on. I picked up Walter Hagen at the Canal. He had the biggest crowd, including the Prince of Wales whom I wormed my way next to in the front row round the green. Hagen was wearing black-and-white shoes, dark blue stockings, dark green plus-fours made of alpaca, a dark blue sleeveless pullover, a white shirt with gold cufflinks and a dark blue-and-white bow-tie. His black hair was patent-leather. The feature of his brown face was a sharp long probing nose. Most of our professionals played in drab shabby old things. The conception of dressing up for golf was new; there had been gibes at Hagen in the press.

Walter Hagen with Archie Compston, the English hero, in their exhibition match at Moor Park Golf Club, Hertfordshire, England in April 1928. Compston defeated Hagen handily in the exhibition, but the Haig came back to win the British Open that year at Royal St. George's, with Compston finishing third, three strokes back

---

* **PATRIC DICKINSON** attended Cambridge University, where he played on the golf team. His autobiography, *The Good Minute*, contains lyrical passages about rounds at Royal St. George's in Sandwich and Royal Worlington and Newmarket in Mildenhall, the Cambridge University home course that is considered the finest nine-hole layout in the world. As for Walter Hagen, the subject of this vignette, he won his third British Open at Royal St. George's in 1928.

Hole 4 at Royal St. George's, Sandwich, England, a course of billowing sand dunes and many songbirds overlooking Pegwell Bay

Now that I saw him I was immediately on his side. I watched his drive and trotted as near as I dared to him. He strolled along laughing, joking, and laying bets. About twenty yards from his ball he fell visibly silent, his gossips took their cue and he advanced, now, rather than walked. His head was erect and still, his nose like a pointer's. He seemed to me to send his eyes physically forward to the distant green, and they reconnoitred minutely the slopes, the position of the guarding bunker, indeed a whole limited area, and I *knew* what he was doing: he was deciding whether to play safely short, or "go for the green." This meant pitching a full brassie shot within a minute area. All this time he was moving on

> *With unperturbed pace,*
> *Deliberate speed, majestic instancy.*

It was an extremely dramatic moment. As he reached his ball the crowd congealed into that almost tangible cold silence unique to the golf links. I was directly behind the line. Hagen selected his brassie with a quick certain flourish that got a gasp of awe, stepped straight to his ball and in a second had hit it. I watched it the length of its flight—the straight rocketing upward trajectory, the beginning of the earthward curve, its steepening fall, the pitch and bounce up. The frozen moment melted. There was a cheer from the green, a scurrying surge of legs, and chatter, and Hagen strolling on, laughing, joking and laying bets. He won the championship. I had followed his play before, as far as I was able to; now I idolised him. He was with Wethered and Tolley.

GEORGE PLIMPTON

A LITTLE NIGHT READING

from *The Bogey Man*, 1967*

I MADE IT A PRACTICE, STARTING WITH THAT FIRST EVENING WHEN I RETURNED TO MY room from the lodge, of dipping into a large green bag full of books on golf, and doing some reading before dropping off to sleep. I had purchased, or borrowed, the books before leaving on the tour, and I brought them with me in a large green laundry bag with a clothesline draw-string. I dipped into it whenever I had the chance, on the principle that saturating myself with the subject of golf whenever possible might have an osmotic effect on my game.

Some of the books were instructive (such manuals as Ben Hogan's *Power Golf*, Sam Snead's *How to Hit a Golf Ball*, Bob Rosburg's *The Putter Book*), illustrated with stop-action photographs of the perfect swing; line drawings of golfers swinging in barrels, red arrows pointing to danger spots such as the crook of the arm, the chin, the hips; metaphorical drawings to associate the golf swing with some other common act. One of these latter showed a man pulling down a window shade with both hands, with the suggestion, I recall, that the motion was the exact fac-simile of the correct way to hit down into the ball. I also had a copy of Phillips B. Thompson's *Simplifying the Golf Stroke*—a very popular book in the twenties, five pages long, with print the size of the lower levels of an oculist's chart—which both begins and ends with a sentence urging the reader to think of the golf club as a "weight at the end of a string."

Other books were discursive; some were reminiscences. Some I had ordered simply because I was intrigued by the titles in the catalogues: *Super Golf with Self-Hypnosis*, by Jack Heise; *Golf-Reflections on Morals*, by John L. Low; *The Happy Golfer*; J. Dunn's *Intimate Golf Talks*; *The Nine Bad Shots of Golf and What to Do About Them*, by Jim Dante and Leo Diegel; *Are Golfers Human?* by R. Murray. One group of books by the same author (Fred Beck) had an intriguing progression of titles—*73 Years in a Sandtrap*, *89 Years in a Sandtrap*, and finally *To H___ with Golf*—which seemed appropriate to my situation—but when the books arrived they turned out to be cartoon collections which did not measure up to the jocosity of the titles.

Golf literature, on the whole, is on a very high level—which is perhaps not surprising

---

* **GEORGE PLIMPTON** (b. 1927) has edited *The Paris Review*, a small but prominent literary magazine, since 1953. A true Renaissance man, his interests range from pyrotechnics, having served as honorary commissioner of fireworks for New York City, to lepidoptery, or the study of butterflies. Plimpton is best known for having invented participatory sports journalism when he wrote *Paper Lion*, recounting his experiences as the third string, rookie quarterback of the Detroit Lions in 1963. In *The Bogey Man*, Plimpton chronicles his travails and triumphs on the pro-am golf circuit.

considering the antiquity of the game and its popularity among the educated classes. No other sport can offer such fine reading—with the possible exception of exploration, or game hunting. Browsing through the book bag I found myself introduced to the works of Bernard Darwin—an absolutely first-rate writer, so good that one can sit with one's feet up and read about matches that took place a half-century before and skip dinner or delay an appointment to find out how it came out in the end. It was a dangerous practice to begin a chapter by Darwin. He wrote with such dedication and erudition about his subject and yet with such ease that it almost seemed a trick; and then one could see that at the base of his skill was a profound, almost mystical awe of the game. Here he is, for example, writing about his fixation with golf:

> I write as one who has been perhaps a fond and foolish devotee, and may have done himself little good by it, but I can look back gratefully on many agreeable hours spent—or even wasted in playing. I think not only of quiet corners of many courses, but of many fields where the grass was so long that almost every stroke required a search; I think of a mountain top in Wales and a plain in Macedonia; of innumerable floors on which I have tried to hit the table legs; I recall rain and wind and mud and the shadows of evening falling, so that the lights came twinkling out in the houses round the links, and the ball's destiny was a matter of pure conjecture. Remembering all these things, I can say that I may have been an unprofitable practicer of the game, but at any rate I have been a happy one.

Bernard Darwin's grandfather was the great naturalist, Charles, but he is mentioned rarely in the Darwin books; Darwin's maternal grandfather appears more frequently—an affectionate portrait of a man who for hygienic reasons of his own never wore socks. He was an amateur phrenologist and had a greenhouse full of skulls with bumps. According to Darwin he was a champion of lost causes. He had an "infallible recipe" for growing strawberries, but annually the strawberry patch would be searched without success for signs of growth. Certainly he was a man closer in character to the Sisyphean aspects of golf than the great scientist. Darwin, who gave up a law practice he despised for golf, was an excellent player himself (he reached the quarter-finals of the British Amateur), and his ABC's of golf as described in his books are marvelous—as candid as the remarks of a hell-fire preacher. He says of faults for example:

> There are certain faults which can only be cured in the most obvious way, namely by trying to avoid them. For example, if a man be conscious of leaping, figuratively speaking, into the air at the top of his swing, and so being far too much on his toes, I know of no remedy, save that he must try not to jump; he must peg his feet down by dint of sheer determination.

Darwin has his successors in golf literature—Henry Longhurst, Charles Price, and Herbert Warren Wind, among others. What is interesting is that the great golfers themelves, with an occasional helping hand from a ghost writer, have a considerable flair for the written word: Harry Vardon, Bobby Jones, Sam Snead, Tony Lema, Ben Hogan. Though their work may not be honed to such a fine degree as the professional writer's (with the exception of the Jones books, which are at Darwin's level), still there is a finesse and distinction which is a refreshing departure from the usual sports literature and certainly distinct from the "as-told-to" books by contemporary athletes in other sports.

I asked someone about this once, and he reflected and said perhaps a game in which euphoria was so short-lived, the bad shot lurking so surely in the future, was conducive to the state of contained melancholy which produced first-rate literature. Dostoevski, for instance. Conrad. Hardy.

Certainly the literature was contained, and even great moments of triumph were described in muted tones, as if excessive smugness would bring on a lengthy attack of the shanks from on high. Always there was great respect for the fellow golfer, however confused his game. Harry Vardon's book *The Complete Golfer* is absolutely fine (he had help from a superb anonymous ghost writer)—written in as easy and effective a style as his golf stroke, which was so effortless that he often hit a ball with a pipe in his mouth. Yet he shows a considerable compassion for the lower echelons of golfers— such compassion, indeed, that he seems one of them in a common struggle against adversity. Here are his subheadings to Chapter III of *The Complete Golfer,* which tell something of his concern: "The Mistakes of a Beginner"; "Too Eager to Play a Round"; "Despair that Follows"; "A Settling Down to Mediocrity"; "The Sorrows of a Foozler"; "All Men May Excel," etc.

This cover from *The American Golfer* unlooses the bogey man that lurks in the mind of every golfer

This last seemed, as I settled into my book-bag reading that night, an idiom common to all the books: there was hope. Of course, some writers were of a gloomy turn of mind. Particularly Sir W.A. Simpson, author of *The Art of Golf,* one of the great classics of the 1880's. In writing of the drawbacks of golf he pointed out that "winds cease to be east, south, west, or north. They are head, behind, sideways, and the sky is bright according to the state of the game." Why, it was even possible, he wrote, "by too much of it to destroy the mind; a man with a Roman nose and a high forehead may play away his profile."

But then, shot through the golf books I read were gentle suggestions that everything was going to work out all right. Even Simpson, the melancholy peer, writes: "All those who drive thirty yards suppose themselves to be great *putters.* . . . The duffer is a duffer merely because every second shot is missed. Time and care will eliminate the misses and then!"

The message of one of the books I looked into called *The Happy Golfer,* for example, was "that the major force of all life is *hope.* The golfer should have 'Spero Meliora' as his coat of arms—and he should strain for 'the faintest note that comes from the one long string that remains on the almost dismantled harp.' " I particularly liked the last image—the analogy of the dismayed golfer struggling off the last green as an "almost dismantled harp."

Bernard Darwin, with a fine classical bent, also had an occasional Latin phrase to brighten the golfer's day. "Nec Temere, Nec Timide" [not rash, not timid], he suggested for those about to step into a bunker.

Darwin would always vow on New Year's Eve that his next year of golf would be a fortuitous one, and he always believed that "a miracle would occur, and the dash and strength and glory of hitting which are vouchsafed to the few might suddenly one fine morning descend on us, too, so that we should be as creatures transfigured and made splendid for evermore."

Even great golfers could not do without such mental bolstering. Darwin reports that Braid, the Scottish champion, "went to bed a short driver and woke up a long one."

That was a good place to stop my first night's reading, I thought. I turned out the light. I could hear the sea moving at the breakwater across the 18th fairway. I tried to remember Darwin's prayer: "Creatures transfigured and made splendid for evermore. . . ." Was that it? I stared into the darkness. In the recesses of my mind there was a gentle murmuring. I strained to hear. . . .

JOHN UPDIKE

GOLF DREAMS

from *Golf Dreams*, 1996*

Winter Dreams: Misquamicut Golf
Club in Westerly, Rhode Island,
under snow (right) and transformed
in summer (below)

THEY STEAL UPON THE SLEEPING MIND WHILE WINTER STEALS UPON THE LANDSCAPE, sealing the inviting cups beneath sheets of ice, cloaking the contours of the fairway in snow.

I am standing on a well-grassed tee with my customary summer foursome, whose visages yet have something shifting and elusive about them. I am getting set to drive; the fairway before me is a slight dogleg right, very tightly lined with trees, mostly conifers. As I waggle and lift my head to survey once more the intended line of flight, further complications have been imposed: the air above the fairway has been interwoven with the vines and wooden crosspieces of an arbor, presumably grape, and the land seems to drop away no longer with a natural slope but in nicely hedged terraces. Nevertheless, I accept the multiplying difficulties calmly, and try to allow for them in my swing, which is intently contemplated but never achieved, for I awake with the club at its apogee, waiting for my left side to pull it through and

to send the ball toward that bluish speck of openness beyond the vines, between the all but merged forests.

It is a feature of dream golf that the shot never decreases in difficulty but instead from instant to instant melts, as it were, into deeper hardship. A ball, for instance, lying at what the dreaming golfer gauges to be a 7-iron distance from the green, has become, while he glanced away, cylindrical in shape—a roll of coins in a paper wrapper, or a plastic bottle of pills. Nevertheless, he swings, and as he swings he realizes that the club in his hand bears a rubber tip, a little red-rubber tab the color of a crutch tip, but limp. The rubber flips negligibly across the cylindrical "ball," which meanwhile appears to be sinking into a small trough having to do, no doubt, with the sprinkler system. Yet, most oddly, the dreamer surrenders not a particle of hope of making the shot. In this instance, indeed, I seem to recall making, on my second or third swing, crisp contact, and

---

* In writing about golf, **JOHN UPDIKE** brings to bear his characteristic perspicacity in describing the familiar and peculiar physical traits of golf and golfers. In this essay, which originally appeared in *The New Yorker,* he provides an appreciation of the deeper emotional appeal of golf.

striding in the direction of the presumed flight with a springy, expectant sensation.

After all, are these nightmares any worse than the "real" drive that skips off the toe of the club, strikes the prism-shaped tee marker, and is swallowed by weeds some twenty yards *behind* the horrified driver? Or the magical impotence of an utter whiff? Or the bizarre physical comedy of a soaring slice that strikes the one telephone wire strung across three hundred acres? The golfer is so habituated to humiliation that his dreaming mind never offers any protest of implausibility. Whereas dream life, we are told, is a therapeutic carica-ture, seamy side out, of real life, dream golf is simply golf played on another course. We chip from glass tables onto moving stairways; we swing in a straitjacket, through masses of cob-web, and awake not with any sense of unjust hazard but only with a regret that the round can never be completed, and that one of our phantasmal companions has kept the score-card in his pocket.

Even the fair companion sleeping beside us has had a golf dream, with a feminist slant. An ardent beginner, she confides at dawn, "I was playing with these men, I don't know who they were, and they kept using woods when we were on the green, so of course the balls would fly miles away, and then they had to hit all the way back. I thought to myself, *They aren't using the right club,* and I took my putter out and, of course, I kept *beating* them!"

"Didn't they see what you were doing, and adjust their strokes accordingly?"

"No, they didn't seem to get it, and I wasn't going to tell them. I kept winning, and it was wonderful," she insists.

We gaze at each other across the white pillows, in the morning light filtered through icicles, and realize we were only dreaming. Our common green hunger begins to gnaw afresh, insatiable.

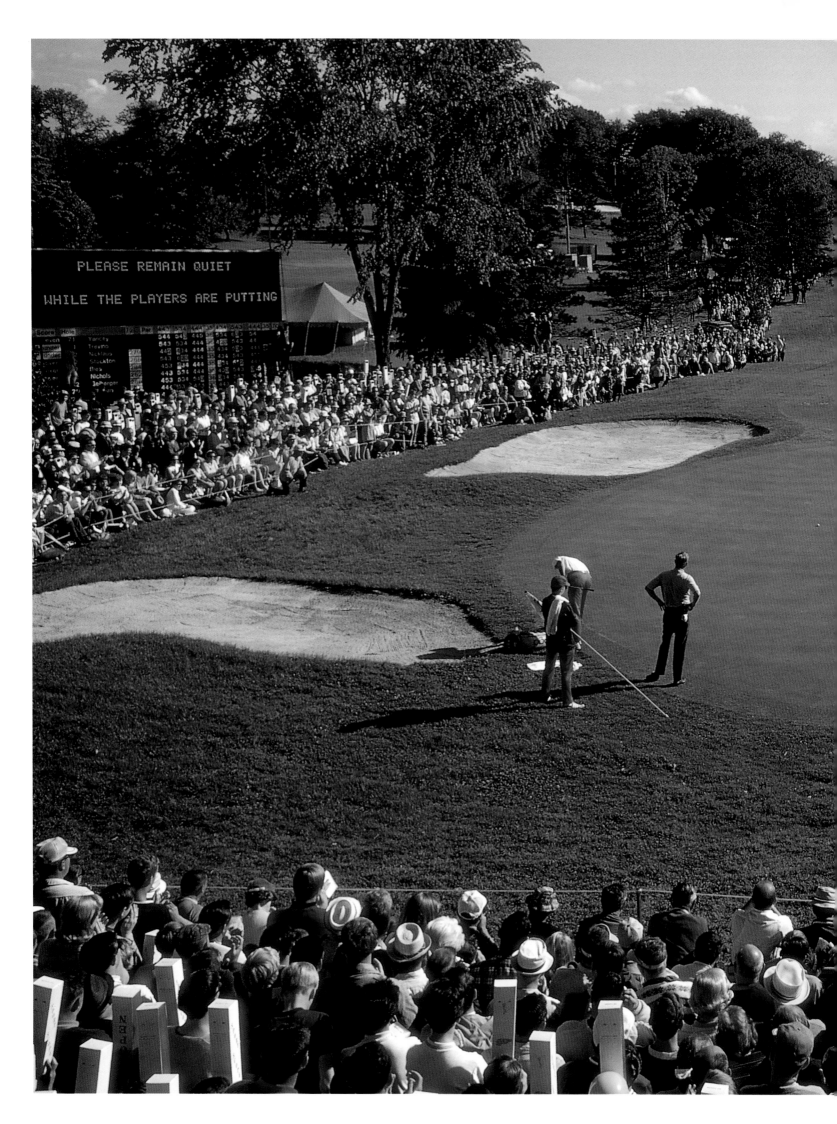

MODERN CONQUERORS *and the* COMING OF TIGER

MODERN CONQUERORS *and the* COMING OF TIGER

Whenwe consider the greatest golfers of recent times, we inevitably find ourselves making comparisons between them—gauging the facets of their respective personalities that made them champions and wondering how they would have stacked up against those who came before them. Jack Nicklaus, Arnold Palmer, and Gary Player were the "Big Three" of the 1960s. Palmer, the oldest of the three, is really the first modern golfer, not in the way he played the game, but in that he was the first champion to play in the modern media age. He was in his prime when golf was beginning to attract a national television audience, and Palmer's persona and style of play spurred the growth of the game. Palmer was handsome, charismatic, hard-charging, and earnest. He was the first grassroots golfing hero and his heroism remains undimmed.

Gary Player was the most unlikely of champions, but he has won all four majors, which puts him in the company of Gene Sarazen, Ben Hogan, Jack Nicklaus, and Tiger Woods. Player is a small man who lacked the physical power of Nicklaus and Palmer, and he had to make his way onto the world stage from South Africa, but he possessed, and still does, the heart of a lion and an incisive intellect. Of all the greats, Player in his mental tenacity reminds us the most of Tiger Woods, or perhaps we should say that Woods reminds us the most of Player. Despite the physical dissimilarities, both entered the cauldron of championship golf completely self-possessed, supremely self-confident, and able to will the shot needed at the moment required for victory.

Bernard Darwin, writing about Harry Vardon, pointed out the difficulty of comparing players of different generations, but concluded that "no one who ever saw Vardon in his best days can doubt that his genius was unsurpassable."

None of us who saw Jack Nicklaus play in his prime could imagine a greater player.

PAGES 244, 245

Lee Trevino getting ready to putt on the final hole at Oak Hill Country Club, Rochester, New York, in his 1968 U.S. Open victory

Jack Nicklaus holes the climactic birdie putt on the 17th hole to seal his storybook victory in the 1986 Masters

Nicklaus, at least until Tiger Woods came along, was generally acknowledged to be the greatest golfer who ever lived, and his record of eighteen major victories remains unsurpassed. Indeed, with the exception of Woods, who as of this writing has won eight majors and is gaining ground, no one has come close.

When Nicklaus came on the scene, he was viewed as something of a stocky, crew-cut pretender to the throne of the hugely popular Palmer. By the late 1960s, Nicklaus had established his ascendancy as a golfer, earned the title of the "Golden Bear," and was well on his way to becoming far and away the game's most popular player. Nicklaus's insuperable strength as a golfer has been his ability to combine a power game, an exquisite putting touch, and a cerebral mind.

Lee Trevino was Nicklaus's chief rival in the early 1970s. Trevino was seen as a comic foil to Nicklaus, a happy-go-lucky prankster with the moniker the "Merry Mex." Inside though, Trevino burned with a deep competitive fire and possessed the intuitive ability to perform under pressure that all great players have. In 1972, Nicklaus came to the British Open at Muirfield in search of the Grand Slam, having already won the Masters and the U.S. Open. Nicklaus was at the height of his powers, but Trevino was to dash his dream. Trevino pulled out a one-shot victory by chipping in from off the green for an improbable five on the par-five 17th hole, and in so doing not only nipped Nicklaus but broke the spirit of his playing partner, Tony Jacklin.

The British Open at Turnberry in 1976 proved to be another epic encounter in the history of golf,

this time between Nicklaus and Tom Watson. Watson's one-stroke victory in a torrid shootout under the shadow of the Turnberry lighthouse symbolized the passing of the mantle from Nicklaus to Watson. With his rifle-like accuracy and fearless putting, Watson continued his run for another seven years. Nicklaus continued to win majors, including the U.S. Open at Baltusrol in 1980, and his rousing and unforgettable career finale at the Masters in 1986, but he would never again be all alone at the pinnacle.

In the late 1980s, and through much of the '90s, we were convinced that there could never be a colossus on the order of Nicklaus. Surely, there was simply too much depth for any one player to dominate so thoroughly. Instead, there would be a handful of outstanding players who would vie for the top spot. We became accustomed to an oligopoly of great players, including Greg Norman, Seve Ballesteros, Curtis Strange, and Nick Faldo.

remained the gut fighter we insisted he be, a man so willing to accept the agonies of pressure and the burdens of fame that for a few years we absolutely forgot that anyone else played the game he was dominating and changing.

He actually started *being* Arnold Palmer in that summer of 1960, a stupidly short time ago it seems. He became the Arnie of whoo-ha, go-get-'em Arnie on a searingly hot afternoon in Denver when, during the last round of the U.S. Open, he exploded from seven strokes and fourteen players behind to win. Two months earlier he had finished birdie-birdie on national television to win the Masters and now he had created another miracle—again on national television.

Much has been written into the lore of golf of how it was that day, of the epic 65 he shot in the final round at Cherry Hills, of the day that really made him, but not by anyone who had lunched with him, kidded him, and then happily marched inside the gallery ropes with him, scurrying after Cokes, furnishing cigarettes, and hoping to put him at ease.

During lunch in a quiet corner of the Cherry Hills locker room before that round, Arnold was cheerful and joking as he ate a hamburger, drank iced tea, and made small talk with a couple of other players, Bob Rosburg and Ken Venturi, a writer named Bob Drum, and myself. He talked of no one else who might win. All he seemed concerned about was Cherry Hills's 1st hole, a comparatively short, downhill, downwind, par four. It bugged him. He thought he could drive the green, but in three previous rounds he had not done it.

"It really makes me hot," he said. "A man ought to drive that green."

"Why not?" I said. "It's only three hundred and forty-six yards through a ditch and a lot of high grass."

"If I drive that green I might shoot a hell of a score," he said. "I might even shoot a sixty-five if I get started good. What'll that bring?"

"About seventh place. You're too far back."

"Well, that would be two-eighty," Arnold said. "Doesn't two-eighty always win the Open?"

"Yeah," I said. "When Hogan shoots it."

Arnold laughed and walked out to the first tee.

For a while I loitered around the big clubhouse waiting for the leaders to go out, as a good journalist should. In the process of milling around, however, I overheard a couple of fans talking about an amazing thing they had just seen. Palmer, they said, had driven the first green. Just killed a low one that hung up there straight toward the mountains and then burned its way through the USGA trash and onto the putting surface. Got a two-putt birdie.

I smiled to myself and walked out onto the veranda and began edging my way through the spectators toward the 1st tee where the leader, Mike Souchak, would be going off presently. But about that time a pretty good roar came up from down on the front nine, and seconds later, a man sprinted by panting the news that Palmer was three under through three.

"Drove the first, chipped in on two and hit it stiff on three," he said, pulling away and darting off to join Arnie's Army. Like the spectator and a few thousand others who got the same notion at the same time, I tried to break all records for the Cherry Hills Clubhouse-to-Fourth Fairway Dash. We got there just in time to see Arnold hole his fourth straight birdie.

Wringing wet and perishing from thirst, I staggered toward the fifth tee, stopping to grab a Coke at a concession stand. I ducked under the ropes as an armband permitted and stood there puffing but excited.

Arnold came in briskly, squinted down the fairway and walked over. He took the Coke out of my hand, the cigarettes out of my shirt pocket and broke into a smile.

"Fancy seeing you here," he said. "Who's winning the Open?"

Palmer birdied two more holes through the 7th to go an incredible six under, working

Arnold Palmer at Harbour Town Golf Club, Hilton Head Island, South Carolina, 1969 on an incorrigible twenty-nine out. But he bogeyed the 8th and had to settle for a 30. Even so, the challengers were falling all around him like wounded soldiers, and their crowds were bolting toward him, and the title would be his. Everything would be his now.

Later on, somewhere on the back nine holes, I remember sizing up a leader board with him and saying, "You've got it. They're all taking gas."

"Aw, maybe," he said, quietly. "But damn it, I wanted that twenty-nine."

There have been other major victories, as we know, and scores of lesser ones, and precisely because of him the professional tour has tripled, quadrupled in prize money. He has become, they say, something immeasurable in champions, something more than life-size, even though he has turned into his forties, the hip hurts, and a lot of other big ones have slipped away.

This is true, I think. He *is* the most immeasurable of all golf champions. But this is not entirely true because of all that he has won, or because of that mysterious fury with which he has managed to rally himself. It is partly because of the nobility he has brought to losing. And more than anything, it is true because of the pure, unmixed joy he has brought to trying.

He has been, after all, the doggedest victim of all.

Arnold Palmer waves farewell as he comes down the 18th fairway at St. Andrews in 1995 in his final appearance at the British Open

JAIME DIAZ

THE ONCE AND FUTURE
GARY PLAYER

from *Memorial Tournament Program,* 1997*

GARY PLAYER HAS WON SO OFTEN OVER SO LONG A PERIOD OF TIME, IT'S DIFFICULT TO pinpoint exactly when his prime occurred. In one of his more zealous moments, he might even argue that it hasn't ended. But it once had a beginning, and it wasn't long after that Player stamped his image on our collective memory: a gymnastic silhouette in all black (with jut a dash of white in his wingtips), biceps stretching the sleeve openings of his Ban-Lon mock turtle, close-cropped pompadour glistening above a face both boyish and rugged, eyes innocent, intense and ruthless all at once.

At the same time, that ageless package—which stays so alive because even at sixty-one and draped in looser fitting earth tones, Player, right down to his thirty-two-inch waist, has hardly changed—conspires against his accomplishments' being appreciated. Player reminds people so much of Jack La Lanne they forget how often he beat Jack Nicklaus.

In golf's history, he's come as close as anyone else to the scope of the Golden Bear's feats, making his selection as a Memorial Tournament honoree, which he is for 1997, inevitable. From 1959 to 1978, Player won nine professional majors, a figure exceeded only by Nicklaus and Walter Hagen. Before his thirtieth birthday, he became only the third man to win all four of the professional major championships, joining Gene Sarazen and Ben Hogan. Nicklaus soon became the fourth, and with one more U.S. Open title Player would have matched Nicklaus as the only person to achieve the professional Slam twice (Jack needs one more British Open to complete four cycles). In every season from 1955 to 1982, Player won at least one sanctioned international professional tournament, a remarkable twenty-seven-year victory streak which is ten years longer than anyone else ever achieved. Since competing on the Senior Tour, he has won eight of that tour's major championships (counting, as he does, two British Senior Opens), which is more than anyone else.

Besides being the first foreign winner of the Masters, Player has won the staggering total of 159 tournaments around the world, making him indisputably the most successful international golfer of all time. He did much of it in an era in which it took him fully forty-five hours to commute from his native South Africa to the United States in a propeller-driven

Gary Player on the 18th hole at Bellerive Country Club. He would win his only U.S. Open the next day in a playoff against the Australian Kel Nagle

* **JAIME DIAZ** (b. 1953) began playing golf at public courses in his native San Francisco at age 12. He began writing about golf after joining *Sports Illustrated* in 1983. He covered golf for *The New York Times* from 1990 to 1993, before returning to *Sports Illustrated*. He is currently a senior writer for *Golf Digest*.

aircraft (sometimes with all six of his children and more than thirty pieces of luggage in tow). He won the British Open three times (in an unprecedented three different decades), the Australian Open seven times, the World Match-play five times, the South African Open thirteen times. He is the only golfer to break 60 in a national championship, with a 59 in the 1974 Brazilian Open. His worldwide record dwarfs the efforts of subsequent globe-trotters, including Seve Ballesteros, Nick Faldo, Greg Norman and Nick Price, all of whom have had the assistance of private jets and appearance fees.

A SCRAPPY STYLE

Yet Gary Player, despite his permanent place in golf's pantheon of champions, has never quite been anointed with the majesty that the names of Nicklaus, Palmer, Hogan, Snead or Nelson carry. Part of it was his five-foot-seven-inch height, part of it was his scrappy style. He has been characterized as doing it with grit rather than genius, with industry more than artistry. Along with Palmer and Nicklaus he made up the "Big Three," but he was always the third member. About the only thing anyone was prepared to call Player the best at was bunker play, which implies a need to scramble, to compensate for a lack of tee-to-green excellence.

As much as he won, there never seemed to be an extended period when he was clearly the best golfer in the world. Instead, in the midst of the American domination of the game in the 1960s and 1970s, Player was the pesky little man from the other side of the world who interceded during the successive primes of Palmer, Nicklaus, Lee Trevino, Johnny Miller and Tom Watson. Player would pop up in bursts, but, at a time when the PGA Tour was truly the center of golf's universe, he rarely stayed on it long enough to be dominant. Although in 1961 he became the first foreign-born golfer to win the American tour's money list, he never did so again. His finest year was probably 1974, when he won both the Masters and the British Open, but his claim to being the best even that year was mitigated by Miller's eight PGA Tour victories. . . .

IN PURSUIT OF GREATNESS

It's a complex picture, one that's tended to blur Player's feats on the course. But in another way, it's easy. All the effort and all the extremes, all the passion, were for a simple aim—to be the greatest golfer who ever lived. So when Player did all those Gary Player things—practicing in bunkers until he had holed five times, convincing himself that the course he was playing that week was among the finest in the world, lugging sixty pounds of barbells with him on his transcontinental travels—it was all part of a grand design. His willingness to go to extremes, to do the unorthodox, to commit to uncharted waters ("there are no half measures," he is fond of saying), is a manifestation of his lifelong adherence to his eighth commandment, borrowed from Winston Churchill: "Trust instinct to the end, though you cannot render any reason." In his incredibly focused mind, Gary Player had no choice.

As the great British golf chronicler, Pat Ward-Thomas, wrote of Player: "No golfer that I have known, not even Hogan, Nicklaus or Palmer, has been more lastingly consumed with the desire to conquer and prove himself the greatest of all golfers."

To those who saw Player early in his career, it seemed an absurd goal. His size, an unorthodox method that included an overly strong grip, a flat swing and a chronically off-balance finish, as well as a stabby putting stroke, all stacked the decks against him. "I remember being quite appalled at his method," said Peter Alliss, who first saw Player in the mid-1950s. "A few well-meaning older pros told him he'd be better off to go back home and get a nice club job." Even after he'd made himself a legend, there remained an unfinished quality to Player's golf that prompted the late golf writer Peter Dobereiner to quip, "No better than a two handicap, really."

But Player had the genius for winning of, in the words of Ward-Thomas, "the natural games player." It involved all the intangibles—courage, resourcefulness, an unerring sense of moment, and, above all, desire.

"There was nothing really exceptional about Gary's game," said Nicklaus of his good friend, "except one thing: his desire to win. I've seen him win tournaments you thought there was no way he could win, just do it on pure guts. I don't think Gary was a great driver of the golf ball. I don't think he was a great iron player. He was a good putter, not a great putter. But, when he really needed to be, he was a great driver, a great iron player, and he made the putt when he needed to make it. Gary, as much as anyone I ever saw, has that thing inside him that champions have."

Gary Player, "the man in black," at Bellerive Country Club, outside St. Louis, on his way to winning the 1965 U.S. Open

Whatever that thing is, those who played against him knew it was there. Arnold Palmer has called Player the fiercest competitor he ever encountered. Nicklaus has called Player's second-place finish by a stroke to Raymond Floyd at the 1969 PGA Championship—when Player was under death threats and antiapartheid demonstrators tried to disturb his rounds by, among

Gary Player teeing off at Royal County Down in the 2001 British Senior Open

other things, throwing cups of ice in his face—the greatest performance he has ever seen on a golf course. "If I ever won a tournament in my life, I own that tournament," says Player. Seve Ballesteros said that being Player's playing partner in the final round of the 1978 Masters, when Player birdied seven of the final ten holes to win, was vital to making him a major championship winner. It's the stuff that allowed Player to defeat Tony Lema in the thirty-six-hole semifinal of the 1964 Piccadilly World Match-play after falling 7 down with seventeen holes to play, a match he later said "contains my whole life story." Lee Trevino, who knows something about overcoming obstacles, understands the essence of Gary Player.

"Everything Gary's ever done in golf probably seemed impossible to most people," said Trevino, "but the man's got more belief in himself than anyone I've ever seen. He's always been David against Goliath. He was small but he was strong, and he worked tremendously hard. Biggest thing, he had—has—a gigantic heart."

TOUGH BEGINNINGS

Player was born November 1, 1935, in Johannesburg, South Africa, the third of three children to Harry and Muriel Player. The family lived in a poor neighborhood built directly over a gold mine called Robinson Deep, where Harry Player was a mine captain who spent most of his working life twelve thousand feet underground. The elder Player was a big man, six feet one inch, more than two hundred pounds, with a gregarious disposition and booming laugh that earned him the nickname Laughing Harry. One of Gary's earliest memories is seeing his father emerge from the mine at the end of his shift, take off his boots, and empty liquid out of them. "I thought it was water," says Player. "It was sweat." By the time Harry Player died in 1977 at the age of seventy-eight, he had been all over the world to see his son win golf tournaments.

Muriel Player was a well-educated woman who mixed affection with an insistence on correct manners. The nurturing environment was one that, early on, made Player feel special. "My parents always encouraged us," he says. "I'm sure it gave me the belief that what I could conceive, I could achieve. It's the greatest gift you can give a child."

At the age of forty-four, Muriel Player succumbed to cancer after a long battle. Gary was eight years old, and he calls his mother's death the key event in his life. "That was the moment my case-hardening started," he wrote in his 1991 autobiography, *To Be the Best: Reflections of a Champion.* "That loss was to breed an independence, a toughness of spirit, and an awareness of adversity and discipline that have never left me. . . . All that I am and all that I have become is in some way a tribute to her. [Her loss] has been a means for me, as it were, to settle some unfathomable debt." . . .

THE TRAVELS BEGIN

In 1953, at the age of eighteen, he turned professional, taking an eighty-dollar-a-month assistant's job at Virginia Park. Two years later, he won his first tournament, the 1955 East Rand Open, near Johannesburg. Funded by a collection from friends and local golfers, plus his father's bank loan, Player took the equivalent of five hundred dollars to play his first foreign tour, which would include his first airplane ride (he's logged an estimated eight million miles since, entailing the equivalent of more than two years of his life in the air). His first stop was Cairo for the Egyptian Match-play Championship on the banks of the Nile. Player beat fellow South African Harold Henning for the title, and three hundred dollars.

Next he went to Great Britain for the first of what this year will be forty-three consecutive British Opens. Upon arriving at St. Andrews, he found the guest houses full and the hotels too expensive for his miserly budget. That first night, he slept in a sand dune off the Firth of Forth.

Early in 1956, Player won a tournament at famed Sunningdale near London by shooting 70, 64, 64, 68, 72—338 for five rounds. Afterward, the great Australian player and teacher, Norman Von Nida, told him, "Kid, you've really got it." Player was fascinated. "I asked him, 'What is *it?*' He responded, 'Well, nobody can define it, but you've got it.' I still don't know what 'it' is. I only know it when I see it. It's a way of moving, a way of carrying yourself. It's what a good thoroughbred horse has. Snead had it. Palmer had it. Nicklaus had it. Tiger Woods has it."

The next year, Player made his first trip to America, where the game's best players made it clear by example that he needed to improve his game. He was particularly struck by his inability to reach the par 5s at Augusta in two shots. So Player continued to strengthen his body, while weakening his hooker's grip and learning how to carry the ball through the air farther. The next year, he won his first American event, the 1958 Kentucky Derby Open.

If Player needed any reinforcement, he got it from his idol, Ben Hogan, in the Southern Hills locker room after finishing second in the 1958 U.S. Open. "Hogan got about an inch from my face and locked me with those cold eyes. I'll never forget it. 'Son,' he said, 'you are going to be a great player.' Can you imagine hearing that from Hogan. Man alive!"

FIRST MAJOR

The next year, Player won the British Open at Muirfield. He started the final day, in which thirty-six holes were played, eight strokes behind the leader, Belgian Flory van Donck. But, partially fueled by van Donck's comment that Player would never make it because his swing was too flat, he played brilliantly. On the seventy-second tee, needing a par for 66 and certain victory, he drove into the rough and made a double-bogey 6. Believing he had blown the championship, he waited for the next two hours as contender after contender fell back. Finally, when van Donck and England's Fred Bullock failed to birdie the final hole, Player at twenty-three was the British Open champion. . . .

Player's greatest attainments came in the 1960s, that magical decade in golf when he, Palmer and Nicklaus were at or near their peaks. His victory at the 1961 Masters is generally remembered as a championship Palmer threw away by making a double-bogey from the middle of the eighteenth fairway to lose to Player by a stroke. It's been forgotten that, down the stretch, Player made a double-bogey on the par-5 thirteenth hole and a bogey on the par-5 fifteenth. But, on the seventy-second hole, he saved par from the same greenside bunker that later victimized Palmer.

The next year, Player won the PGA Championship at Aronomink to give himself three legs of the modern Grand Slam. Palmer and Nicklaus also had three legs when the U.S. Open came to Bellerive in 1965, at that time the longest course ever to hold a U.S. Open, and they were duly made the favorites. But Player realized he had a trancelike concentration that week. A large scoreboard near Bellerive's first tee had the names of the previous winners on it, with a blank after the slot for 1965. The first time Player studied the scoreboard, he says he clearly saw the blank filled by the name Gary Player in gold letters. He went on to defeat Kel Nagle in a playoff. Attaining the career Grand Slam before the age of thirty remains Player's proudest achievement.

CROWNING ACHIEVEMENT

When he came to Augusta in 1978, Player was forty-two and hadn't won in the U.S. since his 1974 Masters victory. He began the final round seven strokes behind, and was still far back after a disappointing par on the par-5 eighth hole. But then he went on a tear in which he birdied seven of the final ten holes, dramatically holing an eighteen-footer on the seventy-second hole. He shot 64, playing the final nine in thirty strokes. When Tom Watson, Rod Funseth and, finally, Hubert Green, all faltered down the stretch, Player, incredibly, had won.

"That Masters is my crowning achievement," says Player. "I was out of the tournament— out of it—but I simply never gave up. My focus was so intense, it was as if I poured every lesson I ever learned into that final nine holes. Do you know, I had two lip-outs on fifteen-footers and missed another birdie from six feet on that back nine? I could have shot 27! I was absolutely possessed! To beat those young players on that course, to convert that opportunity into victory, that was the finest moment of my career. . . . "

THE ULTIMATE SURVIVOR

But even Gary Player's desire is finite. He has vowed that his final appearance in the British Open will come at St. Andrews in the year 2000. He speaks of wanting to spend more time in South Africa, where he has three residences, the thousand-acre primary estate called Blair Atholl outside Johannesburg, a beach home in Pletenburg Bay near Capetown, and his eight-thousand-acre stud farm near Colesburg in the country's Karoo, bordered by the Orange River. Player has named it Mandiba, a term of affection and respect South Africans often use when addressing Nelson Mandela. All three homes are underused, and all beckon.

At the same time, Player remains too much a warrior to simply walk away from competition. He loves the challenge and the age-defying concept of the Senior Tour, where he is known among his peers by the forever-young nickname of "Laddie." And when he returns to Augusta each year, he competes with all his heart, convinced that, if a hot putter could somehow get him into contention on Sunday, he would still thrive on the opportunity.

"I just haven't sorted it out yet," he says. "My life, in a way, is too full."

It's the complaint of a protean force. Player's rewards have been great, but so has his sacrifice. From private struggles, like forcing himself to do his daily exercises and being apart from his family, to public ones like enduring close defeats or being unfairly branded a racist, Player has paid a price. "Those who aim at great deeds must also suffer greatly" is a quotation from Plutarch's *Lives* that could have been Player's eleventh commandment. Of course, he would gladly pay the price all over again.

"I have been so blessed, so lucky with golf, with my family, with my health, all I can be is thankful," he says. "When I was younger, to achieve what I wanted to achieve, I had to be selfish. It's a very selfish game. But I had a wife who was selfless. Can you imagine what it must have been like being married to me? Vivienne is the greatest thing that ever happened to Gary Player.

"As I've gotten older, I've come to understand that fewer things matter. Love is the most important word in our lives. As much as I'm proud of my record in golf, people will forget."

Gary Player exults at the moment of his come-from-behind win in the 1978 Masters. His victory also inspired his playing partner, a young Seve Ballesteros, who would go on to win two green jackets of his own

DAVE ANDERSON

THE GRAND SLAM
THAT ALMOST WAS

from *Golf Digest*, July 1987*

IN TWO DAYS, THE 1972 BRITISH OPEN WOULD BEGIN. BEYOND THE HEATHER AND THE gorse, a chilly wind had put a froth on the Firth of Forth in a niche of Scotland's northeast coast. On the Muirfield moors, Scots in tweeds and turtlenecks swarmed over the linksland as Jack Nicklaus moved through a practice round. Near the 14th green, a ruddy-faced Scot watched the 32-year-old American float an iron to within 15 feet of the cup on the 447-yard hole.

"Aye," the Scot said, "he's something to beat."

Something indeed. In winning the Masters and the U.S. Open at Pebble Beach that year, Nicklaus had either led or shared the lead in every round. He had won the 1966 British Open at Muirfield and now, his blond sideburns thick in the style of the time, he had returned to pursue the modern Grand Slam—winning the Masters, the U.S. Open, the British Open and the PGA Championship in the same year.

Greg Norman discovered in 1986 that the Grand Slam could be so close and yet so far. And this year at the Masters he appeared to have one leg up before Mize chipped in. But 15 years ago Jack Nicklaus had two legs up.

"Take a good look," another Scot was saying now to his small son as Nicklaus approached the 15th green. "There's one of the 10 most famous men in the world."

All week the local newspapers would call it The Grand Slam Open, but what only a few knew was that Nicklaus had awakened with a crick in his neck the previous morning at Greywalls, the small stone hotel near the ninth green. He has never used it as an alibi, then or now. "But my neck wasn't very good," he recalls today, "until halfway through the third round." By then he appeared to be all but out of contention for the title he had won at St. Andrews two years earlier. Despite decent scores of 70, 72 and 71, he was six strokes behind Lee Trevino, breezy and bold at the high noon of his career and the winner of both the U.S. Open at Merion and the British Open at Royal Birkdale the year before. And he was five strokes behind the 28-year-old Tony Jacklin, the elegant Englishman who had won the U.S. Open in 1970 at Hazeltine and the British Open in 1969 at Royal Lytham and St. Annes.

Jack Nicklaus at The Masters in 1972, on the first leg of the Grand Slam

---

* **DAVE ANDERSON** (b. 1929), who played his first round of golf when he was 18 at Dyker Beach in Brooklyn, has had a long and outstanding career as a sportswriter for *The New York Times*. He joined the *Times* in 1966 and has written the "Sports of the Times" column since 1971, which earned him the Pulitzer Prize for distinguished commentary in 1981. He has been a regular contributor to *Golf Digest* since 1973.

"I had the impression that Lee had given up," Jacklin remembers. "Lee never hooks the ball, but he had pulled his tee shot and his third shot. To me, that was an indication he was losing his concentration."

Trevino's 7-iron chip scooted across the green and up into heavy grass on the back slope. There in four, he would be lucky to salvage a bogey. Jacklin then chipped to within 16 feet, a possible birdie, and presumably, a sure par. And in the R&A shed, Nicklaus was checking his scorecard as Trevino's troubles were being shown on television sets near the 18th green.

"Trevino's blown!" somebody yelled.

On the slope behind the 17th green, Trevino stabbed at his ball with a 9-iron. "I think I might have given up," he said later. "I felt like I had. My heart wasn't really in that chip shot." But his ball hopped onto the green and rolled toward the cup. And into it. Another roar, the loudest of the day.

Behind the 18th green, somebody yelled, "Trevino holed his chip!" Nicklaus' caddie, Jimmy Dickinson, flung down his yellow caddie vest in disgust just as Jack emerged form the scorer's shed.

"He holed a chip shot for a 5!" Dickinson yelled.

"What?" Nicklaus said, his voice shrill in shock.

Trevino had stayed one stroke ahead of Nicklaus, but if Jacklin could make his 16-foot birdie putt, the Englishman would take the lead. The headlines in many of the Scottish and British papers that morning had rooted for "Jacko" to win, as he had three years earlier, the first British golfer to win the British Open since Max Faulkner in 1951. And now even Princess Margaret had come to see if Jacko could do it again.

Lee Trevino, "the Merry Mex," shares a laugh with Neil Coles's caddie at the British Open at Muirfield in 1972. Trevino chipped in for an improbable par on the 17th hole to nip Nicklaus by a stroke and end his dream of a Grand Slam

"There was no Seve Ballesteros then, no Sandy Lyle, no Nick Faldo," Jacklin says now. "I was in the pressure cooker. Going into that last day, I told myself, 'Keep your head and hold steady,' I felt like I'd done that all the way through, but when Lee's chip ran in, I ran out of patience. I could have run the ball up close, but my immediate reaction was, 'He's not going to beat me like that.'"

Jacklin stroked his putt firmly. The ball hurried past the left side of the cup and stopped about 2 ½ feet away.

"I wasn't jumpy on that first putt," Jacklin says. "I still felt in control. I wanted to make it so badly. In those circumstances, 2 ½ feet was too much."

Jacklin missed that 2 ½-footer. Instead of a birdie, he had a bogey, which dropped him one stroke behind Trevino.

"Once I three-putted, it was all over," Jacklin recalls. "After that I won a tournament every year to 1982 when I stopped playing, but I never really challenged in the major tournaments again. That finish in '72 kind of knocked the stuffing out of me. I lost a lot of confidence. It was the kind of thing that might not ever happen again. But it doesn't have to happen again. It happened once."

THE FINISHING HOLE

Watching from behind the 17th green, Trevino knew he needed only a par at the 18th to stay ahead of Nicklaus, to win.

"Instead of leading, Tony was out of it," Trevino recalls. "And by the time he finished putting, I had my composure."

Trevino's caddie turned to hurry to the 18th tee, but Lee grabbed his arm. "No, not yet," Trevino said, "let's wait for Tony before we walk back there." As much as Trevino wanted to hit quickly, he knew that if he hurried to the tee, he would be forced to wait until Jacklin walked back there inside the gallery ropes. Instead, he walked back with Jacklin, but as they neared the tee, he turned to his caddie.

"I told Willie to get out of my way because I was going to hit quick," Trevino says. "I grabbed my driver, teed it up, took one look, did my little left-foot shuffle and hit it."

By now, Nicklaus was watching television in an R&A trailer. His arms were folded, his legs crossed as Trevino's ball soared against the blue sky.

"Hit a long drive, didn't he?" Nicklaus said. Long enough for Trevino to float an 8-iron about seven feet behind the cup on the 447-yard finishing hole. "At long last," Henry Longhurst intoned on the BBC, "we have seen the shot that has won the Open." Nicklaus scratched his head and departed. Behind the bleachers he was being escorted to the press tent when he saw his wife, Barbara.

"Hi there," she said softly.

Without a word he kissed her and held her for a moment, then he heard the roar that saluted Trevino's par for 71 and 278—one stroke ahead of him, two ahead of Jacklin, who had bogeyed the 18th after pulling his approach into the left bunker.

"I was there and I let it get away," Nicklaus told his wife. "I felt a 65 would do it. I had a 65 and let it get away."

ODDS ON THE SLAM

If he had finished 3-4-4, as he did in 1966, Nicklaus would have won this British Open, too, but he finished 4-5-4—a two-stroke difference that was all the difference. Suddenly the PGA at Oakland Hills outside Detroit would be just another PGA, not the summit of a Grand Slam. (Nicklaus would finish six shots behind the winner, Gary Player.) When Jack sat behind a microphone in the press tent, the golf writers were trying to phrase a gentle first question when he looked down at Norman Mair of *The Scotsman.*

"Well, Norman," he said, smiling, "I guess I cost you a trip to Detroit."

The writers laughed, then the questions and answers flowed. Asked about the odds on his producing a Grand Slam in the future, Nicklaus grinned. "They're pretty high right now," he said. "I shot 279, and 19 out of 20 times that'll probably win. But it didn't. That's what you're fighting. That somebody will beat you. For 16 rounds, to put it together, that's difficult. I'm disappointed, because I felt I could put it together, but I didn't. I got beat. That's why everybody enters and plays. You don't want to give it to one guy." In those few words he had defined the difficulty of the modern Grand Slam that perhaps no golfer will complete. Then he stood up to go to the presentation ceremony.

"Lee Trevino is some good player," he said. "If I had to lose, I'm glad it was to him."

Maybe if Nicklaus hadn't been quite so cautious in the early rounds, he would have won. But then and now, he has never publicly second-guessed his strategy. "I'll always believe I played the course the right way and just didn't play well," he said that day. "What can I do about a guy who holes it out of bunkers and across greens?" Four times Trevino had holed it from off the putting surface, twice with his 9-iron, twice with his Helen Hicks sand wedge that he presented to British friends who auctioned it for charity. But every so often Jack Nicklaus thinks about how close he came to going to the PGA that year with an opportunity to complete the Grand Slam, how maybe it would have happened if he hadn't awakened with that crick in his neck.

"Not winning that British Open was a very big disappointment then," he says today. "And it seems to have become bigger as the years go by. But that's why the Slam is so tough. You've got to win those four tournaments over a span of four months. When you wake up every day, you never know how you're going to feel."

FRANK DEFORD

THE BEST AGAINST THE BEST

from *Sports Illustrated*, June 1986[*]

It is a rare treat when two superb golfers, each at the peak of his powers, go head-to-head with a major title at stake. Jack Nicklaus and Tom Watson have won eight British Opens in their illustrious careers, but none provided as many thrills as the 1977 Open at Turnberry

AS THEY APPROACHED THE TEE AT THE 72ND HOLE, ALFIE FYLES, TOM WATSON'S CADDIE, spoke up. "Go for the jugular," he said, and Watson broke a small grin and nodded his head and asked for his one-iron. This was it, at last; this would be the final hole in what, even then, people were calling the greatest golf match ever. Watson had gone head to head with Jack Nicklaus—the young lion, the challenger of this decade, vs. the golfer of the ages—in the first British Open ever played on the Ailsa course at Turnberry, on the Ayrshire coast, by the Firth of Clyde, off the North Channel of the Irish Sea. It was July of 1977; Nicklaus was 37, still in his prime, and Watson was 27, the new Masters champion, just coming into his.

On this last hole, Watson's tee shot drifted a bit left, but still clear of the bunker that sat 260 yards out. It was "awfully perfect," said Watson, so Nicklaus didn't hesitate.

For the first time on this hole he yanked out his driver and called up his power. It was incredible what he and Watson had done: identical 68-70s the first two days, matching 65s the third day, playing almost stroke for stroke together the final two rounds, pushing each other higher and higher, driving the gallery into a happy frenzy. They were a shot apart coming to the last hole, but still, either one of them could 10-putt the 18th green and finish runner-up. The winner's 268 would be the best score in British Open history by eight strokes. Two men had never played golf like this before, side by side.

The instant Nicklaus finished his swing he knew he had tried too hard and had hit the ball too full. The 18th fairway bent left just past the bunker Watson had missed, and Nicklaus wanted his drive to drift that way. Unfortunately his drives had been sailing to the right all day, and once again his tee shot flew that way, through the crook in the fairway, into rough as deep as there was anywhere on the course. Nicklaus turned the driver in his hand like a

---

[*] **FRANK DEFORD** (b. 1938) is one of the all-time great sportswriters. Deford did not set out to write about sports, but in 1962, after graduating from Princeton, he went to work for *Sports Illustrated*. He spent the next 27 years at *SI*, receiving national acclaim for his perceptive profiles. In this essay, Deford captures the high Caledonian drama of the greatest head-to-head clash in the history of the game—Tom Watson's one-shot win over Jack Nicklaus at Turnberry in 1977.

baton, took the offending club end and banged the handle down angrily to the turf as he stomped off the tee. To think it would end like this. It had to finish in glory. Nobody should *lose* this match. He or Watson, either one, O.K., but this was a match one of them had to *win*.

Watson walked over to check on Nicklaus's lie. At first he wasn't sure that the ball was even playable; it was buried deep in tall grass, only inches from a prickly strand of gorse. Would Jack be able to bring a club back, much less muscle the ball out? Watson decided Nicklaus would just be able to negotiate a swing, and he returned to his own ball, which lay perhaps 180 yards from the pin.

"What do you think?" he asked Alfie. The caddie fingered the seven-iron. Watson stared at him quizzically.

"What? You know I can only carry 160–65 with a *six*."

"The way your adrenaline's pumpin', Tom. . . ." Was all Alfie said, and his man took the seven. Watson hit it full-blooded to the pin, 30 inches from the cup.

It surely must be over now.

Nicklaus grasped his eight-iron. He took it back right through a branch of the gorse bush, macheted it down with a superhuman swat and sent the ball and a massive divot flying out. Somehow the ball found the right side of the green, 32 feet from the flag. It was impossible. Right away Watson knew—*knew*—that Nicklaus was going to make that putt for a birdie.

on the same order, say, as pinsetters in a bowling alley. British caddies have always had their opinions solicited, and usually valued, even by the grandest and most savvy of golfers. For one thing, the elements are forever shifting in Britain. But much of the status of caddies has to do with the differences between the two societies. In America it's considered beneath oneself to labor as an athletic domestic, yet the British, comfortable with the gentleman-servant relationship, saw that men could make an honorable career out of toting other men's bags. Except for time out as a seaman in the Royal Navy, Alfie has caddied for about half a century.

Alas, there are fewer such stalwarts all the time. Long John, The Wasp, The Lawyer, the one-armed Wingy Eugene, the similarly handicapped Halifax Wingy (who lost his hook in some heavy rough once), Johnny One-Blank (who did have all his limbs but lacked an eye), Mad Mac, Laughing Boy, Yorky Billy have all gone. And disappearing just as rapidly is the caddie's Cockney argot, which featured a rhyming code. A Vera Lynn, for example, meant a gin, a Gregory Peck a check. A beehive was a five (usually used in association with cherry picker, which meant a knicker, which was itself a slang word for pound; thus a caddie with a beehive cherry picker had a £5 note). And St. Louis Blues was shoes, Holy Ghost was toast, and sizzle and strife meant the missus.

But the career boys are a dying breed. "All you've got is your bag-carriers now," Alfie sneers. "All they can do is give the golfer a weather report—not the right club." Nothing sets Alfie's blood to boiling more than the familiar sight of a man who calls himself a caddie throwing grass up in the air to detect the wind direction. In Alfie's view, you might as well have a homing pigeon asking a bobby to show him the way back to the house. "Once it was all eyeball," he explains. Caddying is telling your man to use a seven-iron to carry 180 yards when the most he can hit a six iron is 165. That is caddying, eyeball.

And in a world today where Americans expect to have a little piece of home wherever they go—the English language and the baseball scores, McDonald's and MasterCard—most American pros bring their caddies over to Scotland for greater security. Watson and Alfie are the exception. And even they had one great falling out, right at the beginning, after Alfie eye-balled Watson to his first major, at Carnoustie in '75. When he went up to the Watsons' room to get his pay, Alfie was so disgusted at the figure Watson gave him that he threw the Gregory Peck down on the floor. "You must need this more than me," he snapped. Linda Watson was furious, and Alfie told Watson to have her leave, that he worked for Tom, not for his wife. But Watson wouldn't budge, so Alfie picked the check off the floor—"before Tom could take me literally"—and left in disgust.

The next summer Watson brought his American caddie over to help him defend his title at Royal Birkdale and he missed the 54-hole cut. Both the Watsons began to seek rapprochement after that, and Alfie was waiting for Watson when the Yank arrived at Turnberry. They've been together every July since then, and Watson has the finest British Open record—five championships—of any American.

In 1977 it wasn't until Friday, the third round—when Nicklaus and Watson were first paired together—that they began to outdistance the field. Indeed, when they started off that midday, both having shot par 70s before, they were a stroke behind Roger Maltbie and there were 16 contenders within four shots of the lead.

But on that third day Nicklaus and Watson would both shoot 65s—six birdies and a bogey apiece—and on Saturday they would move off into a realm by themselves. The pattern was set on the 1st hole, too, when Nicklaus struck a wedge to within three feet and made a birdie. Always, over the last two days, Nicklaus would draw ahead and Watson would fight back. On Friday, Nicklaus was two strokes ahead, playing the 8th hole, called Goat Fell, when

Jack Nicklaus, Tom Watson, and Alfie Fyles take shelter during a storm on the rocks below the 9th hole at Turnberry in the third round of their historic shootout at the 1977 British Open

the overcast skies turned electric. Both men were on the green, but Watson wanted to take cover immediately.

Nicklaus, the senior, prevailed, though, and Watson reluctantly went along, but as soon as they both putted out, parring, the golfers and their caddies scurried down to find shelter among the rocks on the beach. Only when they were protected by an overhang did it occur to Alfie that water made the best conductor, so back up the cliff they hustled to take refuge in a BBC trailer. Watson and Nicklaus didn't say much to each other, but rarely does either talk on the course. When the storm passed they put on sweaters and proceeded to the forbidding 9th tee, the one stuck out on an overlook, the one that Herbert Warren Wind has described as "out of a Gothic novel."

They both parred there and sank long birdie putts on 10. Nicklaus took his only bogey of the round with a bad putt on 14, and when Watson sank a 20-footer on 15, they were level once again. Nicklaus should have gained a stroke on 17, but he missed an eagle putt and, like Watson, had to endure a mere bird. Both parred 18. Nicklaus 31-34, Watson 33-32. Both: 203 for 54 holes, seven under par.

Curiously, it still wasn't viewed strictly as a duel. There was Ben Crenshaw, of whom great things were expected, only three shots back, at 206. Nicklaus was near the height of his powers, but even if Watson had won at Carnoustie in '75 and had edged Nicklaus at the Masters three months earlier, there remained something unsubstantial about him. In time Watson would tote up eight majors, but the "quitter" charge still lingered then with Watson, as even now he is being written off early, after only two years of struggling. "It has the same flavor," he says, biting off the words. Pause. "The same smell." Then, too, even at his best, Watson was neither awesome nor mysterious, and while he was invariably described as having "a Huck Finn look," Huck's playful, mischievous aspect was missing. Besides, the British had never held it against Nicklaus, the way the Americans did, that he eclipsed Palmer, so there were more cheers for Jack.

Nobody knew then how great a force Watson would become in the British Isles. "Tom's a good thinker," Nicklaus says, "and you have to think well over there to win. You're playing in adverse conditions, and there are just a lot of our guys who can't do that for 72 holes."

Watson would also develop a peculiar facility for playing his best down the stretch against Nicklaus—better even than emotional characters like Trevino and Palmer, who could sway a crowd. In his entire career, Nicklaus says, "my hardest loss" remains the '82 U.S. Open, when Watson beat him straight-up by chipping in from off the 17th at Pebble Beach. Watson never let Nicklaus's majesty intimidate him. Three months before Turnberry, at the Masters, playing in adjacent twosomes, Watson was on the 13th fairway when he saw Nicklaus raise his putter toward him after he sank a birdie on the green ahead, as if to say, *Take this.* In fact, Nicklaus was only exulting, but Watson upbraided him for his seeming hot-dog action as soon as they encountered each other off the last green. Nicklaus, stunned, didn't have the foggiest idea what he was being accused of, and Watson finally backed off, embarrassed but undaunted.

Watson is not an easy man to characterize. Principled and sensitive, he also bears the rap of being a know-it-all. He is one of the few athletes left who still smoke. While most other golfers play out of planned Sunbelt subdivisions, Watson went off to Stanford to school and has returned to his native Kansas City to celebrate his family, the Royals and the seasons. Some days in January or February he's the only person playing at the Kansas City Country Club. "It's cleansing," he says. After that, Turnberry and the other links may not seem quite so beastly.

The fans at Turnberry were jostling for places when the two men teed off in the final pairing late Saturday morning. It was a bright, sunny day, but for the first time all week a brisk

THOMAS BOSWELL

BUCKING THE SYSTEM

from *Strokes of Genius*, 1987*

JUNE 1981—TEN YEARS AGO THIS MONTH WHEN HE THREW A RUBBER SNAKE AT JACK Nicklaus on the practice tee, then beat him in a playoff at Merion to win his second U.S. Open, Lee Trevino became famous.

Famous, yes; known, no.

Many in golf, including Trevino himself, say that he barely became known at all. In June 1971, there on the Main Line, Trevino became bona fide—two Opens are considered proof of golf bloodlines. That thunderclap of success brought Trevino into the glare of publicity. Every corner of his Dickensian life was lit. His early sufferings were considered uplifting, amusing, heroic. Quickly, the myth of the funny man was profitably put in place. Once Trevino was a public personality, anything at odds with that role was left in shadow. Only with the years have the other parts of Trevino slowly come to light, giving balance and humanity to what we knew and appreciated all along.

Still, Trevino may be the least-fathomed superstar in golf. As a melodramatic example, it's been a Tour whisper for years that when Trevino began his comeback in 1978 after being struck by lightning and undergoing major back surgery for a ruptured disk, the second-leading money winner in golf history was almost broke. "I didn't want to make a comeback; I had to make one," says Trevino now. "It got to a point where I was scared that everything I'd worked for would be gone. I'd invested badly. . . . I had almost everything tied up in one [failed] project and, until I got out of it, it was draining everything. I still had our $300,000 home, but it had a $140,000 mortgage. I had eight antique cars, but that doesn't amount to too much. And I had one piece of commercial property all paid for that was worth maybe $25,000. Other than that, all I had was the rainbow."

The rainbow?

"Sure, you know, the pot of gold that's buried under the end of the rainbow. I've always believed in that. But I had to get my old tools out and dig for it again."

It's hard to find any aspect of Trevino that is not either completely misunderstood, or, at best, half-understood. Trevino needs to be read like some of the late works of Mark

* In addition to this collection of his essays on golf, **THOMAS BOSWELL** is also the author of two collections of baseball essays, *How Life Imitates the World Series* and *Why Time Begins on Opening Day*.

Twain—with trepidation, lest we find that the joke is on ourselves. "People think Trevino's loosey goosey," says Dale Antrum, a veteran PGA Tour official. "In fact, he's tight as a drum. They think he's relaxed. Really, he's so intense he has to talk and joke constantly to relieve the tension. The reason he plays so fast is because he has to. Trevino goes absolutely nuts if play is slow. It can destroy his game and other players know it."

Says Trevino, "There ain't nothin' relaxed about me on a golf course. I'm very tightly wound. All that jabbering is a pressure valve. I couldn't do without it. The competitor inside you knows what has to be done. If the game doesn't eat you up inside, you can't possibly be a great player. I still get mad, but not nearly like I once did. In the last ten years, that's probably the biggest improvement in my game."

An unsung Lee Trevino at the U.S. Open at Oak Hill, Rochester, New York in 1968. Three years later he would win his second Open at Merion Cricket Club, outside Philadelphia

PETER DOBEREINER

FALDO AND THE DEMON

Volvo PGA Championship Program, 1991*

William St. Clair of Roslin, an oil painting by Sir George Chalmers, 1771. Roslin, Captain of the Honourable Company of Edinburgh Golfers, was 70 when this portrait was painted. Sir Walter Scott, who recalled Roslin's exploits from boyhood memories, described him as "thin-flanked and broad-shouldered, built it would seem for the business of war or chase. . . . In all manly sports which require strength and dexterity he was unrivalled, but his particular delight was in archery."

RUDYARD KIPLING DIDN'T HAVE MUCH TIME FOR GOLF. POLO AND PIG STICKING WERE more in his line. It was all the more remarkable, then, that he was able to predict so accurately what was going to happen to the European Tour 100 years later. He even anticipated that golfers would call themselves by the names of animals, great white shark, golden bear and so on, and he therefore used a jungle metaphor for his uncanny prophecy.

You remember his story of How The Elephant Got Its Trunk, of course. Originally all elephants had normal noses not a whit bigger than say, Barry Manilow's. This young elephant, who was much put upon by the bullying adults, went down to the river for a drink and a crocodile grabbed him by the hooter. The beasts of the jungle raced to his rescue and pulled him from behind, the tug o' war ending with rescue for the young elephant who by now had a greatly extended proboscis. Armed with this prehensile appendage, the young elephant returned to the herd and whaled the tar out of his tormentors who in self defence had to go to the river for nose jobs from the crocodile.

In this prophetic parable we have the life story of Nick Faldo, today the dominant leader of the golfing herd while his hapless rivals go trooping off to Florida to get the crocodile treatment from David Leadbetter. But will they have the character, the patience and the sheer guts which Faldo displayed during the long and painful process of acquiring his trunk?

He is a much misunderstood man. But the key to his character is that he is possessed of a demon, the Demon of Ambition.

In this he is in the historic tradition of golfing champions going back to William St. Clair of Roslyn [sic], winner of the silver clubs of St. Andrews and the Honourable Company of Edinburgh Golfers back in the 18th century. This

* **PETER DOBEREINER** wrote and edited several books about golf. Some of his best columns and essays, including this piece on Nick Faldo, are collected in *Golf à la Carte*. Dobereiner's grandfather was John Hassall, an artist who created landmark advertising posters for the British railways, and painted many well-known and highly sought-after golf illustrations and caricatures.

remarkable character, whose red-coated figure is celebrated in one of the most reproduced golfing prints of all time, was so skilled at golf and archery that he was thought to have sold his soul to a witch.

Every great player since then has been the subject of demonic possession, none more so than Jack Nicklaus. These are men apart and they deserve some effort from us to understand,

Nick Faldo runs aground on hole 10 at Shoal Creek, Birmingham, Alabama, during the 1990 PGA. Faldo won both the Masters and the British Open that year

Phil Mickelson hitting out of the trees on the 10th hole during the 2002 Byron Nelson Classic at the Cottonwood Valley Golf Course in Las Colinas, Texas

birthday, he won the first golf tournament he entered, a putting competition against kids as old as thirteen. A few weeks later, in his second tournament, the Pee Wee International in Orlando, Florida, he placed second. Like Woods, Mickelson dominated the junior circuits he competed on and won the U.S. Amateur and the NCAA individual championship (in Mickelson's case, three times). He won his first Tour event, the Northern Telecom Open, while still a junior in college at twenty, younger by a few months than Tiger was when he won his first Tour event.

But the differences between the two child prodigies are more telling than the similarities, and they may shed some light on why Woods, at twenty-five, has won twenty-nine Tour events and six majors, while Mickelson, at thirty-one, has won only nineteen times on Tour and no majors (although to be fair, those nineteen victories are more than any player under fifty has won, except Woods). The most significant difference between them involves the influence of their parents. Tiger's visionary father, Earl, explicitly bred his son to be a champion, instituting concentration drills and exposing him to the glare of public attention from early childhood. Mickelson's parents, in contrast, took a let's-wait-and-see attitude about Phil's future as a golfer and encouraged their boy simply to have fun with his gift.

To make a musical analogy, you might say that Woods grew up to be Beethoven—driven, intense, brooding and prone to grand finishes—whereas Mickelson is like Mozart—playful, light, fun-loving and mischievous. Both players are profoundly competitive, but Tiger by nature seems bent on something like world domination while Mickelson mostly just seems to want a good game. "It doesn't matter whether it's darts, pool or pitching pennies, Phil wants to win," says his frequent practice round companion Andrew Magee. "That's what drives him be so aggressive on the golf course." And as Mickelson himself admits, that aggressiveness is often what gets him into trouble, especially in clutch situations. In the Mickelson-Mozart mind-set, laying up on the eighteenth hole at Pebble Beach is simply not as exciting as going for the green in two with a driver off the deck, which he did last winter in the final round of the AT&T, only to slice his ball into the Pacific and blow the tournament.

There's evidence, however, that Mickelson is getting fed up with such antics. At the start of the 2000 season, aiming to make his game more major-tough, he quietly initiated his first-ever thorough swing revamp, with instructor Rick Smith. He's also striving, against every fiber of his nature, to rein in his risk-taking tendencies. The early results are encouraging. He didn't win a major in 2001, but he came close at both the Masters and the PGA, and statistically his game is now tops on Tour. By mid-September he had more top-ten finishes, more birdies and more eagles than anyone, the best putting average and the best all-around rating. Yet it's an open question whether the new, more resolute Phil will ever totally eclipse the Mozart Mickelson—or whether we should even want him to. . . .

Mickelson's victory at the 1991 Northern Telecom Open in Tucson, Arizona, was the perfect, Mozartean finale to his boyhood. Although he'd won the U.S. Amateur the summer before, no one reasonably expected a pink-cheeked twenty-year-old to prevail in a big-money PGA Tour event—but Mickelson did, in storybook fashion. Unfazed after sleeping with a two-shot lead on Saturday night, he charged into Sunday's round beaming and enthusiastic and got as far as the par-five fourteenth without making any youthful mistakes. There, however, he triple-bogeyed after driving into trouble and then making an unwise decision on his recovery shot. Suddenly Mickelson was three shots back—the classic opportunity for a newbie pretender to totally collapse. But Mickelson, feeding off the crowd's support and clearly having fun, birdied the final two holes to win by a stroke and claim the silly silver helmet that every victor at Tucson must don.

Better results began to show up almost immediately. He won four times in 2000 and twice more through September of this year, and he has had more top-ten finishes this year than anyone, including Tiger. He still makes the occasional bad decision, such as hitting that driver off the deck at the AT&T, and suffers spells of erratic play. But when he struggles, Smith often shows up the next day, or they e-mail videos of his swing back and forth. "There has been a huge, a *huge* difference in my ball striking, iron play and driving in the last year and a half," says Mickelson.

This season, he also did better in the majors. He didn't win one, but he was within three shots of the lead after three rounds in every major but the British Open and contended until late in the final round at both the Masters and the PGA. At the PGA, in fact, his final score 266 was the lowest ever recorded at a major and two strokes clear of the field—except for the 265 that David Toms threw up to win.

And if you need a visible sign of Mickelson's newfound determination, he provided it after chipping in for birdie on the fifteenth green at that event, to pull even with Toms. Mickelson's traditional reaction after a brilliant shot is a half-apologetic, hayseed shrug of the shoulders and a goofy, anybody-could-a-done-it grin. ("It's almost as if he is embarrassed the ball went in," his father describes it.) But at the fifteenth he stalked toward the pin with a series of steely fist pumps and a look of resolve on his face that could have frozen Ray Floyd.

Even so, there's no guarantee that Mickelson will ever win a major. Despite his progress, the 2001 season included a couple of embarrassing final-round blowups while in contention—one at Colonial (he missed three short putts) and one at New Orleans ("pathetic," he called the round)—and a final-round seventy-five at the U.S. Open after starting the day only two strokes off the pace. Collapses are new for Mickelson. Through 2000, he won ten of eleven times he held the fifty-four-hole lead. Through September of this season, he was one for four.

The truth is, a struggle is going on within Mickelson's soul. In accepting that he needs to make changes in his game if he wants to win majors, he puts at risk the fearless prodigy spirit that got him to where he is. Take his penchant for attempting risky shots. I asked Mickelson why, despite knowing intellectually that the odds favor a more conservative shot selection, he sometimes still takes the gamble. After pondering for a second, he blurted out, "Because I know I can make the shot!" This is the confidence that Mickelson grew up with and that is still intimidating to other pros on Tour. "The rest of us have a lot of doubts and fears out there, but I don't know if Phil has any at all," says Magee. "Either that or he's very, very good at masking his feelings."

Unshakeable confidence helps on routine shots as well as risky ones. And under the klieg-light pressure at the majors, anything that impinges on confidence, such as thoughts of recent swing changes or the need to refrain from playing the go-for-it golf of one's youth, can wreak havoc. It may ultimately be that Mickelson's style of golf has less in common with the grim, hyper-intense, fireproof games of Hogan, Nicklaus and Woods than with the lighter, more sublime games of Sam Snead and Byron Nelson—men who did win a few majors in less competitive times but became legends more on the basis of their syrupy swings and, in Nelson's case, an otherworldly, nonmajor winning streak. Mozart's compositions may not be as earth-shaking as Beethoven's, but to the music-loving public they have given every bit as much pleasure.

And who knows? Mickelson may yet find the right on-course balance between the golf-playing joy of his past and the more complicated ambitions and distractions of adulthood. He has his own jet now and is starting a course-design business. The trick for him will be having fun and feeling secure even as he tries to push his genius to the limit.

DAVID OWEN

CREATING TIGER WOODS

from *The Chosen One*, 2001*

A FEW HOURS BEFORE WOODS'S OKLAHOMA CITY EXHIBITION, I SAT WITH THE ALL-BLACK congregation of the St. John Missionary Baptist Church (Motto: "We Strive to Be 'The Best Church This Side of Judgement' ") while Tiger's father gave a guest sermon. Earl's talk was preceded by hymns, prayers, and half a dozen full-immersion baptisms, which were conducted in a large tank that was visible through an opening in the wall above the altar. His subject was his only subject. "Tiger was not created to be a golfer," he said. "Tiger was made to be a good person, and that was first and foremost in our family."

Earl is shorter and considerably wider than Tiger, and he is a walking anthology of alarming health problems. He is a heavy and largely unapologetic cigarette smoker; it's a habit he picked up in the Army, and one that his son finds disgusting and has pushed his father to shake. ("I know smoking is wrong," Earl himself once told Rick Reilly of *Sports Illustrated,* "but I contend there's no cholesterol in a cigarette.") He suffers from advanced heart disease. He underwent quadruple bypass surgery in the 1980s and was hospitalized with coronary problems again in October 1996 while Tiger was competing in the Tour Championship at Southern Hills Country Club, in Tulsa, Oklahoma. Concern about his father's condition distracted Tiger during that tournament and contributed to his shooting his worst score ever as a member of the PGA Tour: 78 in the second round. Four months later, Earl underwent triple bypass surgery, then had surgery again after ripping out the grafts with hiccups. Earl has also undergone radiation treatment for prostate cancer and has endured a variety of lesser medical emergencies. His brushes with death have not inspired him to transform his lifestyle, however, and he often appears to be struggling when moving under his own power; he has to catch his breath after almost any significant physical exertion.

He has a good speaking voice, though—a preacher's voice. It caught in his throat a couple of times during his sermon, despite the fact that he has given essentially the same presentation dozens if not hundreds of times before. "Sometimes when I talk about my son I get very emotional," he explained. "So bear with me." He often rambles in puzzling directions when speaking extemporaneously—I once heard him refer to Tiger as "brain-damaged," a

---

* **DAVID OWEN** is the author of several books, including *The Making of the Masters. The Chosen One* is an expanded version of an essay about Tiger Woods that appeared in *The New Yorker* in August 2000.

jarring remark that he made in passing and didn't explain—but he was in good form that morning in church.

Earl Woods was born in Manhattan, Kansas, during the Great Depression. He had an older brother and four older sisters. His mother had earned a college degree, but because she was black she could find work only as a housemaid. His father was a brick mason and a gardener and a frustrated athlete, and he dreamed of a baseball career for his son. (The father's closest personal contact with baseball in adulthood was as a scoreboard operator at a local park where only white teams were allowed to play.) The family was poor—Earl remembers receiving charity food baskets from the local Rotary Club at Thanksgiving—but the Woods children did not feel impoverished. His mother was loving and protective, and she was evangelical on the subject of education. She forbade Earl to stay home from school during snowstorms, asked his teacher to increase his workload when he showed signs of slacking off, and admonished him, in connection with one of his early athletic heroes, "Don't you dare talk the way Joe Louis talks when you grow up!" Earl, in turn, passed versions of these lessons along to Tiger, who had a distinguished record at every stage in his education and, unlike most other students with athletic scholarships, took a full load of regular academic courses when he was in college, at Stanford.

Earl's secure world came apart when he was eleven: his father died suddenly of a stroke, and his mother died two years later, at least partly of grief. (Earl recalls the pain of watching her ceaselessly rocking in a rocking chair while humming the hymn "What Are They Doing in Heaven Today?") He was raised from that point by his eldest sister, who had absorbed her mother's powerful example and who succeeded in keeping the children together in the home in which they had grown up. Earl attended a mostly white high school and played catcher on an otherwise all-white American Legion baseball team. He endured numerous racist taunts when he was on the ball field—as did the other members of his family, who were often the only black fans in the grandstands. In high school he was a popular candidate for "king of the prom," but he says that the election was rigged against him by adults who did not want to see a black king kiss a white queen. He got through it all with the support of his siblings and with the help of a powerful sense of self-worth, which he attributes to his mother. She had taught him—as he would later teach Tiger—that racism is evidence of a defect in the racist, not in the racist's victim. He needed to apply the same lesson when he attended his hometown college, Kansas State University, on an athletic scholarship, and became the first black baseball player in the conference known today as the Big Twelve. He lived at home and commuted by bicycle.

After graduation, Earl briefly played semiprofessional baseball, then reluctantly turned down a chance to play in the Negro Leagues—a job that would have fulfilled his father's dream for him—and spent twenty years in the Army, where he felt he would have a bigger and better future. The day before he entered the service, he married Barbara Hart; they eventually had three children, two sons and a daughter, to whom he was a remote father at best. (Those children, who now have children of their own, are named Earl, Kevin, and Royce.) He served two widely separated tours of duty in Vietnam, the second as a Green Beret, and later taught military history at the City College of New York. It was in Southeast Asia that he met two of the most important figures in his adult life: Vuong Dang "Tiger" Phong, a South Vietnamese lieutenant colonel, who was his colleague, close friend, and protector during the war; and Kultida Punsawad, a Thai office receptionist, who would later become his second wife. After the fall of Saigon in 1975, Earl vowed to himself that if he and Kultida had a son, he would give the boy the nickname of his old friend Colonel Phong, whom he credited with having more than once saved his life.

Earl retired from the Army in 1974, with the rank of lieutenant colonel, and he and Kultida moved out of New York, where Earl had been teaching, and settled in California. Eldrick Tiger Woods was born on December 30, 1975. His parents selected his first name because it began and ended with the initials of their own names, an orthographic reminder to themselves of their total commitment to this child.

Earl was determined to be a better parent to the last of his four children than he had been to the first three, and his retirement from the Army gave him more time to be attentive. His one significant distraction—other than his job, as a contract administrator and materials manager at McDonnell Douglas, in Huntington Beach, California—was golf, a game at which he had become remarkably proficient despite having taken it up little more than a year earlier, at the age of forty-two. (Playing mostly on a scrappy military golf course near their home, he quickly reduced his handicap to zero—a rate of progress almost unheard of in golf, whose players often require a decade or more of hard work to become even mediocre.) He tuned his swing in the evenings by hitting balls into a net in his garage, and he often placed his infant son in a high chair beside him, so the two of them could commune while he practiced. "It was a way of spending time together," he said—a typical golfer's rationalization, although in this case it appears the baby was a more than willing spectator. Far from being bored, Tiger was captivated by the motion. One momentous day, when he was still young enough not to have mastered all the finer points of walking, he astonished his father by climbing down from his high chair, picking up a baby-sized plastic club, and executing a passable imitation of Earl's quite good golf swing. Tiger made that first swing left-handed—a mirror image of his right-handed model. A few days later, he stepped around the ball, correctly reversed his grip, and made an equally precocious swing from the opposite side. At that moment, Earl realized he was the steward of an extraordinary talent.

Signs that the new child was special had been evident from before the beginning, according to Earl. "When Tida was seven months pregnant with Tiger," he has written, "I was invited to play in a golf tournament at Lake Shastina in northern California. We drove there, and Tida walked the golf course with me." The baby squirmed and kicked, except when the Woodses drew close to any putting green. "Then, whenever a golf ball hit the green, it reverberated against the volcanic surface and produced a thumping sound, similar to a drum. Tiger apparently reacted to these vibrations. He would be very still and quiet"—as well-behaved spectators always are when golfers are preparing to putt. Earl's conclusion: "He seemed to know golf protocol while he was still in the womb."

As the years went by, this incident and others led Earl to believe that the birth of his son had been—as he told the St. John congregation—"the plan of the man upstairs." Looking back on his life, he detected a pattern of trials and tests and close escapes from tragedy, and he decided that God had been grooming him all along for something big. He remembered a day in Vietnam when his life had been spared twice: first, when a sniper's bullets narrowly missed him; and later, when his friend Tiger Phong warned him about a poisonous snake lurking inches from his head. He came to view his first marriage as a sort of providential dry run for his second, and to think of his first two sons almost as rough drafts for his third. (In Earl's autobiography, the chapter concerning this period is called "Marriages and Mulligans.") He blamed himself for not taking an active role in the upbringing of his first three children, but he also decided that his negligence had been a necessary phase in his preparation for what he now believed to be the true purpose of his life: the creation and nurturing of Tiger Woods. He hadn't been a good father, he realized, but without those early failures he would never have learned how to become a better father now.

As young Eldrick grew, Earl was struck more and more by what he described in church that day as "the charismatic power that resides in my son Tiger"—a power that he had otherwise noticed only in Nelson Mandela, Mahatma Gandhi, and a handful of other figures. (Tiger has met Mandela, an encounter that Earl described this year in a quote in *TV Guide:* "It was the first time Tiger met a human being who was equal to him, who was as powerful as Tiger is. He told Tiger he had a lot to give the world. He saw himself in Tiger.") Golf, Earl began to believe, was not the true purpose of Tiger's life, but was merely one of the instruments by which he would one day influence the course of civilization. The boy's talents were too astonishing not to have some deeper purpose; how else could his father make sense of this remarkable prodigy? Earl saw manifestations of divine influence in Tiger's competitive record, his golf swing, his work ethic, his ease in front of television cameras, and in Earl's own ability at critical moments to transmit encouragement and advice to his son by means of mental telepathy. (Earl says that he communicated telepathically with Tiger—and urged him to trust his putting stroke—at a crucial moment during the 1999 PGA Championship, which Earl was watching on TV and which Tiger went on to win.) Earl even came to view his own ill health as a God-given gift; its purpose, he says, was to teach him (so that he, in turn, could teach his son) that life is short: seize the day.

Tiger Woods tees off on No. 4 at the Bethpage Black Course, Bethpage, New York, en route to his U.S. Open victory in 2002

"Tiger has already transcended the game of golf," Earl has said. "He is a world figure, not just a world golf figure. He has transcended athletics already. He is a spokesperson. He is a world celebrity. The next step is to be someone on the world scale who makes an impact on humanity, and that is what he is going to be doing. He is going to make a difference in people's lives all over the world. In what areas? I don't know yet, because it hasn't come. But it's coming."

Even to someone sitting in a church pew, this might sound mystical and wacky—and yet the more you learn about Tiger Woods's preternatural relationship to the game of golf, the easier it becomes to understand why terrestrial interpretations seem inadequate to Earl. Of course, Earl's explanation has the substantial benefit for him of making his early failures as a parent seem to have been divinely ordained: he is, in effect, forgiving himself for not being a better person. But when he speaks or writes in this vein he doesn't seem cynical, or even particularly self-serving. He is as mystified by the scale of his son's achievements as everyone else is, and he is too much in awe of them to take full credit for himself. As he told the congregation, "I'm good, but I'm not that good."

When Tiger was still a toddler, Earl says, the child was able to identify the swing flaws of adult players. ("Look, Daddy," Tiger would say, "that man has a reverse pivot!") Tiger putted with Bob Hope on the *Mike Douglas Show* at the age of two, broke 50 for nine holes at the age of three, hit golf balls on *That's Incredible!* at the age of five, and received his first autograph request when he was still too young to have a signature. (The television performances grew out of a chance appearance on a local news show in California.) He was aware of his gift, and remarkably comfortable with it. In one frequently shown piece of old footage, a smiling and impossibly young-looking Tiger Woods, his golf cap pushed back high on his head, happily says, "I want to win all the big tournaments—the major ones—and I hope to play well when I get older, and beat all the pros." He looks so cute and innocent that his comment would break our heart if you didn't know what he's done since then. Before he had learned to count to ten, Earl says, Tiger could tell you, on any golf hole, where each member of a foursome stood in relation to par. While his grade school contemporaries drew pictures of racing cars and robots, Tiger sketched the trajectories of his irons. He came from behind to win the Junior World Championship, in San Diego, against an international field, when he was eight.

"Something that I think no one really knows," Woods said shortly before his exhibition in Oklahoma, "is that the Junior World was where my confidence started—knowing that I could play this game against a high level of players—and from then on I felt like I could compete against the best players anywhere around the world." He won the same tournament four more times as well, at the ages of nine, twelve, thirteen, and fourteen.

The Changing of the Guard: Tiger and Jack cross paths at the 2000 PGA Championship at Valhalla Golf Club in Louisville, Kentucky. Tiger would win his third major of the year

More than anything else, Woods loved to compete. "He gets that from me," Earl says. "We were very competitive when he was a little kid. We had fun through competition. Tiger is the ultimate competitor, always has been, always will be. And we just enjoyed competitive situations. Every practice was a competition. We played games—and it's still that way. When I drive a ball now, Tiger says, 'Is that the best you can do?' And I tell him, 'Well, I can beat your butt on the putting green.' And he says, 'No, you can't—not anymore.' You see, I used to have an advantage, because I was taller, and my lag putting was a lot better than his. Now he's taller than I am, and his lag putting is better than mine." As Tiger's skills grew, Earl helped him mentally prepare for competition by putting him through (with Tiger's advance consent) what he called his "Finishing School"—an extended period of psychological hazing on the golf course, which was intended to harden Tiger's nerves for tournament play and gradually inoculate him against a broad spectrum of distractions. When the two played together, Earl would tee up his own ball on the wrong side of the markers, improve his lie, jingle change in his pockets as Tiger was preparing to putt, clap his hands, make rude noises, and do everything he could think of to break his son's concentration. Earl's program helped to hone Tiger's ability to remain focused while competing—one of the most impressive of his many athletic talents, and one that is probably unequaled in sports. Tiger's concentration is so acute that he probably receives less credit for it than he deserves, because he makes it seem easy. No athlete in history has ever competed day in and day out under the burden of such intense public fascination. His appearance remains so serene as the pressure mounts that you tend to forget about the trying conditions under which he performs. Golf fans simply assume that he is going to win, and time and again over the years he has found startling new ways to exceed their expectations. Earl has said that Tiger simply doesn't feel pressure—that he "has no comfort level," as he once

MICHAEL BAMBERGER

NOT SO FAST

from *Sports Illustrated*, July 2002

TO THE PREDICTION IN THIS SPACE, AFTER BOTH THE MASTERS AND THE U.S. OPEN, THAT Tiger Woods will win the Grand Slam, we now offer this addendum: some year. The soaking seaside blow last Saturday afternoon robbed him of his 2002 Grand Slam bid. When was the last time you saw him playing without a cap? Never. The raindrops were pouring off the brim, and he could not go backward, Griffey-style, as he did at Bethpage. His lid would have gone flying in the 30-mph gusts. When was the last time you saw Woods shoot 81 in a major? Never.

Don't look for him to win the PGA Championship at Hazeltine next month either. The emotion of the year has been robbed from him now. Woods is the king of the grinders, but his greatness is rooted in his desire to make history. Three majors in one year? He's already done that. The wait for next year has begun.

God bless Scotland, the Royal & Ancient, the craggy linksland and the weather. Muirfield was short for a major, a pitch shot more than 7,000 yards and playing much shorter. But when the fairways are narrow and fast, when the rough is knee-high, when the skies go from blue to gunmetal gray, when the tents rattle in the wind, when the players bundle up in two lawyers of cashmere and rain suit, 49-year-old Des Smyth of Ireland is as good as Tiger Woods, at least for a while. Nick Price, always smart, looks smarter yet right about now. All through the Tiger Era he has been saying that if you want to bunch the fields, make the courses shorter and tighter and the greens a touch slower. Last week, Price, 45, Scott Hoch, 46, and Mark O'Meara, 45, were all better than Woods. Remember when the Masters used to be an exciting tournament—a couple dozen trees, a few hundred yards and two inches of rough ago? The British Open is still a thrill. Price says the U.S. Open should go back to bony old Merion. He has the right idea. Pine Valley should be perfect, too, if only the club admitted women.

Tiger has been using Jack Nicklaus's 18 major titles as his mile marker since boyhood. (Woods is at eight and holding.) But at Muirfield last week he showed how much more he has learned from Nicklaus. Woods's disappointment was profound in Saturday's gloaming. A chance to win the Grand Slam had come and gone, but like Nicklaus before him, he never

Tiger Woods celebrates under the giant yellow scoreboard on the final hole of the 2000 British Open at St. Andrews. Woods demolished the defenseless Old Course and the competition with a winning score of 19 under par

---

*MICHAEL BAMBERGER (b. 1960) grew up in Patchogue, Long Island, and started playing golf at the public course in Bellport. After graduating from the University of Pennsylvania, he was a staff writer for the *Philadelphia Inquirer*. Bamberger joined *Sports Illustrated* in 1995 and is senior writer. His books include *To the Linksland*.

Tiger Woods heads for the 18th hole in the second round of the British Open at Muirfield, East Lothian, Scotland in 2002. The Big Gale that blew the next day cost Woods his chance for the single-season Grand Slam, and the Big Easy, Ernie Els, won in a riveting four-man playoff

made an excuse. After enduring an afternoon in which he took 81 whacks and went through a dozen gloves, he showed grace. "I tried on each and every shot," he said. "That's the best I could shoot." Yes, fellow grownups, you may put his poster up in your bedroom.

Last week at Muirfield the refrain from the long bombers—some of them, anyway— was, "They're taking the driver out of my hands." Woods lodged no such complaint. All he'll do is work harder and get straighter off the tee. Woods shot an easy 65 playing with Jeff Maggert, his accuracy god, on Sunday. Mags, as Woods calls him, trying to sound like one of the boys, hits more fairways than Woods, hits more than just about anybody. Not for long.

American golf has always had a keeper of the flame, an ancient who teaches by example. O'Meara is that player today. O'Meara and Woods made the slog through the Muirfield links together on Saturday. Marko, as Woods calls him, shot a 77. It has been noted before that Woods doesn't play his best when paired with O'Meara, his neighbor and friend. It really doesn't matter. There was an important observation to be made last week, and only O'Meara was in a position to make it. O'Meara: "I said to him on Saturday, 'Look, we're both struggling here. But at least you're acting in the proper manner.' I know he was down because he'd love to win the Grand Slam, but he's only 26."

O'Meara had it exactly correct. You can do all the right exercises, eat all the right foods, work the hardest and have the best coaching, but in the end, some weeks the wind, the rain or the age-old rub of the green will have the final say. There is a real God, there is the accuracy god and then there are the golfing gods. They had a message for Tiger, and for us, straight from the black Scottish night: Not just yet.

BIBLIOGRAPHY

The American Golfer. Edited by Charles Price. New York: Random House, 1964.

Balfour, James. *Reminiscences of Golf on St. Andrews Links*. Edinburgh: David Douglas, 1887.

Boswell, Thomas. *Strokes of Genius*. Garden City, N.Y.: Doubleday, 1987.

British Sports and Sportsmen: Sportsmen of the Past. Compiled and edited by "The Sportsman." London: Sports and Sportsmen, 1908.

Collett, Glenna. *Ladies in the Rough*. New York and London: Alfred A. Knopf, 1928.

Cortissoz, Royal. *Nine Holes of Golf*. New York: Charles Scribner's Sons, 1922.

Darwin, Bernard. *Green Memories*. London: Hodder & Stoughton, 1928.

——. *Mostly Golf*. London: A. and C. Black, 1976.

——. *Out of the Rough*. London: Chapman, 1932.

——. *Playing the Like*. London: Chapman & Hall, 1934.

——. *Rubs of the Green*. London: Chapman & Hall, 1936.

Dickinson, Patric. *A Round of Golf Courses: A Selection of the Best Eighteen*. London: Evans Brothers, 1951.

——. *The Good Minute*. London: Victor Gollancz, 1965.

Dobereiner, Peter. *Golf à la Carte: The Best of Dobereiner*. New York: Lyons & Burford, 1991.

Farnie, H.B. *The Golfer's Manual; Being an Historical and Descriptive Account of the National Game of Scotland, by 'A Keen Hand.'* London: Dropmore, 1947; originally published in 1857.

Finegan, James W. *Blasted Heaths and Blessed Greens: A Golfer's Pilgrimage to the Courses of Scotland*. New York: Simon & Schuster, 1996.

Golf Digest: Golf's Greatest Players, Courses and Voices. New York: Hugh Lauter Levin Associates, 2000.

Hagen, Walter. *The Walter Hagen Story*. New York: Simon & Schuster, 1956.

Haultain, Arnold. *The Mystery of Golf*. Boston and New York: Houghton Mifflin, 1908.

Herd, Alexander. *My Golfing Life*. London: Chapman & Hall, 1923.

Houghton, George. *Golf Addict Invades Wales: The Account of a Crusade*. London: Pelham Books, 1969.

Jenkins, Dan. *The Dogged Victims of Inexorable Fate*. Boston: Little, Brown, 1970.

——. *Fairways and Greens: The Best Golf Writing of Dan Jenkins*. New York: Doubleday, 1994.

Jones, Jr., Robert T., and O. B. Keeler. *Down the Fairway: The Golf Life and Play of Robert T. Jones, Jr.* New York: Minton, Balch, 1927.

Keeler, O.B. *The Bobby Jones Story*. Edited by Grantland Rice. Atlanta: Tupper & Love, 1953.

Laney, Al. *Following the Leaders*. New York: Ailsa, 1991.

Lang, Andrew, and others. *A Batch of Golfing Papers*. Edited by R. Barclay. London: Simkin, Marshall, Hamilton, Kent, 1892.

Leach, Henry. *The Happy Golfer, Being Some Experiences, Reflections, and a Few Deductions of a Wandering Player*. London: Macmillan, 1914.

Lee, James P. *Golf in America: A Practical Manual*. New York: Dodd, Mead, 1895.

Longhurst, Henry. *It Was Good While It Lasted*. London: J.M. Dent and Sons, 1941.

McKinlay, S.L. *Scottish Golf and Golfers*. New York: Ailsa, 1992.

McCallen, Brian. *GOLF Magazine's Top 100 Courses You Can Play*. New York: Harry N. Abrams, 1999.

Milne, A.A. *Not That It Matters*. New York: E.P. Dutton, 1920.

Murray, Jim. *The Jim Murray Collection*. Dallas: Taylor Publishing, 1988.

Nash, Ogden. *The Face Is Familiar: The Selected Verse of Ogden Nash*. Boston: Little, Brown, 1940.

Nicklaus, Jack, with Chris Millard. *Nicklaus by Design: Golf Course Strategy and Architecture*. New York: Harry N. Abrams, 2002.

Owen, David. *The Chosen One: Tiger Woods and the Dilemma of Greatness*. New York: Simon & Schuster, 2001.

——. *My Usual Game: Adventures in Golf*. New York: Villard Books, 1995.

Pennink, Frank. *Homes of Sport: Golf*. London: Peter Garnett, 1952.

Plimpton, George. *The Bogey Man*. New York: Harper & Row, 1967.

Price, Charles. *A Golf Story: Bobby Jones, Augusta National, and the Masters Tournament*. New York: Atheneum, 1986.

Sampson, Curt. *Hogan*. Nashville: Rutledge Hill Press, 1996.

Sassoon, Siegfried. *The Weald of Youth*. New York: Viking, 1942.

Simpson, Sir Walter. *The Art of Golf*. Edinburgh: David Douglas, 1887.

Smith, Garden G. *The World of Golf*. London: A.D. Innes, 1898.

Smith, Red. *Strawberries in the Wintertime: The Sporting World of Red Smith*. New York: Quadrangle/The New York Times Book Co., 1974.

Sports Illustrated Golf. Birmingham, Alabama: Oxmoor House, 1994.

Taylor, J.H. *Golf: My Life's Work*. London: Jonathan Cape, 1943.

Tillinghast, A.W. *Reminiscences of the Links*. Edited by Richard C. Wolffe, Jr., Robert S. Trebus, and Stuart F. Wolffe. Basking Ridge, New Jersey: Tree Wolf Productions, 1998.

Tufts, Richard S. *The Scottish Invasion, Being a Brief Review of American Golf in Relation to Pinehurst and the Sixty-Second National Amateur*. Pinehurst, N.C.: Pinehurst Publishers, 1962.

Tulloch, W.W. *The Life of Tom Morris, with Glimpses of St. Andrews and Its Golfing Celebrities*. London: T. Werner Laurie, 1908.

Updike, John. *Golf Dreams*. New York: Alfred A. Knopf, 1996.

Vardon, Harry. *My Golfing Life*. London: Hutchinson, 1933.

Ward-Thomas, Pat. *The Long Green Fairway*. London: Hodder & Stoughton, 1966.

——. *Masters of Golf*. London: Heinemann, 1961.

Wethered, H. N. *The Perfect Golfer*. London: Methuen, 1931.

—— and Simpson, T. *The Architectural Side of Golf*. London and New York: Longmans, Green, 1929.

Wind, Herbert Warren. *Following Through*. New York: Ticknor & Fields, 1985.

INDEX

Note: Page numbers in italics refer to illustration captions. Page numbers followed by *n* refer to the biographical note at the bottom of the page.

SOURCE ACKNOWLEDGMENTS

Dave Anderson, "The Grand Slam that Almost Was," from *Golf Digest,* July 1987, reprinted with kind permission of the author; Michael Bamberger, "Not So Fast," from *Sports Illustrated,* July 29, 2002, copyright © 2002 Time Inc. All rights reserved, reprinted courtesy of *Sports Illustrated;* Thomas Boswell, from *Strokes of Genius,* copyright © 1987, reprinted with permission of *The Washington Post;* Royal Cortissoz, "On Dufferdom," from *Nine Holes of Golf,* copyright © 1923 by Charles Scribner's Sons, reprinted with permission of Scribners, an imprint of Simon & Schuster Adult Publishing Group; Bernard Darwin, "James Braid: Divine Fury," "Touching Wood," and "Gene Sarazen: The Man From Titusville," reprinted with permission of A.P. Watt Ltd. on behalf of Ursula Mommens, Lady Darwin, and Paul Ashton; Bernard Darwin, "The Links of Eiderdown," from *The Times* (London), February 3, 1934, and "Harry Vardon," from *The Times* (London), March 22, 1937, © Times Newspapers Limited, London 1934 and 1937, reprinted with permission; Frank Deford, "The Best Against the Best," from *Sports Illustrated,* July 14, 1986, copyright © 1986 Time Inc. All rights reserved, reprinted courtesy of *Sports Illustrated;* Jaime Diaz, "The Once and Future Gary Player," from *Memorial Tournament Program,* 1997, reprinted with kind permission of the author; Peter Dobereiner, from *Golf à la Carte,* copyright © 1991 by Peter Dobereiner, reprinted with kind permission of Globe Pequot Press; James W. Finegan, from *Blasted Heaths and Blessed Greens,* copyright © 1996 by Aberdovey, Inc., reprinted with kind permission of the author; James W. Finegan, "Eternal Oakmont," from *U.S. Open Magazine,* 1994, reprinted with kind permission of *GOLF Magazine;* Rhonda Glenn, "A Friend Remembers Babe Zaharias," from *Golf Journal,* July 1984, reprinted with permission of the author; Robert Green, "Pine Valley," from *Golf World* (U.K.), August 1985, reprinted with kind permission of *Golf World* (U.K.); Walter Hagen, from *The Walter Hagen Story,* copyright © 1956 by Walter Hagen, reprinted with permission of Simon & Schuster Adult Publishing Group; George Houghton, from *Golf Addict Invades Wales,* copyright © 1969 by George Houghton, reprinted with kind permission of Sean Arnold; *Dan Jenkins,* from *The Dogged Victims of Inexorable Fate,* copyright © 1970 by Dan Jenkins, reprinted with permission of Little, Brown and Company, Inc.; Dan Jenkins, "The Mother of All Streaks," from *Fairways and Greens,* copyright © 1994 by D&J Ventures, reprinted with permission of Doubleday, a division of Random House, Inc.; *Robert T. Jones, Jr.,* from *Down the Fairway,* copyright © 1927, reprinted with permission of the family of Robert T. Jones, Jr.; O.B. Keeler, from *The Bobby Jones Story,* reprinted with permission of Sidney L. Matthew/I.Q. Press Corporation; S.L. McKinlay, "Watching and Suffering," reprinted with kind permission of *The Glasgow Herald;* Brian McCallen, from *GOLF Magazine's Top 100 Golf Courses You Can Play,* copyright © 1999 by Brian McCallen, reprinted with kind permission of the author; A.A. Milne, from *Not That It Matters,* copyright © 1919 by A.A. Milne, reprinted with permission of Curtis Brown, London.; Jim Murray, "An American Legend," from the *Los Angeles Times,* March 15, 1981, copyright © 1981, *Los Angeles Times,* reprinted with permission; Ogden Nash, "The Strange Case of the Ambitious Caddie," copyright © 1938 by Ogden Nash, renewed, reprinted with permission of Curtis Brown, Ltd. and Andre Deutsch Limited; John Paul Newport, "Phil Mickelson: The Prodigy vs. the Genius," from *T&L Golf,* November 2001, reprinted with kind permission of the author; Jack Nicklaus, from *Nicklaus by Design,* copyright © 2002 by Harry N. Abrams, Inc., reprinted with kind permission of the publisher; David Owen, from *My Usual Game,* copyright © 1995 by David Owen, reprinted with permission of Villard Books, a division of Random House, Inc.; David Owen, from *The Chosen One,* copyright © 2001 by David Owen, excerpted by permission of Simon & Schuster Adult Publishing Group; George Plimpton, from *The Bogey Man,* copyright © 1967 by George Plimpton, reprinted with kind permission of Globe Pequot Press; Charles Price, from *A Golf Story,* copyright ©1986 by Charles Price, reprinted with kind permission of Laurie Roche-Price; Curt Sampson, from *Hogan,* copyright © 1996 by Curt Sampson, reprinted with permission of Rutledge Hill Press,

Nashville, Tennessee; Siegfried Sassoon, from T*he Weald of Youth,* copyright © 1942 by Siegfried Sassoon, renewed 1969 by Hester Sassoon, reprinted with permission of Viking Press, a division of Penguin Putnam Inc., and kind permission of George Sassoon; Red Smith, "70 Is Two Under Par," copyright © 1972 *The New York Times,* reprinted with permission; A.W. Tillinghast, from *Reminiscences of the Links,* copyright © 1998 by Tree Wolf Productions, reprinted with kind permission of the publisher; Richard S. Tufts, from *The Scottish Invasion,* copyright © 1962 by Richard S. Tufts, reprinted with kind permission of Peter V. Tufts; John Updike, "The Bliss of Golf" and "Golf Dreams" (originally published in *The New Yorker*), from *Golf Dreams,* copyright © 1996 by John Updike, reprinted with permission of Alfred A. Knopf, a division of Random House, Inc., and Penguin Books Ltd.; Pat Ward-Thomas, from *The Long Green Fairway,* copyright © 1966 by Pat Ward-Thomas and *Masters of Golf,* copyright © 1961 by P.A. Ward-Thomas, reprinted with kind permission of Patricia Guintrand de Peyre; Herbert Warren Wind, "North to the Links of Dornoch," originally published in *The New Yorker,* June 6, 1964 and "Robert Tyre Jones, Jr.," originally published in *The New Yorker,* April 29, 1972, reprinted with kind permission of Gertrude Scheft

PHOTOGRAPHY CREDITS

Stuart Abraham, 60; courtesy of the Atlanta History Center, Berckmans Collection, Cherokee Garden Library, 190; courtesy of George Bahto, 163; Royal Blackheath Golf Club, 35; Aidan Bradley, 84-85, 201, 213, 226-27; Christie's Images, 90, 100; Emory University, Bobby Jones Collection, Special Collections and Archives, Robert W. Woodruff Library, 125, 138, 141; Getty Images/David Cannon, 53, 170, 247, 252; Getty Images/Jonathan Ferrey, 283; Getty Images/Harry How, 284; Getty Images/Ross Kinnaird, 296; Getty Images/Andrew Redington, 256; Getty Images/Paul Severn, 220, 294; Getty Images/Jamie Squire, 291 and back cover; Matthew Harris/The Golf Picture Library, 29, 88, 91, 93, 96, 103, 105, 173, 175, 185, 235, 238, 265, 279, 288, 292; John and Jeannine Henebry, 160-61, 176, 181, 195; High Museum of Art, Atlanta, Georgia, 136; Hobbs Golf Collection, 121; Hulton Getty, 55, 133, 151, 217, 237; Leonard Kamsler, 244-45, 249, 250, 253, 255, 258, 259, 261, 275; Russell Kirk/Golflinks, 58, 66, 106, 271; Mike Klemme/Golfoto, 225; courtesy of Kohler Resort, 198, 199; L.C. Lambrecht, 2, 12-13, 17, 20, 32, 49, 90, 109, 115, 117, 122-23, 145, 148, 165, 167, 168, 171, 178, 180, 187, 189, 193, 196, 242, 243; courtesy of Royal Mid-Surrey Golf Club, photography by Mark Morosse, 54; New York Public Library, Photography Division, 64, 69, 94, 102, 232; reproduced by kind permission of the Royal and Ancient Golf Club of St. Andrews, 46; courtesy of the University of St. Andrews Library, 41, 42, 43, 45, 52; Scottish National Portrait Gallery, 18, 44, 87; National Gallery of Scotland, 19; Phil Sheldon Golf Picture Library, 157, 219, 262, 268 and Dale Concannon Collection/Phil Sheldon Golf Picture Library, 47, 50, 53, 57, 59, 63, 113, 154, 186, 202-03, 205, 212; collection of Robert Sidorsky, photography by Bruce Schwarz, 16, 23, 24, 26, 33, 34, 36-37, 75, 78-79, 81, 83, 89, 99, 231, 278 and collection of Robert Sidorsky, photography by Mark Morosse, 8, 86, 233; courtesy of Tillinghast Association, 140, 166, 179; courtesy of Tufts Archives, Given Memorial Library, 174; courtesy USGA, 28, 30, 70, 73, 74, 77, 128, 130, 131, 143, 146, 147, 149, 150, 152, 155, 156, 159, 183, 206, 207, 211, 216, 223; courtesy USGA Museum and Library, photography by Mark Morosse, front cover, 25, 27, 68, 120, 135, 192, 229, 241; courtesy Walton Heath Golf Club and Phil Sheldon Golf Picture Library/Gary Prior, 65

For my mother, Rhoda Sidorsky

Editor: Margaret L. Kaplan
Designer: Gary Tooth and Carrie Hamilton/Empire Design Studio, NYC
Production Manager: Justine Keefe

Library of Congress Cataloging-in-Publication Data

Golf's greatest moments : an illustrated history by the game's finest
writers : a literary anthology of golf / introduced and edited by Robert
Sidorsky ; with selections by Dave Anderson ... [et al.].
      p. cm.
Includes bibliographical references and index.
 ISBN 0-8109-4631-9 (hardcover)
 1. Golf—History. 2. Golf stories. I. Sidorsky, Robert. II.
Anderson, Dave.

 GV963.G65 2003
 796.352'09—dc21

                                        2003007423

Copyright © 2003 by Robert Sidorsky

Published in 2003 by Harry N. Abrams, Incorporated, New York.
All rights reserved. No part of the contents of this book may be reproduced without written
    permission of the publisher.

Printed and bound in Singapore

10 9 8 7 6 5 4 3 2 1

 Harry N. Abrams, Inc.
100 Fifth Avenue
New York, N.Y. 10011
www.abramsbooks.com

Abrams is a subsidiary of LA MARTINIÈRE GROUPE